Saturday Afternoon
AT THE MOVIES

3 VOLUMES IN 1

Alan G. Barbour

Saturday Afternoon
AT THE MOVIES

3 VOLUMES IN 1

BONANZA BOOKS
New York

This omnibus edition was originally published in separate volumes under the titles: *Days of Thrills and Adventure, A Thousand and One Delights, The Thrill of It All*.

This 1986 edition is published by Bonanza Books, distributed by Crown Publishers, Inc., by arrangement with Macmillan Publishing Company.

Printed and Bound in the United States of America

Library of Congress Cataloging in Publication Data

Barbour, Alan G.
  Saturday afternoon at the movies.

  Contents: Days of thrills and adventure—The thrill of it all—A thousand and one delights.
  1. Moving-pictures—United States—History. I. Title.
PN1993.5.U6B297   1986   791.43'75'0973   86-2332
ISBN: 0-517-60898-7

h g f e d c b a

CONTENTS

VOLUME 1

DAYS OF THRILLS AND ADVENTURE

Dedicated to the memory of

ROY BARCROFT, 1902-1969

in grateful appreciation for

presenting all of us with so many wonderful

Days of Thrills and Adventure

ACKNOWLEDGMENTS

The author wishes to express his sincere thanks to the individuals and organizations listed below who supplied, through the years, the stills and information which have made this book possible.

The Individuals:
Roy Barcroft, Spencer Gordon Bennet, John Cocchi, Edward Connor, Homer Dickens, William K. Everson, Phil Glickman, Eric Hoffman, Henry Kier, Al Kilgore, Ernie Kirkpatrick, Paula Klaw, William Lava, Milton Luboviski, Louis McMahon, Bob Miller, Gray Morrow, Sloan Nibley, Bob Price, Mark Ricci, Gene Ringgold, Stephen Sally, Samuel M. Sherman, Jim Shoenberger, Tom Steele, Chris Steinbrunner, Linda Stirling, and Bud Thackery.

The Organizations:
Cinemabilia, Collector's Bookstore, Columbia Pictures Corporation, Fawcett Publications, Inc., Kier's, King Features Syndicate, Larry Edmunds Bookshop, Marvel Comics Group, The Memory Shop, Movie Star News, The Museum of Modern Art, National Periodical Publications, Inc., National Telefilm Associates, Screen Gems, Inc., United Features Syndicate, Inc., Universal Pictures Corporation, and Vista Productions.

With Special Thanks to:
Jean Barbour and James Robert Parish.

Contents

Preface

ALAN BARBOUR's BOOK is thoroughly enjoyable, and I am happy
and proud to have been a part of those *Days of Thrills and
Adventure* he describes so well.

In page after page I was treated to a pleasantly nostalgic
backward look at friends and acquaintances, actors and actresses
with whom I share the common bond of those hectic but
happy days of movie-making.

I cannot recommend the book highly enough. It is accurate,
interesting, and entertaining. It should find an enthusiastic audience
of remember-those-good-old-days moviegoers, as well as
serious film buffs and students.

BUSTER CRABBE

Author's Note

"It seems like only yesterday!" I wonder how many people have uttered that now-trite phrase as they fondly recalled the wonderful memories of years gone by. I had always assumed that it was a phrase reserved for those "senior citizens" who had little else to do with their time but spend it recalling the glorious days they would never see again. But now I find that at the ripe old age of thirty-seven I am already uttering that same woeful cry myself.

It does, indeed, seem like only yesterday that a freckle-faced, red-haired boy by the name of Alan G. Barbour practically ran those few short blocks from his home on Linden Street to the Broadway Theatre in downtown Oakland, California, every Saturday, timing his arrival so that he could get his two bags of fresh popcorn and still be seated in time to see the serial at twelve-twenty and again about three-thirty.

Yes, they were wonderful days. And, of course, the serials didn't end with those two screenings. I lived every episode for a full seven days until the next one flashed on the screen. I made my Captain Marvel cape and my Spy Smasher cape and I fought a thousand mock battles with boyhood companions.

Those days, perhaps the most enjoyable of my life, are gone now—and the serials are gone, just as the pulp magazines and the radio adventure shows vanished before them. The serials brought me, and millions like me, pleasure beyond verbal description— and now they're gone, forever, and I feel sorry, not for myself, for I enjoyed them all, but for all those future generations of young boys who will never experience the joy of sharing those wonderful Saturday afternoons with bigger-than-life heroes on the screen and reliving all those unforgettable *Days of Thrills and Adventure.*

Alan G. Barbour

Introduction

Days of Thrills and Adventure seems a particularly felicitous title for Mr. Barbour's excursion into the color and history of the American chapter-play. Were the book called, for example, "The Art of the Serial," the author would be in the defensive position of having to prove that there *is* an art to the serial! But I think the key word is "Days"; when all is said and done, no American serial really lives up to its reputation, or to our own nostalgic recollections of it. The good serials—and there are some *very* good ones—more often than not survive on merits that we didn't even dream existed when we first saw them. To be enjoyed to the full, the serial had to be seen in those days paralleling our own days of innocence, when the movies truly had magic, when we believed everything that we saw on the screen, and when, in our happy ignorance of critical standards or technical knowledge, the serial was judged by the same standards as a box-office blockbuster or an artistic masterpiece—and usually survived the comparison rather well.

It is sometimes surprising what aspects of the serial (or any film, for that matter) can impress themselves indelibly on the mind of a child. My own most vivid recollections of serials from the early thirties are not of the chases and fights and marathons of action, but rather of climaxes that approached moments of near-horror. One jungle serial reached its climax with the hero being buried alive by natives in a deep pit; the framing of the shot and the rising crescendo of beating drums are details as vivid in my memory now as they were nearly forty years ago, and I can still sense the feeling of claustrophobic horror that the scene created. (I have never seen that chapter again, nor have I ever tried to trace the serial, although since the period is so clearly defined, it would have to be one of a mere half-dozen titles. But some memories are too delicious to disturb, and why take the risk?) In that same period, Universal's science-fiction serial *Vanishing Shadow* (1934) was productive of a similar traumatic experience. One of the "good" scientists had perfected some kind of electrical death-ray which was installed at the door to his laboratory. After it was tried out amid a shower of sparks, the scientist told his cohort that the ray would certainly kill any crook who came through that door. Needless to say, within the reel either the heroine or the hero blundered through that door, to be enveloped in electrical sparks for the fadeout. I never had a chance to see the follow-up chapter, but I was comforted by the preparatory remark that the death-ray was designed to kill "crooks"; that was the obvious escape clause, and I imparted to that death-ray the ability to distinguish between good and evil, the right to exercise judgment on who should live and who should die. I am sure that the ultimate solution was a much more mechanical one—yet again, my own innocence and awe made those few seconds of film immortal. Later on, when violence and horror were less common in the serial—and less likely anyway to create such deeply etched impressions on the mind of a maturing ten-year-old—the memories formed were rather different.

Curiously, I remember *The Lone Ranger,* one of the best Western serials, not for its action or even for its quite strong story-line. The impression that lingers is a rather stylistic one revolving around the dominance of the color white: the white stetsons, white silk shirts, and white horses of the rangers, the white chalk cliffs and white sands of the locations. The serial has been unavailable for reappraisal for some time, but logic insists that Republic undoubtedly used their standard locations in and around Hollywood, and that white sands and cliffs were no more predominant in *The Lone Ranger* than in their other Westerns of the period.

If these introductory reminiscences are essentially personal rather than critical, it is to emphasize that almost *all* appreciation of the serial has to be largely personal, and based to a very great degree on one's age at the time and the conditions under which one saw it. Moreover, the serial is a branch of film unique and exclusive unto itself, and has to be judged and regarded accordingly. Mr. Barbour is generous with his use of such words as "classic," "masterpiece" and "superb"—and within the confines of his text, he is quite justified. By serial standards, a film like *The Adventures of Captain Marvel is* a masterpiece; the juxtaposition of the best serials of Republic (for example, *Mysterious Dr. Satan* or *Drums of Fu Manchu*) next to the worst of the independents (*Custer's Last Stand* or *The Black Coin*) automatically makes "classics" of the Republics. A bravura performance by Lionel Atwill or Eduardo Ciannelli as a Republic villain certainly is "superb" acting compared with the listless and thoughtless reading of lines by a Jack Ingram or a Gene Stutenroth in a Columbia serial. But everything in film is relative: to term a serial a "masterpiece" is in no way to imply that it can stand side by side with such genuine film masterpieces as *Sunrise, Intolerance*, or *Citizen Kane*. There are perhaps only a handful of true film masterpieces which can hold their own as independent works of art with the other great masterpieces of the art world: painting, sculpture, poetry, music. There is no film serial (or at least, no *American* serial) which can call itself a masterpiece outside of its own little world. With full regard for the skill of the serials, the money they made, and the entertainment they brought to millions, the serials have not added one iota of development

to either the art or the history of the film. One could sweep them all away, blot them out totally, and the blow to film history would not be a major one. Indeed, if the serial had never evolved at all, it is unlikely that the course of film would have been changed or diverted in any way.

This may seem like a very harsh judgment, especially from one who is an admitted devotee of the serial. Obviously one can't just sweep away four full decades of serials—some 3,000 hours of film—nor do I wish to. But unlike the two-reel comedy or even the B-Western, the serial was never innovational. Everything it had, everything it did, represented a kind of brain-picking from what had gone before. The best serials were the ones made by the directors who loved their craft, loved film—and had seen a lot of it. They knew what had been done before, and how best to adapt it to their own work. The most common element of all serials was the steady building of suspense to climaxes via speed, action and, cross-cutting—devices that D. W. Griffith had explored in his Biograph shorts of 1908–1913 and had brought to fruition in *The Birth of a Nation* and *Intolerance* in the mid-teens, just as the serials were getting under way. Serial directors, who would be the last to call themselves artists, probably knew more about the true art of film than many a more pretentious and acclaimed director of features. How else can one explain the frequent references to classic silent work that one finds scattered throughout the best of even the talkie serials? *Flash Gordon* (1936) uses designs and prop-machines in its "atom furnace" set that obviously derive from Fritz Lang's *Metropolis* of a decade earlier. Their presence is not vital to either set or story-line, but it is one of those intangible assets that makes all the difference between a good serial and a mediocre one. Another more striking example is provided by *Undersea Kingdom*, a serial of the same period. On a smaller scale, of course, one battle sequence is based exactly on the monumental battle in 1916's *Intolerance*, complete to such details as the destruction of the scaling towers and the utilization of a fanciful flame-thrower.

In view of the structure of the serial and the nature of its production methods, it is not surprising that its makers have pursued ingenuity rather than creativity. The director of a B-Western has probably more "artistic freedom" than any other director in the world. His product isn't important enough to warrant front-office supervision, nor does anybody care very much if he deviates from his script. Moreover, much of the time he is away from the studio—either on location, or at the studio ranch—away from even nominal interference. As long as he brings in a salable product, on time and under budget, nobody is going to care whether he delivers five reels of action or a five-reel masterpiece. Admittedly, shooting has to be fast, and the average director is more interested in shaving time off an already tight schedule than in exploring the niceties of camera composition or shooting a scene so that it is, in a sense, edited in the camera. Yet a director who really cares, and who has ambitions beyond B pictures, will take precisely that care. A case in point is Joseph H. Lewis, who directed some of the best of the Bob Baker and Johnny Mack Brown Westerns for Universal before going on to big-budget thrillers. The style and finesse that he brought to films like *Courage of the West* and *Arizona Cyclone* really paid off and lifted them well above formula level. It's unlikely that his efforts increased their box-office yield in any way, but at least he had the personal satisfaction of seeing a one-hour film in which his style was consistent and recognizable, and also, probably, the more commercial satisfaction of knowing that a film that good might well attract the attention of production higher-ups who could promote him to bigger and better properties.

No such incentives exist with the serial, nor would they be practical to pursue if they did. By its very nature, the serial is mechanically constructed to fit a set pattern, a set running time, and a set audience. Given a rudimentary story-line, it has to be developed to encompass as much action as possible, to avoid dramatic entanglements which entail careful writing and acting, and to utilize such budget-paring ingredients as stock footage and standing sets as frequently as possible. Moreover, because of the great length of footage involved—some five hours per average complete serial—and the frequent re-utilization of the same key sets and locations, production is always broken down mathematically so that all the shots involving a given set or a key player are filmed at the same time. Further, two (and often more) directors are usually

involved in the average serial, one handling action scenes, particularly fights, another directing the purely dialogue sequences, and perhaps a third doing the second-unit location work (car chases, Indian–cavalry encounters, and so forth). As a result, no one director exercises total control over a serial or is able to impose a definite style. (Admittedly, two directors working together as a team could, in time, evolve a kind of style—and some did.) In addition, with production at such breakneck speed, the kind of niceties that Joseph Lewis could afford in a humble Western were sheer luxuries in a serial; moreover, they would be wasted, since an adroit piece of editing or careful attention paid to the way an actor handled his lines would just be lost in such a morass of footage. Audiences wouldn't remember little moments of artistic endeavor—and unless they were spotted within the first couple of chapters, the chances were that studio executives would never get to see them at all. So the shrewd serial director aimed not so much at artistry as at gimmickry, at making his serial look far more expensive than it was, dreaming up original little bits of business that could make his audience sit up and take notice because they were getting something new—and all this, if possible, without any increase in budget or shooting time. A typical example is provided by a Universal serial of the mid-thirties, *Scouts to the Rescue*, in which a lost tribe of Indians was given a most impressive and undecipherable guttural language. Certainly the gimmick worked on me as a child, and it wasn't until years later, when I ran off a print on a projector that also worked in reverse, that I tumbled to the trick. The Indians spoke perfectly normal dialogue—which was then printed in reverse. Very often they were physically motionless, so that the *picture* could be printed in reverse too, and a perfect lip-synch maintained!

None of this is meant to imply that there was no artistry in the serial: there *was*, but it was all devoted to areas where it really counted (and could be reused!), and again, it was merely an extension of techniques and styles that existed outside the serials. Republic, for example, lavished great care on their miniatures; they were often incredibly realistic, putting to shame a lot of the miniature work in million-dollar specials. The miniatures in MGM's sound *Ben Hur* are positively amateurish compared with the work done by the Lydecker brothers for Republic. There is artistry too in the choreography (and the word is used here deliberately) of fight scenes, and in the slick utilization of running inserts in chase scenes. But it is a kind of mechanical artistry, honed to perfection through years of polishing, nonetheless exciting for being so efficiently manufactured, but still mechanical.

It's significant, I think, that while many major directors emerged from the ranks of two-reel comedies and Westerns (among them Charlie Chaplin, Buster Keaton, Mal St. Clair, Frank Capra, John Ford, William Wyler), graduates from the serial were far less impressive. Only two really major directorial names got their start in serials, George Marshall and W. S. Van Dyke, and even Van Dyke had had an apprenticeship with Griffith prior to his serials. Both Marshall and Van Dyke learned how to keep their pictures constantly on the move, and how to bring their films in on time and under budget —a particularly useful lesson for Van Dyke, who made his best pictures at MGM in the thirties, where the prevailing *modus operandi* was to shoot slowly and to retake (or remake) as much as necessary. His lightning methods made him the envy of other directors, the delight of the budget-conscious front-office, and, sadly, an object of genial derision by most critics who couldn't believe—*Trader Horn, White Shadows in the South Seas,* and *The Thin Man* notwithstanding—that pictures made quickly, and by an ex-serial director, could be any good! Most directors who proved adept at serial-making—Ray Taylor, Ford Beebe, Spencer Gordon Bennet—tended to stay with the genre throughout their careers. And, too, the serial proved a useful haven for once-leading directors (primarily of action material) who, in their later days, found themselves short on good assignments: Lambert Hillyer, Elmer Clifton, James Horne. Writing for serials is such a specialized field that relatively few of its scenarists ever left it; none certainly made any major marks in movies outside of the chapter-play area. Even the number of stars who were discovered in the serial is few: Warren William, George Brent, Jennifer Jones, Carole Landis. (John Wayne was a minor but established player well before his three early sound serials). As with the directors, however, the serial was a welcome refuge for many of the veteran stars who were having problems finding suitable roles but whose names still meant something to the patrons of serials—Herbert Rawlinson, Hoot Gibson, Francis X. Bushman, Clara Kimball Young, Kenneth Harlan.

On the whole, however, actors were always somewhat handicapped by the production methods of the serial, and they rarely had a chance to perform at their best. Most of the straight dramatic scenes were shot even more out of context than is usual in films, and the actors—especially the bit-players—rarely knew to what set of circumstances they were reacting, or into what context their scenes would be cut. Many supporting "roles," not accounted for in the script, would be created on the spot to provide instant justification or explanation for a situation and the actor would usually be a bit-player doing half-a-dozen other "roles" in the serial, sometimes with just a moustache or a pair of spectacles to "disguise" him, and often not even that. There was rarely time to establish any real kind of characterization, let alone the "motivation" so beloved by method actors. Of course, the action star personalities—Ralph Byrd, Buster Crabbe, Kane Richmond—had little trouble breezing through their familiar roles in dashing style. Not so successful were the less experienced, off-beat actors, who were often used by Republic in many of their leads partly because they worked at cheaper rates, and partly because their somewhat nondescript appearance made the matter of doubling easier. Such players as Robert Wilcox, Walter Reed, and Harry Lauter were far too dour and colorless to be a consistent match with the dashing image created by their doubles for the action scenes. For sheer lethargy and absence of get-up-and-go, however, some prize should surely be awarded to Ralph Graves for his performance as the G—man hero of the singularly dull *The Black Coin.* Not once did Graves (normally quite a good and pleasing actor) seem to snap out of his sleepy-eyed coma, and the apex of his inertia was reached in an early chapter when he looked out of the window of his plane (safely on the ground) to note that one wing and a fuel tank were merrily blazing away. "The plane's on fire" he remarked in a conversational tone of total disinterest, lazily forcing himself to rise from his seat as though in doubt whether to leave or not!

In contrast to his nonchalant "cool," the casts of Columbia serials were rushed about from situation to situation in a state of perpetual frenzy. It seemed almost a matter of policy to keep the players in such a state of non-stop motion that neither they nor the audience had time to stop and think about the absurdity of it all. This hectic activity was by no means limited to the fight scenes, where such stalwarts as Warren Hull (*The Spider's Web*) or Jack Holt (*Holt of the Secret Service*) would cheerfully take on (and vanquish) half a dozen heavies in fights of Keystone Cop speed and animation, but also to simple dramatic or transitional scenes. Nobody ever walked from a cabin to a car in a Columbia serial, they *ran*—and when they reached their destination they tumbled out like the Marx Brothers in the stateroom sequence of *A Night at the Opera,* and started running again. This breathless lack of decorum was inflicted on leading ladies and dignified character actors as well as mere hoodlums, and was emphasized by undercranked camerawork which gave their haste an even more frenzied appearance—to say nothing of the furious *agitato* music (usually by Lee Zahler) which helped to speed them on their way. Under such circumstances, subtlety in acting was an impossibility: players had neither the time (nor, probably, the breath) to deliver lines with care or respect, and simply had to hurl them out before being whisked off to something else. Small wonder that even the simplest line of dialogue seemed to be delivered amateurishly, with all the emphases on the wrong words. In fairness to Columbia, however, it would seem that this deliberate stress on artificial speed was part of an overall scheme to "camp" up their serials long before that absurd, much-abused (and happily now dying) term came into common usage. Although the studio made a handful of good early ones, Columbia rapidly lost interest in turning out quality serials, abandoning both the superior production values and action content of the contemporary Republic serials and the more reasonable and logical story values of the Universals. The Columbia serials directed by James Horne were clearly tongue-in-cheek, with exaggerated melodramatic gestures, derisive and sarcastic end-of-chapter narrations, and moments of truly lunatic comedy involving the villains. Serial purists understandably resented this and have never liked Horne's serials. Yet he was too good a director, too much a past master of great silent

and sound comedy (*The Cruise of the Jasper B,* Laurel and Hardy's *Big Business*) not to know precisely what he was doing. Undoubtedly he reasoned that to play the scripts straight, with their stereotyped stories and meager budgets, could only result in serials spectacularly inferior to the competitive ones issued by Republic and Universal. Playing them for comedy didn't make them better, but it did keep them lively, distinctive, and different. Their speed and constant changes of pace, however, and their intermingling of melodrama and farce, to say nothing of their frequent elements of what we would now call black comedy, made them even more of a challenge for actors, who could do nothing but go along for the ride. For the most part, the actors who fared best in serials (and *not* in Columbia serials, let it be added) were the well-established character actors (Irving Pichel, Ralph Morgan) and the bravura villains (Bela Lugosi, Lionel Atwill, Eduardo Ciannelli), players who had the expertise to go through their familiar paces with polish and aplomb, utilizing every bit of business at their disposal, employing every nuance of expression and delivery to build and magnify the quality of what they had to work with. Polished and suave villains like Atwill even managed to get away with audience-acceptance of that oldest and silliest of serial clichés, the villain's foolhardy reluctance to dispose of the hero while he has him in his power. After episodes of the most elaborate (and expensive) attempts to have the hero blown up, incinerated, guillotined, or eaten by crocodiles, there always arrives a moment when the hapless hero has pulled a boner and lies unconscious at the feet of his enemy. One of the smarter and more farsighted hoodlums aims a gun point-blank at his head. "Don't waste a bullet on him!" admonishes the mastermind, preferring to leave the hero's disposal to the mechanical contrivance which forms that week's chapter title—and chapter ending. Needless to say, such a priceless opportunity rarely arises again—or if it does it is similarly muffed for the sake of self-indulgent sadism!

Perhaps the least sung of all serial heroes is the editor: not only was he responsible for putting the mass of repetitious footage together, and creating as exciting a tempo as possible, but in many cases he had to salvage the mistakes or omissions of directors who, working at top speed, might understandably have left out minor scenes or found it impractical to go back to reshoot scenes that turned out badly. With very little to work with, for serial budgets didn't allow for the luxury of protection shots or standby footage, the editor often performed near-miracles. The salvage work might be apparent, but the show went on! Universal, always a little more concerned with story values than with action for its own sake, often neglected in the script stage to plant sufficient motivation or explanation in the dialogue. As a result, the end product often looked much like the extension of a comic strip, action flowing too facilely from point A to point C without the intermediate justification or logical explanation at point B. *Flash Gordon,* with its welter of scientific gimmickry, was especially guilty of this, and since the film was a major serial in its day, designed for more than just the kiddie trade, it obviously bothered Universal production heads. The solution was to dub in quick, pithy lines all the way through—a masterly compression of scientific data into one sentence here to explain a complicated bit of rocketship wizardry, or an expository line there to justify everybody's knowing exactly what to do without having to discuss it first. Unfortunately, the same deep booming voice was used for these lines (an average of four or five such lines appeared in each episode) throughout the entire serial. Whether it was the villainous Ming, the heroic Prince Barin, or the enterprising Dr. Zarkov who was supposed to be speaking, the voice was always the same—and the unintended result was the seeming omnipresence of a benign Deity, forever booming out instructions and helpful advice at the frequent moments of crisis!

There was usually little that the editor could do to bolster belief in the solutions to the previous week's climaxes: either they tended to be too cut-and-dried and formularized to be really exciting, or they cheated outrageously, banking rather forlornly on the audience's faulty memory. An example that comes readily to mind is a giant ore-crusher falling on Bob Livingston's chest in *The Vigilantes Are Coming,* the hero groaning in agony at the fadeout—but the following week he manages to remove himself from harm's way in ample time. Similarly, in *Winners of the West* Dick Foran lies unconscious in the path of an onrushing locomotive which thunders *over* his inert form at the end of one episode,

while in the next he staggers to his feet and wanders away while the train is still a good hundred yards down the track! Once in a while serials were so haphazardly shot that *no* "rescue" footage was delivered at all; thus, Johnny Mack Brown came to the end of one episode of *The Oregon Trail* under a herd of stampeding horses. Nothing was shot to save him from his predicament, so the editor had simply to ignore the whole thing and start the following chapter as though nothing had happened. Such lack of logic was, unfortunately, too often a hallmark of the American serial. The early chapters of *The Secret of Treasure Island* made a great to-do about a pirate's ghost, a lively skeleton that, among other enterprising activities, engaged the hero in a sword-fight or two. He was conveniently dropped several chapters before the end, and then explained away in the fifteenth episode as merely an image thrown by a projector! Even a first-class editor was comparatively helpless against such odds.

Another obstacle—particularly at Universal—was the musical director's apparent unwillingness to see the film he was scoring! For the most part *Flash Gordon* is a well-edited serial, but many of its highlights are lessened by the too-casual application of stock music and themes from earlier films. A pastorale theme may drone on through an exciting fight scene, while potentially gripping episodes of transitions from suspense to action are let down by musical scoring which does not punctuate those changes in mood. Perhaps all of these rather petty criticisms fall under the general heading of a lack of showmanship. Given that the serial is an unambitious branch of the art, geared to a set pattern with predictable costs and returns, too many directors forget that a basically juvenile audience follows a serial with loyalty and respect. Showmanship, sadly, has been too often limited to the opening three chapters, which are the ones shown to the trade for review purposes and to get bookings. A disproportionate amount of the budget usually goes to these opening chapters, along with the more imaginative elements of the plot too. Tom Mix's *The Miracle Rider* offered all sorts of elaborate gimmicks, some of a semi-science-fiction nature, in its first few episodes; thereafter both the gimmicks and often Mr. Mix too were conspicuous by their absence. Strong plot-lines, too, have a habit of dissolving after they have been established at the very beginning. Columbia serials were notorious for bogging down in single situations which never developed, and thus they were merely a loosely connected string of fights and chases. Worst of all were the "tug-of-war" plots as exemplified by the Buck Jones serial *The Roaring West,* in which practically the entire continuity was devoted to an old prospector and his map: they were captured by the badmen, rescued, captured by Indians, rescued; then his daughter was captured by badmen, he went to the rescue and was recaptured—ad infinitum, all against the background of a wagon train that lumbered from nowhere to nowhere, much like the plot itself.

Most inexcusable of all of course was the betraying of juvenile loyalty by coming up with a last chapter which shunned spectacular action in favor of wrapping it all up as economically as possible. The studios saw no point in ladling out largesse for a climactic episode, yet audiences who had been following the serial faithfully for fifteen weeks had a right to feel cheated when the unspeakable villain was brought to book without a chase or a fight. While certainly some studios did finish up their serials with a bang and/or imaginative twists in the ultimate unmasking of the villain, too many took the easier and less exciting path.

The history of the American serial is a frustrating one of missed opportunities, perhaps because of its own self-imposed limitations. Even in the earlier silent days, when the serial enjoyed its biggest box-office boom and was designed for adult approval, it stuck rigidly to the two-reel format. The Europeans on the other hand, respected the serial tradition and developed it with care and imagination, giving it the kind of running time and story sense that they thought it warranted. The German serials of Fritz Lang and Joe May had wildly extravagant—and romantic—plot-lines, and the episodes (which were complete in themselves, yet ended on the thresholds of obviously greater adventures) often ran for more than an hour. Moreover, they were totally unformula in concept and thoroughly unpredictable: one episode of Joe May's *Mistress of the World* suddenly turned itself into a kind of Lubitsch self-satire, playing entirely for comedy, at the same time establishing the fact that more traditional adventure fare was forthcoming the following week. And the early

French serials of Louis Feuillade are unreservedly film classics. His *Les Vampires,* constructed more like a feature than a serial, spends almost two of its seven hours in relatively tame establishment of characters and plot, then follows with a dizzy succession of thrills and sensations that mount to a fantastic crescendo. *Les Vampires* has thrill upon thrill, but it also presents fascinating character and story development, plus real beauty, poetry, and an odd intermingling of documentary values with surrealism. Even today, well over half a century after it was made, it stands as a model of what the serial should be—and what it could have been in this country. But Hollywood was developing so quickly in the years before the twenties: so many great directors—Griffith, Tourneur, Ford, Chaplin, von Stroheim—were maturing so rapidly, understandably bypassing the humble serial in favor of more challenging technical and story innovations. Apart from Abel Gance, a director whose genius rivaled Griffith's, the comedian Max Linder, France could muster few names in the 1910–1920 period (the great Méliès, of course, belonged to the earlier decade) to match the staggering outpouring of creative talent from Hollywood in those formulative years. So we can afford to be generous to France and acknowledge that Feuillade and his masterly serials led the field then—and still do.

Yet while the American serial was entertaining us and bringing healthy profits to its promoters, it was also performing several other valuable if unwitting sociological and historical functions. First of all, the serial always depended on speed —speed that was as up to the minute as possible— which meant a maximum reliance on automobiles and locomotives at first, and later on speedboats, racing cars, and airplanes. Since it was economically desirable to shoot out of doors as much as possible, and since, too, these props demanded it, many serials (particularly in the silent period) stressed a maximum of location shooting on busy city streets and country roads, thus capturing on film an invaluable record of a changing America as it was emerging into a rapidly more automated age. And since serials were so concerned with a direct confrontation between good and evil, they were always careful to spell out the moral standards of the day; to later generations these unintended and therefore quite honest depictions of the moral, racial, sexual, and other climates of their day can be both revealing and valuable. The casual acceptance of interracial humor and homosexuality (Ben Wilson serials made a genial running gag out of transvestism in the mid-twenties) reminds us how less hot and bothered we all got in those days about facets of everyday life that are now considered controversial. And although *Flash Gordon* seems to encourage a healthy interest in sex—the fetchingly underclad Dale Arden (Jean Rogers) is energetically pursued by a number of outer-space lechers, ranging from the winged King Vultan to the arch-fiend Ming himself—the script makes it quite plain that an unmarried male hero must be ignorant of such matters. Buster Crabbe as Flash seems naïvely unaware of Princess Aura's carnal interest in him as she runs her fingers over his rippling muscles; and when Flash and Dale are the guests of a lesser interplanetary ruler, he sends them to their retirement with the rather pointed remark, "Take them to their *separate* quarters!" (Universal seemed especially anxious to assure audiences of the total morality not only of heroes and heroines but even of complete crowds; who can forget burgomaster E. E. Clive dismissing a huge mob in *The Bride of Frankenstein* with the admonition, "It's high time every decent man *and wife* was home in bed"?) *Flash Gordon* offered a further contemporary reference: although the decidedly unroyal decor in Ming's palace was an odd combination of old and new—ray guns juxtaposed with Roman swords and armor, a rather tatty fur rug flung on the floor before the imposing altar-like throne—it was an Oriental motif that dominated. Sculptures of dragons, Ming's

tapering fingernails, his long thin moustache, his kimono-like robes, all of these were reminders that the personification of satanic evil was still to a degree associated with the only slowly disappearing image of the "yellow peril."

In the past, serials have served as a useful training ground for directors and stars, and through them valuable lessons in production economy have been learned and applied in the mainstream of film production. In the present, the now-defunct film serial has come to be regarded (with condescension by some, overawe by others) as a definite and acceptable kind of pop-art culture, so much so that on the open black market a print of *Flash Gordon* or *Captain America* will fetch more than an *Intolerance* or a *Citizen Kane!* In the future, as well as serving as a kind of signpost to contemporary tastes and mores, the American film serial may well find acceptance as a serious branch of American film art. If this seems unlikely, just recall how long it took for the Western—or for the comedies of Laurel and Hardy—to be afforded the respect they deserve.

These notes, written with fondness and genuine affection for the genre, *are* written "looking back," and thus carry the perspective and perhaps reluctant realism that has to come with time. As you read through Mr. Barbour's recapitulation of the serials, however, I suggest that you don't "look back," but instead try to see them with the eyes of youth, as we saw them in those less complicated and certainly more innocent days—when the serials were as guileless and perfect and free of flaw and blemish as we were ourselves!

WILLIAM K. EVERSON

VOLUME 1

DAYS OF THRILLS AND ADVENTURE

Pearl White, the most famous of all serial heroines, in a 1918 portrait.

1. The First Episode

WHILE THIS VOLUME deals almost entirely with the sound serial, I should, nevertheless, devote some space, however slight, to explaining the origin of the format in its embryonic stages.

Mention the silent serial and the name that automatically comes to mind is that of Pearl White. Somehow Pearl, with her singularly daring exploits in *The Perils of Pauline*, has managed to overshadow the stars of more than two hundred and fifty serials produced during the eighteen years between 1913 and 1930 to the point where most people are hard put to name *any* other star of that period.

However famous Pearl White may have become, she was not the first serial queen. That honor belongs to two long-since-forgotten screen heroines, Mary Fuller and Kathlyn Williams.

The serial format was one of the last experiments to be tried in those early days of film-making. William K. Everson, one of the most knowledgeable film historians in the United States, explained the birth of the new form superbly in the first issue of *Screen Facts Magazine*, published in 1963:

Curiously, the serials were late in reaching the screen. By 1913, when the first one was tried out, almost everything else had already been done. There were established, or rapidly-forming, filmic traditions in melodrama, Westerns and comedy. 1912 had seen the feature film (of five and six reels) accepted as normal; there had been experiments in wide-screen, color and even in sound. And like sound and wide-screen, the serials came in initially as a gimmick. They were tied in with newspaper serials, the idea being that the film would boost newspaper circulation, and the newspaper-readers would flock to see their linotype heroes and heroines come alive in celluloid. It was a good stunt and it worked.

The first tie-in between the screen and the printed page was *What Happened to Mary?*, released by the Edison Company in 1912. Unlike the serials we remember so fondly with their cliff-hanger endings, the first serial more closely resembled a television series, with each episode telling a completely resolved story within its relatively short running time. Of course the events that happened to Mary Fuller were pretty tame compared with what Pearl White had to go through only two years later, but it *was* a beginning. One episode climaxed with poor Mary escaping the villains by tying bedsheets together, climbing down from a window, and running to join the Salvation Army!

The pace picked up considerably a year later when Kathlyn Williams starred in an exciting jungle serial called *The Adventures of Kathlyn*, and 1914 brought *The Perils of Pauline*. The basic story running through the twenty self-contained episodes of this most famous of all silent serials was relatively simple. The villains, headed by Paul Panzer, were trying to kill Pauline in order to gain her inheritance. The adventures found the principals traveling all over the world trying everything from time-bombs to murder by snakebite to get rid of the plucky heroine, but Pauline survived every delicious intrigue and danger. Following on the heels of this tremendous film success, Pearl starred in *The Exploits of Elaine*, which ran for thirty-six episodes and found our heroine matching wits against the mysterious Clutching Hand, a power-mad demon bent on world domination. Pearl continued to thrill audiences in subsequent better-made, but less famous, serials like *The Lightning Raider*, *The Iron Claw*, and *The Black Secret*, among others.

But Pearl's cinema success was not to go unchallenged by other attractive screen lovelies who felt they could match, if not exceed, the exploits of the reigning serial queen. Helen Holmes gained a noteworthy reputation for her action-packed train sequences in films like *The Hazards of Helen* and *A Lass of the Lumberlands*, and Ruth Roland gave Pearl a run for her crown when she thrilled audiences in *Ruth of the Range*, *The Avenging Arrow*, *White Eagle*, and others. And there were many others: Eileen Sedgwick, Arline Pretty, Grace Cunard, Neva Gerber—girls who thrilled millions, but never gained the fame attached to Pearl White.

And the men? There were so many of them, such as Joe Bonomo, Ben Wilson, Crane Wilbur, Herbert Rawlinson, Eddie Polo, Jack Mulhall, Jack Mower, Charles Hutchinson, Elmo Lincoln, Francis Ford, William Duncan, and William Desmond.

And, on rare occasions, the serials would pair two performers whose screen magnetism had audiences begging for more joint appearances. Such was the case with pert Allene Ray and stunt man-actor Walter Miller, each of whom had made numerous serials on his own or teamed with others. Films like *Play Ball*, *The Black Book*, *Snowed In*, and *Sunken Silver* showed the couple at their exciting best.

Once in a great while the serials were able to attract celebrity stars. Harry Houdini appeared as the lead in *The Master Mystery* in 1919, but the film was not an overwhelming success, even though the master escape-artist did provide numerous thrilling trick escapes. Much more successful was the appearance of Jack Dempsey, the famous heavyweight boxing champ, in 1920's *Daredevil Jack*.

Because sound had not yet entered into serial production, the stress had to be on visual action; thus the real stars of the silent serials were those who could perform most of their own stunts. This accounted for the tremendous success of men like Walter Miller and Joe Bonomo in the twenties, as it had accounted for similar success of the ladies in the previous decade.

And if the great serial stars on the screen garnered all the fame and attention, no less credit should be given to the men behind the camera who helped them earn it, men like Frank Leon Smith, who turned out screenplay after screenplay (*Snowed In*, *The Green Archer*, etc.), incorporating new and thrilling escapades in each to amaze and entertain a serial-hungry public, and Spencer Gordon Bennet, the king of the serial directors, whose total output is deserving of a book in itself (he directed the final sound serial made in 1956). They are truly two remarkable men in serial history.

But all good things, as the saying goes, must come to an end, and so it was with the silent serial. By the end of the twenties interest in serials had waned considerably. Perhaps it was over-saturation. After all, nearly three hundred productions in eighteen years provided more than just a casual amount of movie excitement. Or, perhaps, audiences living in that wild era of the twenties found their screen heroes less heroic than the real-life heroes who made headlines daily as they waged war against real rather than "reel" gangsters. The serials still had an audience, even if it was limited, and the coming of sound really didn't increase its size by much. The Depression of the early thirties took care of that. It wasn't until the middle thirties that the serials once again found overflow crowds cramming their local theatres to see a new type of screen hero—Buster Crabbe as *Flash Gordon*. A new golden age of the serial had begun.

Pearl White and Buster Crabbe. The mention of their names conjured up visions of a Saturday-afternoon world that no longer exists, except in our fondest memories—that wonderful world of the serial.

right: Lafayette McKee and Kathlyn Williams in the first true serial, *The Adventures of Kathlyn* (Selig 1913). *below:* Pearl White is about to be rudely awakened by the Clutching Hand in *The Exploits of Elaine* (Pathé 1914).

right: Ruth Roland, another popular
favorite, gets the drop on a typical
Oriental menace in *The Adventures
of Ruth* (Pathé 1919). *below:* Pearl
White seems to have her hands full in
this scene from *Plunder* (Pathé 1923).

Helen Holmes' spectacular railroad heroics made her rank as a top serial queen in films like *The Hazards of Helen* (Kalem 1914).

above: Truman Van Dyke was the athletic hero of *The Jungle Goddess* (Export-Import 1922). *left:* Walter Miller and Ethlyne Clair are about to unmask the mysterious Wolf-Devil in *Queen of the Northwoods* (Pathé 1929).

above: That's Lionel Barrymore glowering at Pearl White while another mystery man listens in *The Romance of Elaine* (Pathé 1915).

below: Howard Estabrook is trapped by a secret society in *The Mysteries of Myra* (Pathé-International 1916).

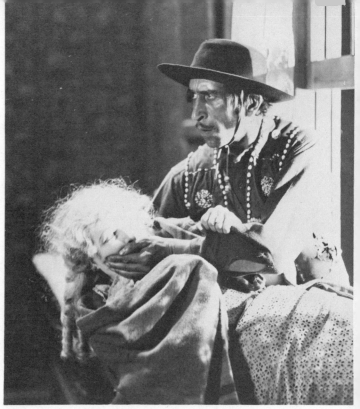

above: Frank Lackteen, one of the most famous of all serial villains, obviously has plans for Allene Ray in *Hawk of the Hills* (Pathé 1927). *left:* Gladys McConnell gets an unhelping hand in *The Tiger's Shadow* (Pathé 1928).
below: The most famous serial team of the twenties was **Allene Ray and Walter Miller**, here trying to solve the mystery of *The Black Book* (Pathé 1929).

Heavyweight champion of the world Jack Dempsey in his serial appearance as *Daredevil Jack* (Pathé 1920).

Onslow Stevens seems at a distinct disadvantage in *The Vanishing Shadow*
(Universal 1934).

2. The Early-Talkie and Independent Serials

ALTHOUGH SEVERAL INDEPENDENT PRODUCERS tried to invade the serial territory dominated by Mascot and Universal in the early and mid-thirties, their efforts, on the whole, were most unsatisfactory. They simply did not have the financial resources to do an adequate job, and the cheapness of their production was only too evident to the audiences who had come to expect much more in their Saturday cinema adventures.

RKO's solo entry in the field was *The Last Frontier,* an utterly pedestrian Western in which Lon Chaney, Jr., portrayed a pseudo-Zorro avenging victimized frontiersmen. Weiss Productions turned out two mildly entertaining thrillers, *The Clutching Hand* and *The Broken Coin.* The former had silent leading man Jack Mulhall playing Craig Kennedy, a famous fictional detective, on the trail of a ruthless band of kidnappers headed by the Clutching Hand who were trying to acquire a secret formula for making synthetic gold; the latter featured Ralph Graves and Dave O'Brien, who were searching for secret papers believed to contain information that could be of value in trapping smugglers. Many background sets utilized in *The Clutching Hand* were re-used in *The Broken Coin.* Another long and tedious affair was the Weiss production of *Custer's Last Stand,* which, the advertising proudly proclaimed, was actually "based on historical events leading up to Custer's Last Fight."

Rex Lease led an enormous cast through the fifteen seemingly endless episodes.

One of the more interesting independents was the Edgar Rice Burroughs-produced *The New Adventures of Tarzan.* Starring Herman Brix (later known as Bruce Bennett) as the famous ape man, the film was photographed on location in the jungles of Guatemala. The story found Tarzan joining an expedition trying to locate the fabulous Green Goddess, a priceless Mayan relic containing a fortune in rare gems. Brix was an ideal choice to play the strenuous role. Buster Crabbe had been less successful in portraying the same character in *Tarzan, the Fearless* two years earlier in 1933. Released through Principal Pictures, this adventure of the legendary jungle lord found him searching for co-star Jacqueline Wells' father, who was studying ancient tribes and had been captured by the mysterious people of Zar, God of the Emerald Fingers, headed by Mischa Auer playing an evil high priest. *The New Adventures of Tarzan* was edited into two feature versions which frequently played double-feature houses in the forties and early fifties, and a feature version of *Tarzan, the Fearless* is included in the current television package of Tarzan films.

Another favorite independent serial was *Return of Chandu,* also re-edited and released in two feature versions by Principal Pictures. With

11

Bela Lugosi in the title role, the chapter play was a delight on every count as the master magician fought against a secret cult of idol worshipers.

While the independents fought a valiant fight to attract box-office attention, Universal was turning out exciting action fare on its own. Richard Talmadge, that stunt ace of the twenties and thirties, finally got his own starring serial, *Pirate Treasure*, and filled it full of his own personal brand of screen heroics. Onslow Stevens managed to oppose a really antagonistic robot and persevere in *The Vanishing Shadow;* Frank Albertson dared a thousand thrills aboard *The Lost Special;* Evalyn Knapp tried to bring back *The Perils of Pauline* with dismal results; Tim McCoy fought Indians in the first talking serial, *The Indians Are Coming*, and arsonists in *Heroes of the Flames;* and Tom Tyler took turns hunting in the jungle in *Jungle Mystery*, riding in the North Country in *Clancy of the Mounted*, and flying through the air in *Phantom of the Air*. More than a dozen other heroes helped the years pass quickly until the most famous hero of them all emerged from the studio—*Flash Gordon!*

Not to be outdone by Universal, Mascot Pictures managed to turn out a number of fine serials starring some of the most popular screen heroes of the day, and some who rose to spectacular fame in later years.

John Wayne starred in three popular serials produced by the company. *Shadow of the Eagle* found him battling a mystery man known only as the Eagle who was out to wreak vengeance on several men he suspected of cheating him. When the script called for a plane to sky-write a message from the Eagle the miniature used was so toylike that it was hard to watch the sequence without breaking up with laughter. In *Hurricane Express*, big John was battling the mysterious Wrecker who was doing his best to wreck everything in sight, including John. The final film in the trilogy, *The Three Musketeers*, had him helping Jack Mulhall, Raymond Hatton, and Francis X. Bushman, Jr., uncover the mysterious El Shaitan.

Mystery Squadron found cowboy star Bob Steele temporarily hanging up his guns and spurs long enough to uncover the mysterious Black Ace in an exciting aerial thriller, and

Burn 'Em Up Barnes had Jack Mulhall and Frankie Darro fighting a gang of racketeers bent on taking over their transportation business.

One of the really superb films in the series was Mascot's 1935 *The Fighting Marines*, featuring Grant Withers and Adrian Morris (brother of Chester Morris). The thrilling plot had the two men battling a mysterious enemy known only as the Tiger Shark. The Shark operated from a remote island and traveled by means of a huge flying "wing," later re-used by Republic in *Dick Tracy* when Mascot merged into the new Republic Pictures Corporation.

Other popular Mascot favorites were *Phantom Empire*, which brought stardom to its singing cowboy star, Gene Autry; *The Last of the Mohicans*, with Harry Carey in a very loosely based version of the James Fenimore Cooper story; *The Whispering Shadow*, with Bela Lugosi slinking around in his best Dracula-like fashion, and which had a thrilling climax to its first chapter featuring a miniature autogiro; *Mystery Mountain*, with cowboy star Ken Maynard taking twelve episodes to discover the Rattler when we knew the truth in chapter one; *The Miracle Rider*, featuring Tom Mix in his only starring serial, and his final film; *The Galloping Ghost*, with football hero Red Grange chasing bad men instead of pigskin; *Fighting with Kit Carson*, featuring Johnny Mack Brown in the first of his five starring Western serials; and the Rin-Tin-Tin, Jr., epics, *The Wolf Dog, Adventures of Rex and Rinty, Lightning Warrior* (ably assisted by future star George Brent), and *The Lone Defender*.

If there was a common flaw in most of these early serials, it was a lack of pacing. They all seemed to drag on interminably, and even chase sequences, which should have been thrilling, were stretched beyond normal patience. Adding to the problem was an almost complete absence of background music. Even the dullest possible serial can be tolerated if an accompanying musical score is sufficiently interesting, but the only music in these early vehicles was played behind the opening credits. But, for all their faults, a re-viewing of many of them still finds us enjoying them for what they were.

And the golden age of the serial was just about to begin!

above: Bela Lugosi seems to be getting the upper hand against Herman Brix (later Bruce Bennett) in *Shadow of Chinatown* (Victory 1936). *below:* Herbert Rawlinson as Blake helps assistant, Ralph Byrd, in *Blake of Scotland Yard* (Victory 1937).

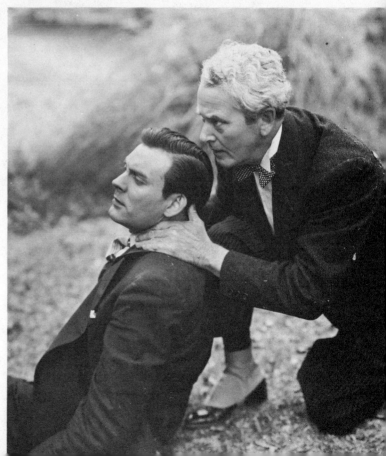

left: Grant Withers and Adrian Morris were excellent in *The Fighting Marines* (Mascot 1935). This serial had all the superb ingredients that became Republic's trademark when Mascot merged into the new Republic Pictures Corp. *below:* Bela Lugosi is up to something mysterious, as usual, in *The Whispering Shadow* (Mascot 1933).

above: George Brent was one of the few major stars who appeared in early serials. That's Rin-Tin-Tin watching Bob Kortman cover Brent in *Lightning Warrior* (Mascot 1931). *left:* Frankie Darro is about to take care of Bob Kortman who was about to take care of Jack Mulhall in *Burn 'Em Up Barnes* (Mascot 1934).

right: Lucile Browne and James Flavin (Mr. and Mrs. in real life) were the stars of *Airmail Mystery* (Universal 1932). *below:* Tom Tyler tries to pry the gun loose from the hand of LeRoy Mason in *Phantom of the Air* (Universal 1933). *bottom:* When two top stunt men go at it serial fans are really getting their money's worth. Yakima Canutt and Dave O'Brien went at it in *The Black Coin* (Weiss-Mintz 1936).

above: Harold "Red" Grange, one of the great football heroes of all time, played himself in the title role of *The Galloping Ghost* (Mascot 1931), his famous nickname. In this scene Grange is about to surprise veteran serial star-stunt man, Walter Miller. *left:* It was a youthful John Wayne who played the flying hero in *The Three Musketeers* (Mascot 1933). *below:* John Wayne has his hands full battling Al Ferguson, Charles King, and Glenn Strange in *Hurricane Express* (Mascot 1932).

A montage of favorite Republic serial heroes and villains drawn by noted artist Al Kilgore. The bell tower in the upper left-hand corner was Republic's trademark in the thirties and early forties before they switched to an eagle.

3. Republic Enters the Scene

WHEN REPUBLIC PICTURES CORPORATION started producing serials in 1936, few people expected anything of real merit to emerge from "that little studio out in the valley." Quite to everyone's surprise, after only a few short years they had perfected their screen action formats to a degree that was not to be matched by any other existing studio, major or minor. For Republic it was simply a matter of combining all the ingredients necessary to provide the best action recipe obtainable. Republic had unjustly earned the denigrating appellation of "Repulsive Pictures," and it was felt by most of Hollywood that working for "that" studio was the final step down the ladder to obscurity and unemployment. Like most underdogs, the Republic production staff refused to believe the charges leveled at them and, combining all their respective skills, they banded together to produce the finest product possible with the means available to them. That they succeeded so magnificently is a fitting tribute to all of them.

Much of the studio's serial success must be directly attributed to three superb action directors, William Witney, John English, and Spencer Gordon Bennet. Each of these men was able to portray on the screen action sequences of unparalleled excellence not readily envisioned in what appeared to be routine scripting. They instinctively knew how to "keep things moving,"

something Columbia and Universal were never able to do. Action and more action! That was what a serial needed, and that is what they contributed to it.

Witney and English co-directed seventeen consecutive masterpieces of serial entertainment that form what most of us nostalgically like to refer to as the golden age of serials. Starting in 1937 with *Zorro Rides Again*, the duo turned out, in succession, *The Lone Ranger, Fighting Devil Dogs, Dick Tracy Returns, Hawk of the Wilderness, The Lone Ranger Rides Again, Daredevils of the Red Circle, Dick Tracy's G-Men, Zorro's Fighting Legion, Drums of Fu Manchu, Adventures of Red Ryder, King of the Royal Mounted, Mysterious Dr. Satan, The Adventures of Captain Marvel, Jungle Girl, King of the Texas Rangers*, and finally, in 1941, *Dick Tracy vs. Crime, Inc.* Each serial, without exception, was crammed with action and visually excellent. The team split up in 1942, with English going into B-Western production at the studio, something Witney was similarly to do shortly thereafter. However, Witney was able on his own to continue to turn out exciting work like *Spy Smasher, Perils of Nyoka, King of the Mounties, G-Men vs. The Black Dragon*, and, after a three-year absence, *The Crimson Ghost*. English's only efforts during this period were *Daredevils of the West* in 1943, one of the most action-packed Western serials ever made, and, the following year, *Captain America,* the latter co-directed with Elmer Clifton.

With Spencer Gordon Bennet's arrival on the serial set came that great period of set destruction that is so closely identified with Republic films. While earlier fight choreography was inventive, it never equalled the heights obtained by Bennet. Working closely with his team of ace stunt men, usually headed by Tom Steele, with Dale Van Sickel, Eddie Parker, Duke Green, Ken Terrell, and Fred Graham joining in, Bennet literally reduced huge, ornately decorated, and liberally prop-laden sets to rubble in fight after fight, chapter after chapter. As he fondly recalls, "the bills for balsa wood were enormous." His very first serial for the studio, *Secret Service in Darkest Africa,* made in 1943, has to contain more fight sequences than any other serial ever made. Almost every one of the film's fifteen episodes contains three slugfests. To a somewhat lesser degree, but not *that* much less, his other Republic efforts were also filled with excitement enough to raise the pulse of even the most reserved serial viewer: *The Masked Marvel, The Tiger Woman, Haunted Harbor, Zorro's Black Whip, Manhunt of Mystery Island, Federal Operator 99, The Purple Monster Strikes, The Phantom Rider, King of the Forest Rangers, Daughter of Don Q, Son of Zorro,* and lastly, in 1947, *The Black Widow.* Although he received solo credit on only the first two serials (the remainder had Wallace Grissel, Yakima Canutt, and Fred Brannon alternately sharing the billing), all thirteen serials bore his unique stamp of quality. Bennet then joined Columbia Pictures, and one has only to view one of his epics there to determine how valuable Republic production was in creating top-notch screen fare.

A later chapter in this book will deal in detail with the superb stunt men who formed the Republic action team so necessary in creating the thousands of thrills which appear in the studio's sixty-six serial productions. Of major importance also was the studio's special-effects department, headed by Howard Lydecker, later assisted by his brother, Theodore. The hundreds of exploding cars, buildings, barns, planes, dams, and what-have-you turned out by this outstanding production unit were an integral factor in giving Republic its distinctive superiority in the serial field. Unlike Universal and Columbia with their cheaply done table-top miniatures, the Lydeckers used large-scale, meticulously detailed models and photographed them outside against natural skies. They were so lifelike that most of us really believed they were the actual full-size items. One has only to view the end of chapter one of *King of the Texas Rangers,* in which an entire miniature oil field goes up in flame, with huge, billowing balls of fire rising within the derrick frames, or the end of chapter one of *The Masked Marvel,* in which a blazing miniature truck blows up igniting a gas-filled model of a gigantic fuel storage tank, which in turn blows up, to realize the quality of work the Lydeckers turned out.

To single out one factor as being more important than any other is, under most circumstances, unfair when so many elements combine successfully to form a superior product. True, the fights, direction, and special effects *were* important, but so was the set decoration, editing, lighting, and photography, the latter accomplished primarily by William Nobles, Reggie Lanning and Bud Thackery during the golden age. And important also, to a greater degree than most people would realize, was the music. Republic was the only studio to utilize elaborately written original scores. William Lava's superb compositions for *Zorro's Fighting Legion, Dick Tracy's G-Men,* and *Daredevils of the Red Circle,* among others, are outstanding examples of film music that can strengthen the intrinsic values of the material it accompanies. Mort Glickman took over the music reins when Lava left to work at RKO and Warner Brothers, and quickly earned the title "King of the Chase Writers" with his superb scores for *Mysterious Dr. Satan, Spy Smasher, The Masked Marvel, Captain America,* and others. The music of both men was so good that Republic re-used the scores numerous times in subsequent serials, B-films, and Westerns. Lava referred recently to the writing of those early scores as turning out "music by the yard." It is an apt phrase, for the men were paid surprisingly little money for their work and ground it out at an amazing pace, often writing pieces while the recording sessions were in progress. It is a tribute to both men that, under these trying conditions, both were able to turn out such consistently outstanding material.

When the quality of Republic serials declined in the years after World War II, it was for economic reasons rather than professional deterioration of the producing staff. Herbert Yates knew the market for serials was declining, and he decided to spend as little as possible on their production, so that at the end, with *King of the Carnival* in 1955, there was hardly any comparison between the final efforts of the company and the greatness of the studio's serials of the thirties and early forties. It was a sad sight to witness.

Yet Republic's track record for success over the twenty-year period was meritorious enough to forget the few failures. From *Darkest Africa* in 1936 through sixty-five subsequent serial productions one can be enormously thankful for countless, and unforgettable, days of thrills and adventure.

A winged Bat Man attacks Clyde Beatty in the premier Republic serial, *Darkest Africa* (Republic 1936). Even in their first serial effort, some of the wonderful Howard Lydecker effects were brilliantly used and served as a generous preview of the greatness that was to emerge from the studio.

above: The Painted Stallion (Republic 1937) was a typical example of Republic's excellence in outdoor action films. The cast included (*left to right*) Ray Corrigan, Hoot Gibson (in a much smaller role than he deserved), Sammy McKim and Hal Taliaferro. *below:* Ray Mala, *left,* was of limited help to Herman Brix (later Bruce Bennett), who portrayed Kioga in the highly successful *Hawk of the Wilderness* (Republic 1938). Adding to the film's excitement was an exciting musical score by William Lava. *opposite page:* Ralph Byrd, in his only non-Dick Tracy role at Republic, is about to take a dangerous plunge with the assistance of Richard Alexander in *S.O.S. Coast Guard* (Republic 1937).

above: Herman Brix and Lee Powell were the *Fighting Devil Dogs* (Republic 1938) who battled one of the most famous of all serial villains, the Lightning. Although many regard it as a favorite, much of the serial is done in a rather routine fashion, but the music and special effects help to counteract the excessive use of stock footage. It certainly has to rank as one of the top-ten serials of all time. *below:* Another of Republic's all-time serial hits was *Daredevils of the Red Circle* (Republic 1939). The three leads were perfectly cast as circus performers who were on the trail of the escaped convict 39013 (Charles Middleton) as he attempted to sabotage various properties of the man he held responsible for his being sent to prison. The ending of chapter one is one of the greatest serial thrills yet seen on the screen, with Charles Quigley fleeing through a rapidly flooding tunnel on a motorcycle. In the scene below, David Sharpe, Herman Brix, and Charles Quigley find a clue which leads them to a daredevil climax at an oil refinery.

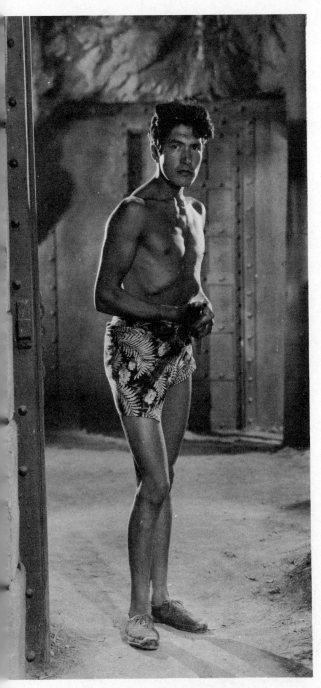

above: With daredevil stunt ace David Sharpe doing the action scenes for Robert Wilcox (as the Copperhead), *Mysterious Dr. Satan* (Republic 1940) was a serial-goer's delight. In this scene the Copperhead releases Ella Neal with the aid of William Newell from a death trap set by Dr. Satan (Eduardo Ciannelli).

above: Ray Mala, whose acting was horribly inept, was nevertheless chosen for the lead in *Robinson Crusoe of Clipper Island* (Republic 1936). The serial holds interest because of the superb photography, music and special effects, but is far from memorable. *right: Drums of Fu Manchu* (Republic 1940) was more of a plot serial than an action serial, and as such it was tremendously successful. Henry Brandon was perfectly cast as the Oriental villain and William Royle was his competent adversary, Sir Nayland Smith. It was one of the few serials in which the chief villain was neither caught nor killed. It is quite possible that a sequel was planned, but it never materialized.

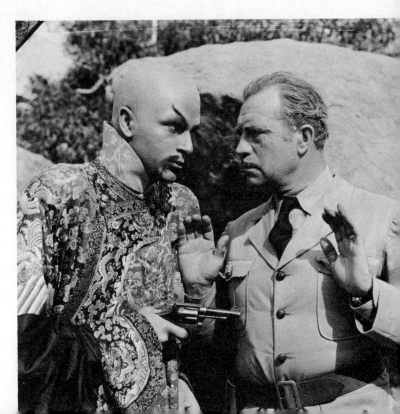

Tom Tyler was a perfect choice to portray the superhuman cartoon favorite in *The Adventures of Captain Marvel* (Republic 1941).

4. Comic Strips on the Screen

THE TREMENDOUS GROWTH in popularity of the newspaper adventure comic strip in the mid-thirties was bound to inspire the serial-producing film companies to bring America's new fictional heroes to the screen. Universal Pictures began the cycle with the popular airplane daredevil Tailspin Tommy, in two thrilling sky adventures in 1934's *Tailspin Tommy* and 1935's *Tailspin Tommy in the Great Air Mystery*. Using visually exciting stock shots from earlier Universal flying epics plus thrilling new footage, serial fans were delighted to see a favorite pencil-and-ink hero brought to vivid life. In 1936 Universal entered into an arrangement with King Features and obtained motion picture rights to an impressive list of Sunday newspaper favorites. Heading the list was Flash Gordon, who was brought to life by Buster Crabbe in three outstanding attractions, *Flash Gordon* (1936), *Flash Gordon's Trip to Mars* (1938), and *Flash Gordon Conquers the Universe* (1940). Viewed today, the three serials seem routine, rather cheaply produced and poorly acted, but to audiences who saw them in their original releases they were pure imaginative delight. Other popular action heroes brought "to life" by Universal included: *Ace Drummond*, another popular flying strip originally created by Captain Eddie Rickenbacker and starring John

King; *Jungle Jim*, with Grant Withers portraying Alex Raymond's creation; *Radio Patrol*, again with Withers playing the lead, this time as Pat O'Hara as he tried to solve a mystery surrounding an invention of "flexible steel"; *Tim Tyler's Luck*, with young Frankie Thomas chasing through the jungle in search of the elephants' graveyard, and being thwarted by the notorious Spider Webb; *Red Barry*, starring Buster Crabbe, on temporary leave from the planet Mongo, playing a detective investigating a Chinatown mystery; *Buck Rogers*, also with Crabbe in the title role, but decidedly cheaper in production values and excitement; *Don Winslow of the Navy* and *Don Winslow of the Coast Guard*, two wartime entries, both inexpensively mounted and using excessive quantities of newsreel stock footage. Don Terry as Winslow was an effective hero, however. Universal also brought Alex Raymond's agent-hero to the screen in two versions: the 1937 *Secret Agent X-9* had Scott Kolk battling conventional villains, while the 1945 *Secret Agent X-9*, portrayed by Lloyd Bridges, opposed the wartime Nazi menace. One of Universal's better film adaptations was the picturization of Zack Mosley's popular flying hero in *The Adventures of Smilin' Jack*, with young Tom Brown giving an excellent performance. In all, Universal adapted sixteen comic-strip heroes for screen serial treatment.

Running a close second, with fifteen adaptations, was Columbia Pictures. They began in 1939 with Warren Hull's imaginative portrayal of the famous King Features' top-hatted hero, *Mandrake the Magician*. The following year a most unsatisfactory version of *Terry and the Pirates* was made by the studio with William Tracy playing Terry and Granville Owens playing Pat Ryan. Directed by James Horne, as were so many of these early Columbia efforts, the result was childish and ineffective. Horne was tremendous at directing two-reel comedies, but he was completely out of his element in bringing thrills to the serial devotee. *The Batman* made his first appearance on the screen in 1943, portrayed by Lewis Wilson in the most ill-fitting costume one could imagine. Douglas Croft as Robin was equally unappealing. That same year, however, Tom Tyler brought a visual acceptance of his characterization of *The Phantom*. And the ladies finally got a chance to see one of their own get screen-time when *Brenda Starr, Reporter*, played by one of the darlings of the B-film crowd, Joan Woodbury, helped rid the big town of criminal elements. Ralph Byrd, trying once again to shed his Dick Tracy image, took to the saddle wearing a mask as *The Vigilante*, a popular character appearing in *Action Comics*. Kane Richmond, one of the more capable serial performers, tried to bring some kind of realism to the characterization of *Brick Bradford*, but the script defeated him, as it had defeated so many others at Columbia. When *Superman* finally made it to the serial screen in 1948, it was one of the few serials to play A theatres rather than the standard "scratch" houses. The showcasing really wasn't justified: Kirk Alyn was not effective in the title role, and the flying sequences, instead of being imaginably staged with miniatures, were simply cartoon dots jumping ludicrously around. The sequel two years later, *Atom Man vs. Superman*, was similarly ineffective. The remaining strips brought little distinction to the studio. *Tex Granger* was a weak Western starring Robert Kellard; *Congo Bill*, with Don McGuire, should have disappeared in one of its own quicksand bogs; *Bruce Gentry*, with Tom Neal, did have a little action, thanks to Tom Steele and Dale Van Sickel, who did the action work, but the serial provided more laughs than excitement; *Batman and Robin*, this time with Robert Lowery and Johnny Duncan in the roles of the Dynamic Duo, was a sorry se-

quel to the 1943 version; *Blackhawk* gave Kirk Alyn more to work with and wasn't half bad, and Buster Crabbe finished his serial career as the Mighty Thunda, who appeared to be considerably less than mighty in this stock-filled, back-lot jungle travesty based on the comic-strip hero, *King of the Congo*. In reviewing the total output, one would be hard put to consider more than three or four Columbia serials even adequate. However, the kids loved them all! They were fun, and, their poor quality notwithstanding, they brought the audiences back week after week to watch every one of them.

Republic only brought ten comic strips to life on the theatre screen, but their track record for success was almost one hundred percent. Dick Tracy was active in four separate thrill-packed adventures. *Dick Tracy*, the first of the four, was the slowest-moving of the group but was fascinating because of the superb mystery man, the Spider. *Dick Tracy Returns*, *Dick Tracy's G-Men*, and *Dick Tracy vs. Crime, Inc.* were all creative masterpieces, filled with location photography and imaginative action sequences. *Adventures of Red Ryder* brought screen stardom to its lead, Don "Red" Barry. Barry recently admitted that he hated doing the role because he felt that his physical appearance was not adequate to portray the tall, lanky red-haired cowboy on the screen. He was grateful, however, for the success it brought him, and the film was extremely successful. *King of the Royal Mounted* and *King of the Mounties* were both based on a character created by Zane Grey, which later found a large following on the comic pages across the country. Allan Lane was a perfect choice to play the leading role in both films, and Republic know-how made both films action-packed hits. Republic had tried to acquire screen rights to Superman but, when the copyright holders demanded too much control over the script, settled on the Fawcett Publications hero, Captain Marvel, in *The Adventures of Captain Marvel*. With Tom Tyler in the leading role, and David Sharpe providing all the stunt thrills, this serial was second only to Universal's *Flash Gordon* in popularity. Fawcett also gave Republic *Spy Smasher*, its second most popular character, and Kane Richmond brought more than an average amount of talent to the screen characterization of the spy-chasing hero. *Captain America* was Republic's final entry in the comic-strip sweepstakes, and it was superb in all aspects of production. Dick Purcell was ideal in the role and would have been an excellent choice to star in subsequent roles had he not died shortly after completing this film.

All three studios took liberties in the scripting of their films based on comic strips. The first *Flash Gordon* serial was the only one to even remotely follow the actual scripts used in the newspaper adventures. *Captain America* lost his regular partner Bucky, *Spy Smasher* suddenly acquired a twin brother, and *Dick Tracy* lost Pat Patton, Junior, and Tess Trueheart as that series progressed. But no one really cared. Each serial was judged on its own merits, and even though some had *no* merit, they were enjoyable film fare.

above: Continuing in the comic-strip vein, Tom Tyler also gave a strikingly acceptable image as *The Phantom* (Columbia 1943). *left:* Don McGuire, who went on to become a television director, was *Congo Bill* (Columbia 1948).

above: Grant Withers barely escapes being crushed to death in an elaborate trap in his role as Pat O'Hara of the *Radio Patrol* (Universal 1937). *right: Captain America* (Republic 1944) found Dick Purcell leaving behind his shield and companion, Bucky, as he battled the evil Scarab. *below:* Al Ferguson (*left*) and Charles "Slim" Whitaker get the drop on Maurice Murphy as *Tailspin Tommy* (Universal 1934) and Grant Withers.

Donald Barry became "Red" Barry after he starred in *Adventures of Red Ryder* (Republic 1940).

Frankie Thomas as Tim and Frances Robinson try to escape from someone, or something, in *Tim Tyler's Luck* (Universal 1937).

left: John King was *Ace Drummond* (Universal 1936), a flying ace created for the newspaper strip by Captain Eddie Rickenbacker. *below, left:* Kane Richmond played a dual role in *Spy Smasher* (Republic 1942). Frank Corsaro was his Free French assistant. *below, right: Mandrake the Magician* (Columbia 1939), based on the popular King Features strip, had Warren Hull in the title role matching wits with the mysterious Wasp.

above: Irving Pichel and Walter Miller (*far left and right*) apparently have Ralph Byrd as Dick Tracy and his partner, Ted Pearson, finally trapped in *Dick Tracy's G-Men* (Republic 1939). *left:* Tom Brown had to contend with many perils like this in *Adventures of Smilin' Jack* (Universal 1943).

Kirk Alyn rescues Noel Neill as Lois Lane with a minor show of strength in
Superman (Columbia 1948).

above: Scott Kolk was Alex Raymond's famous *Secret Agent X-9* (Universal 1937), ably assisted by the lovely Jean Rogers. *right:* Buster Crabbe, among other comic favorites, was also *Red Barry* (Universal 1938). *below:* Buster Crabbe as Flash protects Jean Rogers from the evil spells cast by Beatrice Roberts in *Flash Gordon's Trip to Mars* (Universal 1938).

above: Robert Lowery as the Caped Crusader and John Duncan as Robin point out some facts to Lyle Talbot in *Batman and Robin* (Columbia 1949). *below:* Granville Owens as Pat Ryan lends a helping hand to William Tracy as Terry Lee in *Terry and the Pirates* (Columbia 1940).

This is how Zorro made his first serial entrance in chapter one of *Zorro Rides Again* (Republic 1937). John Carroll played the popular masked hero of early California.

5. The Descendants of Zorro

Of all the masked heroes who graced the serial screen, none was more durable than that masked avenger of the Old West, Zorro. The character was originally created by Johnston McCulley for his story, *The Curse of Capistrano*, which appeared in installments in 1919 in the pulp magazine *All-Story*. The story was a simple tale of a masked man who went about early California avenging the wrongs committed upon the peons by an unscrupulous governor. The hero's identity was not revealed until the conclusion, but Don Diego Vega was the only logical choice from nearly the beginning.

The story was first brought to the screen in 1920 as *The Mark of Zorro*, starring the athletic Douglas Fairbanks, Sr., and was full of action and thrills in the well-known Fairbanks tradition. In 1925 *Don Q, Son of Zorro* had Fairbanks playing Cesar de Vega, the son of the original Zorro. Although in essence a sequel, it was not based on McCulley's work, but on a story written by K. and Hesketh Prichard called *Don Q's Love Story* and adapted by scriptwriters Jack Cunningham and Lotta Woods. In 1937 Republic brought the character to the screen for the first time in a sound film called *The Bold Caballero*, starring the likable Robert Livingston as an "original" masked Zorro in the studio's first film photographed in "Natural Color."

Finally, in 1937 Republic decided to feature the famous character in one of their serial adventures. They chose a relative newcomer named John Carroll to play the role of James Vega, who was the great-grandson of the original Don Diego Vega. He was excellent in the role, with the possible exception of the few times he was required to burst into song. A singing "masked avenger" was too much! The exciting story found villains Noah Beery, Sr., and Richard Alexander out to destroy the California–Yucatan Railroad. Particularly effective were scenes actually photographed at a dam site and other superior outdoor locations. Handling the stunt chores for Carroll was veteran daredevil Yakima Canutt, who provided many thrills and handled the bullwhip in superlative fashion. Released under the title *Zorro Rides Again*, the serial was also edited into a feature version under the same title, and was re-released in the late fifties to cash in on the interest in the character generated by Walt Disney with his television series.

As fine as *Zorro Rides Again* was, *Zorro's Fighting Legion*, released two years later, was even better. Reed Hadley (whose voice was so outstanding that Twentieth Century-Fox was later to use him as the narrator for such quality films as *Guadalcanal Diary* and *The House on 92nd Street*) was in superior form portraying alternately the foppish Diego and Zorro, the dashing masked rider who appeared whenever danger threatened. One of the primary reasons for the serial's success was the incorporation into the screenplay of one of the better mystery villains, Don Del Oro. This reincarnation of a Yaqui god was, in reality, one of the four members of a Council. Contrary to good ethical conduct, this metal-helmeted devil was inciting the Indians to revolt, and it took all his courage, as well as twelve full episodes, for Zorro to unmask the villain, who was ultimately destroyed in a fiery pit by the very Indians he had duped. Contributing to the overall effect of the film was a magnificent score largely composed by William Lava.

Five years went by before Zorro was again to appear, or rather *seem* to appear, in another Republic serial. In *Zorro's Black Whip* there was never any mention of Zorro in the entire serial. Linda Stirling played a character called the Whip and certainly dressed in an outfit resembling the famed avenger's, but no direct tie-up was ever made. Perhaps the writers felt that the name should never be used for the female of the species. Johnston McCulley was given a credit line stating that he created the Zorro character, but that was all there was to it. The story itself was a rather routine Western tale with scheming Francis MacDonald out to control the entire territory and being thwarted at every turn by luscious Linda and George J. Lewis, the latter seen in a welcome change of pace from his usual villainous roles.

In *Son of Zorro,* made in 1947, the mystery man, called the Chief, was out to grab some territory for himself and misused various public offices to further his schemes. Riding to the aid of the town after returning from the Civil War was George Turner (a likable performer whose career was surprisingly brief). Recalling that one of his ancestors had dressed as Zorro many years before to right wrongs, he decides to bring the masked man back once again to help solve the current situation. Peggy Stewart was the damsel in distress, and the mystery man turned out to be—well, either Edmund Cobb, Ken Terrell, Tom London or Edward Cassidy.

The final entry in the Zorro series was *Ghost of Zorro,* released in 1949. Chosen for the lead this time was Clayton Moore, who was just beginning his long-running role as television's Lone Ranger. Moore was a popular leading man at Republic and was particularly effective in Westerns. As Zorro, he cut a striking figure in the

saddle in this tale of a community trying to build a telegraph line and being besieged by Eugene Roth's savage henchmen, including Roy Barcroft. A fair amount of stock footage from earlier Zorro films was used and, in chapter one, a complete sequence was used from the studio's 1943 success, *Daredevils of the West.* For some strange reason, they dubbed in a "mystery voice" for Moore, something they had not bothered to do in any of the other films in the series. At the same time *Zorro Rides Again* was released in feature form in the fifties, *Ghost of Zorro* was also edited and released as a companion film to fill neighborhood theatre double bills.

Although the series had been officially concluded with *Ghost of Zorro,* Republic did release two serials which utilized a masked hero who looked exactly like Zorro, and contained a considerable amount of stock footage from the earlier Zorro serials. *Don Daredevil Rides Again* in 1951 had Ken Curtis, now of television's *Gunsmoke* fame, playing a routine Western hero wearing a Zorro costume in order to match old and new footage. The same was done by Richard Simmons in 1954's *Man with the Steel Whip.* It was a sad finish for the dashing avenger.

Through the years there were a great many pseudo-Zorros who rode the Western range dealing out swift justice. Robert Livingston may have been called the Eagle in *The Vigilantes Are Coming,* but he certainly looked like Zorro. And the Lone Ranger might very easily be termed an Americanized version of the avenging rider.

When Disney brought Zorro to the home audience he reduced the action elements and increased the comedy. He did give the character a more dashing costume, with a silken black cape flowing in the breeze as Zorro rode through the night. None of the Republic Zorros had worn a cloak. One of the strange coincidences that occasionally occur in film-making happened when William Lava, who almost twenty years before had written the background music for *Zorro's Fighting Legion,* was signed to compose the music for the new television series. Alas, if only they could have gotten Reed Hadley to play the role of Zorro in the series instead of Guy Williams.

All in all, though, the masked avenger did all right for himself on the screen.

Don Del Oro, the mysterious masked villain, orders the death of Paul Marian and Zorro (Reed Hadley) in *Zorro's Fighting Legion* (Republic 1939). Holding the gun on Zorro in the center of the picture is Jim Pierce, one of the many stars who played Tarzan on the screen.

above: Zorro's primary opponent in *Zorro Rides Again* (Republic 1937) was veteran badman Richard Alexander. That's John Carroll under the mask. *left:* Reed Hadley's was most likely the best of all the serial Zorro characterizations. His voice, used frequently for narration in Twentieth Century-Fox semidocumentary films, lent the proper authority to the masked hero and was subtly used to portray the foppish alter ego, Diego Vegas. *Zorro's Fighting Legion* (Republic 1939) also had a superb musical score by William Lava to add to the film's overall success.

above: George Turner was a satisfactory Zorro, assisted here by
lovely Peggy Stewart in *Son of Zorro* (Republic 1947).
right: The complete facial covering used by George Turner in
Son of Zorro (Republic 1947) made it easy to substitute stunt
man Tom Steele for all the action sequences. *below:* Linda
Stirling played the "Whip" in *Zorro's Black Whip* (Republic
1944), but no mention of Zorro was ever made in the film.
George Lewis played the principal male hero, a change from
his usual villainous roles.

Ken Curtis wore the Zorro costume for stock-footage purposes, but was called Don Daredevil in *Don Daredevil Rides Again* (Republic 1951).

above: in *Ghost of Zorro* (Republic 1949), Clayton Moore, under the mask, rescues Pamela Blake and uncovers the villainy of Roy Barcroft and Eugene Roth. *left:* Richard Simmons was also "matched up" for stock in *Man with the Steel Whip* (Republic 1954).

Buster Crabbe had the help of young Jackie Moran in combating the evil
Killer Kane in the twenty-fifth century in *Buck Rogers* (Universal 1939).

6. Science Fiction

IN THE PRESENT WORLD where atomic bombs and men traveling to the moon are commonplace, it is hard to imagine that young viewers only thirty-five years ago were going into ecstasy over some toy rocketships and balloon-like artificial planets portrayed on a motion picture screen. However, such was the case when Universal presented Buster Crabbe in 1936 as *Flash Gordon*. Here truly was adventure on a grand scale, previously pictured only on the Sunday comic pages or in the novels of such creative writers as Jules Verne. Here were no ordinary G-men cracking down on racketeers or marshals rounding up outlaws; instead, there was Ming the Merciless, a dweller of the planet Mongo, out to destroy the world, and only one man, Flash Gordon, capable of battling the scheming devil. And it wasn't just Ming poor Flash had to worry about. Along the way there were Shark Men, Hawk Men, Orangapoids, Octosacs, and other assorted monstrosities to deal with, and deal with them he did, to everyone's satisfaction. *Flash Gordon* was so popular that Universal brought Crabbe back to play Alex Raymond's fantastic hero in two subsequent serials, *Flash Gordon's Trip to Mars* and *Flash Gordon Conquers the Universe*, each time battling Ming, who seemed to be indestructible. It was fun in the grand style.

A year earlier, Mascot had introduced Gene Autry to stardom in *The Phantom Empire*. Gene played a singing cowboy who suddenly found himself journeying, via a secret cave entrance, to the futuristic city of Murania far below the surface of the earth, where he met the beautiful queen Tika (Dorothy Christy), who was bent on world domination. Murania was peopled with the mysterious Thunder Riders, who frequently ventured aboveground, much to the consternation of Gene, Frankie Darro, and Betsy King Ross. Adding to the confusion were robots (used again many years later in the Columbia serial, *Captain Video*) and assorted death-dealing devices. The exciting finale had a wildly gyrating ray-gun destroying the entire underground city accompanied by the rousing strains of "Storm and War," a thrilling piece of music often used in Westerns and serials of the thirties. The "destruction" of the city was accomplished by printing a photo of it on a film with thick emulsion, then photographing it in slow motion while the print was heated; the heat of course caused the emulsion to run. This same effect was used in several later Republic serials whenever a mountain had to melt, as in *The Adventures of Captain Marvel*, *S.O.S. Coast Guard*, and *King of the Rocket Men*.

Republic, obviously trying to cash in on the

enormous success expected from Universal's release of *Flash Gordon,* came out with their own science-fiction adventure, *Undersea Kingdom,* the very same year. With the advanced special effects of Howard Lydecker, the undersea city of Atlantis had much more eye-appeal than Murania or Mongo. The story found Ray "Crash" Corrigan playing a naval officer who is sent in a newly developed submarine to discover the underwater cause of a series of devastating earthquakes terrorizing the world. The mystery is solved, after twelve action-packed chapters, and the underground city destroyed. One chapter ending found Crash tied to the front of an armored vehicle which Lon Chaney, Jr., intended to plunge into the heavy gates of an enemy fort. When threatened with death unless he cooperated, Crash heroically shouted, "Go ahead and *ram!*" Now *that* was really a *hero!*

With Buster Crabbe's outstanding success as Flash Gordon, it was only natural that Universal would cast the handsome leading man as Buck Rogers in 1939. By all standards of previous production, this serial should really have been a quality product. However, it turned out to be a rather routine effort, with Buck battling his traditional newspaper foe, Killer Kane (Anthony Warde), who spent most of his time converting humans into robots via a powerful helmet he had developed. Henry Brandon, who was to portray Fu Manchu a year later, was excellent as Kane's chief henchman, and David Sharpe could be seen playing roles on both Kane's side and Buck's team, as well as doubling for young Jackie Moran.

Brick Bradford, with Kane Richmond as the comic-strip hero, started out in its early episodes with several interesting gimmicks including a "crystal door" which, when passed through, could transport one molecularly to the moon, and a "time top" which could send its occupants back in time to earlier centuries. The ideas were inventive enough to hook audiences for the first half of the serial, but after those early thrills the remainder of the serial turned into a straight everyday action drama. This was a rather poor showing from Columbia in 1947, but *Superman* was on the way.

The Purple Monster Strikes was an action-packed Republic serial of 1945 with a most interesting plot. The Purple Monster arrives on Earth from the planet Mars in a small spaceship which is consumed in flames shortly after he

leaves it. He locates Dr. Cyrus Layton, a renownéd scientist, and informs him that he has been sent to Earth in order to learn how to build a much more sophisticated spacecraft. When Layton refuses to cooperate, the Monster takes a small vial of Martian gas and kills the scientist. With this same gas the Monster is able to "enter" the body of the dead man and assume his personality. The remainder of the serial is strictly action and more action as the Monster seeks all the necessary supplies needed to build the spaceship. Roy Barcroft was superb as the Monster and Dennis Moore and Linda Stirling played effectively as the protagonists.

Radar Men from the Moon, made seven years later, found Barcroft in his same Purple Monster costume, but now portraying Retik, a leader of Moonmen intent on conquering the world. Obviously he had been taking lessons from Ming the Merciless. The serial utilized quite a bit of footage from *The Purple Monster Strikes,* including the entire finale, which depicted the aliens' spaceship being blasted from the skies.

Flying Disc Man from Mars and *Zombies of the Stratosphere,* two serials released by Republic in the fifties, also dealt with aliens from other planets landing on Earth. In the former, the Disc Man was seeking aid in building atomic-powered planes and bombs to take over Earth and make it a satellite of Mars; the latter found the Zombies trying to build a hydrogen device capable of blowing the Earth out of its orbit, thus allowing them to let their planet "inherit" the orbit to take advantage of our superior atmosphere. Worthy ambitions, but completely thwarted by the noble heroes.

And how about all those lost civilizations, active and inactive, sought after in serials like *Terry and the Pirates, Darkest Africa, The Lost City,* and *Call of the Savage?* They deserve mention, as do all those serials which utilized mad inventions to further their inventor's wildest dreams: serials like *The Phantom Creeps, Mysterious Dr. Satan, The Vanishing Shadow,* and *The Monster and the Ape,* which had incredible robots doing their master's bidding; and *The Crimson Ghost* with his "cyclotrode," Dr. Vulcan in *King of the Rocket Men* with his "decimator," and so many others. They made it very plain that, perhaps, Earth wasn't so bad after all if our heroes were able to successfully challenge so many attempts to conquer and destroy civilization.

left: Buster Crabbe as Flash Gordon rescues Carol Hughes from one of the perils on Frigia in *Flash Gordon Conquers the Universe* (Universal 1940). *below:* Kane Richmond and Claudia Dell discovered the mysterious city in the jungle in *The Lost City* (Krellberg, 1935). That's Joseph Swickard, Eddie Fetherstone, and Sam Baker in the background.

right: Jules Verne's *Mysterious Island* (Columbia 1951) came to the screen in serial form with Leonard Penn, Eugene Roth, and, in the lead, Richard Crane.
below: The robot from *Mysterious Dr. Satan* (Republic 1940) made a return appearance in *Zombies of the Stratosphere* (Republic 1952). That's Judd Holdren (or his stunt double) under the helmet.

left: Captain Video was a popular television hero in the early fifties. He was portrayed by, among others, Al Hodge, who had played the Green Hornet on radio. When *Captain Video* (Columbia 1951) was transferred to the screen, Judd Holdren played the title role. *below:* Judd Holdren seemed to have a monopoly on playing science-fiction heroes in the early fifties. In this scene from *The Lost Planet* (Columbia 1953), Holdren, *right,* gets some scientific information from veteran character actor Forrest Taylor.

In *The Phantom Empire* (Mascot 1935) singing cowboy Gene Autry discovered
the underground city of Murania. In this scene he gets the drop on Stanley
Blystone.

left: Gregory Gay in an absurd publicity shot for *Flying Disc Man from Mars* (Republic 1951). *below:* C. Montague Shaw and Lon Chaney, Jr., seem to have Ray "Crash" Corrigan at a disadvantage in the *Undersea Kingdom* (Republic 1936).

above: Roy Barcroft as the mysterious alien from Mars is about to inhabit the body of James Craven in the exciting serial *The Purple Monster Strikes* (Republic 1945). *right:* The pursuers they've spotted will not prevent Kane Richmond and Linda Johnson from taking a ride in the "time top" in the serial version of the popular King Features' comic strip *Brick Bradford* (Columbia 1947).

left: Millburn Stone demonstrates one of the mysterious devices uncovered in *The Great Alaskan Mystery* (Universal 1944). *below:* George Wallace is under the mask in *Radar Men from the Moon* (Republic 1952).

above: Bela Lugosi demonstrates one of his inventions to henchman Jack C. Smith in *The Phantom Creeps* (Universal 1939).
right: Tristram Coffin was the unlikely hero in *King of the Rocket Men* (Republic 1949). This was Republic's last really noteworthy serial, and stock from this film was used in three subsequent serial adventures: *Flying Disc Man from Mars* (Republic 1951), *Radar Men from the Moon* (Republic 1952), and *Zombies of the Stratosphere* (Republic 1952).

Tom Mix, in his last starring film, takes care of Tom London in *The Miracle Rider* (Mascot 1935).

7. Hit the Saddle

ALMOST WITHOUT EXCEPTION, the production schedule of each studio's annual serial output would include at least one Western serial. The primary reasons for this were economy and popularity. Westerns were relatively inexpensive to produce: few costly and involved interior sets had to be built, and exteriors could be easily photographed on appropriate sites within a few miles of the studio, if indeed not right on the producing company's back lot. And, of course, Westerns were popular, tremendously popular, during those Saturday-afternoon adventure orgies. Cowboy stars like Buck Jones, Ken Maynard, Tim McCoy, and Tom Tyler were money in the bank to the companies, and so it was to their advantage to have them appear in serials that would bring their fans back for twelve or fifteen consecutive weeks to follow their adventures.

Of all the heroes who hit the saddle on behalf of justice, none was more popular than Buck Jones. A no-nonsense performer who was a capable actor and an excellent rider, Buck gave robust performances in *Gordon of Ghost City*, *The Red Rider*, *The Roaring West*, *The Phantom Rider*, *White Eagle*, and *Riders of Death Valley*. Many more titles might have been added to the list if Buck had not died so tragically in the Coconut Grove fire in 1942, in which he

became a real-life hero by rescuing trapped patrons time after time until he was overcome by the smoke.

Johnny Mack Brown started his film career playing romantic leads. Fortunately, he very quickly found his niche in films as one of the most popular of Western performers on the screen. Beginning with Mascot's 1933 production of *Fighting with Kit Carson*, Johnny moved to Universal and starred in four more action classics: *Rustlers of Red Dog*, *Wild West Days*, *Flaming Frontiers*, and *Oregon Trail*. In the case of both Jones and Johnny Mack Brown, the earlier serials were well photographed and inventively done, and the later ones showed obvious signs of cheapness, including many stock shots from the previous efforts.

Tom Tyler was one of the few cowboy stars who was able to leave his horse behind from time to time in order to play non-Western heroes. Although he is thought of primarily as a Western star, only two of his seven starring serials were Westerns: *Phantom of the West*, made by Mascot in 1931, and *Battling with Buffalo Bill*, a Universal release that same year. His popularity, due to B-Westerns, was such, however, that in 1932 and 1933 Universal starred him in three out of four consecutively produced chapter plays: *Jungle Mystery*, *Clancy of the*

Mounted, and *Phantom of the Air.* In the forties he had the distinction of playing two of the most famous comic-strip characters on the serial screen in *The Adventures of Captain Marvel* and *The Phantom.*

Tim McCoy, or, as many like to refer to him today, Colonel Tim, has the unique distinction of having been the star of the first all-talking serial, *The Indians Are Coming,* which also was released in an all-silent version to accommodate those theatres that had not yet converted to the new sound system. The serial had a great many thrills but also a considerable amount of stock, which seriously detracted from its effectiveness. Still, it was an outstanding success and played at major theatres all over the country. Tim only made one other serial, the non-Western *Heroes of the Flames* in 1931.

William Elliott, another popular Western star, got his start in films by playing "society" extra roles, usually wearing a tuxedo. When he did venture into Western production, he was usually the heavy rather than the hero. However, with Columbia's 1938 production of *The Great Adventures of Wild Bill Hickok,* Elliott was on his way to the "Western Hall of Fame" and had acquired his famous "Wild Bill" nickname. He starred in two other Western serials for Columbia, *Overland with Kit Carson* and *The Valley of Vanishing Men,* as well as a popular series of B-Westerns, before moving over to Republic where he became a top Western favorite but made no serials.

Several top-drawer Western stars made appearances in serials produced by Mascot Pictures in the early thirties, including an old pro, Tom Mix, and an upcoming troubadour named Gene Autry. For Tom Mix, *The Miracle Rider* was his final starring film as well as his only serial. As a Texas Ranger in the film, Tom was trying to prevent scheming white men from stealing Indian land containing rare mineral deposits which they wanted for use in a new explosive, X-94. The aging star was showing his years, and much of the serial was very routine.

Gene Autry fared a great deal better in *The Phantom Empire.* Here was an exciting serial tale that had Autry bouncing like a rubber ball above ground and below to the underground scientific city of Murania. It seems the poor radio cowboy had to make a singing appearance every day on his radio show or lose a valuable contract. The sets were imaginative and the performances above average, and Gene was launched on the road to a successful Western career.

Ken Maynard also had his chance to ride his horse Tarzan into thrilling mystery adventure when he took twelve thrilling episodes to uncover the menacing Rattler and solve the riddle of *Mystery Mountain.* Ken, a very pleasant personality, was beginning to put on weight, and his earlier fame was beginning to wear a little thin. No future serials turned up for the once-outstanding range ace, although he continued to turn out some surprisingly good Western features.

Harry Carey, whom more people remember as a character actor than as a Western star, also received Mascot exploitation in vehicles like *The Devil Horse* and *The Vanishing Legion.*

And among the many other stars and personalities who made one or more forays into the Western field were: Lon Chaney, Jr., as a Zorro-type avenger in RKO's solo serial effort, *The Last Frontier,* and at Universal in *Overland Mail;* Dick Foran, another popular singing cowboy starring in Warner Brothers features, in *Winners of the West* and *Riders of Death Valley;* Clayton Moore, television's Lone Ranger and a popular serial star at Republic in *Jesse James Rides Again, Adventures of Frank and Jesse James, Ghost of Zorro,* and *Son of Geronimo;* Jock Mahoney, a superb stunt man and one of the many Tarzans, in *Roar of the Iron Horse, Cody of the Pony Express,* and *Gunfighters of the Northwest;* Don "Red" Barry, in the serial that made him a star and gave him his nickname of "Red," *Adventures of Red Ryder;* Ray Corrigan, one of Republic's famous "Three Mesquiteers," in *The Painted Stallion;* and all the leading men in the Lone Ranger and Zorro series of chapter plays. The list seems endless, but of all the Western serials, perhaps the most action-packed among them was the Republic thriller of 1943, *Daredevils of the West.* Starring Allan Lane and Kay Aldridge, this serial had all the ingredients necessary to provide a dozen exciting episodes. Directed by John English, the film had a thrilling Indian chase in chapter one (later re-used in a cut-down version in *Ghost of Zorro*), top-notch fight sequences, including a masterpiece in which heroine Aldridge apparently fell into a refining vat, and an excellent script which allowed the leads to move from thrill to thrill with little letup. Add to that combination an exciting Mort Glickman musical score and inventive Howard Lydecker miniatures, and you had to have a perfect serial.

right: Johnny Mack Brown, one of the most popular of all the Western serial stars, in *Wild West Days* (Universal 1937). *below:* Buck Jones comes to the aid of Madge Bellamy in *Gordon of Ghost City* (Universal 1933).

right: Johnny Mack Brown would like a little information from Edward Hearn in *Fighting with Kit Carson* (Mascot 1933).
below: William Haade, taking a hint from Tom Mix in the scene below, tries to get away from Allan Lane in *Daredevils of the West* (Republic 1943).

above: Ken Maynard had able help from Syd Saylor and Verna Hillie in trying to track down the Rattler in *Mystery Mountain* (Mascot 1934). *top:* Duncan Renaldo was "Slingin' Sammy" Baugh's Mexican confederate in *King of the Texas Rangers* (Republic 1941). Baugh was a popular football star, but his acting left quite a bit to be desired.

Harry Carey, one of the most beloved of all Western heroes and character actors, played the lead in *The Vanishing Legion* (Mascot 1931). In this scene Bob Kortman, *right,* is about to get an unexpected surprise.

above: Buck Jones' next to last serial was *White Eagle* (Columbia 1941) with Dorothy Fay. *below:* William Elliott earned his "Wild Bill" nickname in *The Great Adventures of Wild Bill Hickok* (Columbia 1938); here he is with Frankie Darro and Chief Thundercloud.

above: Clayton Moore gets the drop on David Sharpe, stunt man extraordinaire, and George J. Lewis in *Adventures of Frank and Jesse James* (Republic 1948). Moore played Jesse, out to right his name by paying back some of the money he had stolen earlier. *right:* Dickie Moore, former child star, was young Bill Cody, assisted by Jock O'Mahoney in *Cody of the Pony Express* (Columbia 1950).

Dick Foran, *right,* one of the screen's first singing cowboys, argues a point with veteran badman Harry Woods in *Winners of the West* (Universal 1940).

Paul Guilfoyle was supposedly under the hood in *The Scarlet Horseman* (Universal 1946), one of Universal's last serials.

above: Very few serials had an Indian hero, but one of the better ones was *Black Arrow* (Columbia 1944), starring Robert Scott, *right,* and Chief Thundercloud. *below:* The "Million-Dollar Serial," so called because of the tremendous cast, was *Riders of Death Valley* (Universal 1941) and starred Buck Jones, Noah Berry, Jr., Dick Foran, Guinn "Big Boy" Williams and Leo Carrillo. Also featured were Charles Bickford and Lon Chaney, Jr.

Robert Livingston was the Eagle, a semi-Zorro character in *The Vigilantes Are Coming* (Republic 1936) assisted by Guinn "Big Boy" Williams.

Robert Livingston was the "masked rider of the plains" in *The Lone Ranger Rides Again* (Republic 1939). This second, and final, serial based on the popular radio show was closer to the character than the first, also made by Republic, but it still lacked the "integrity" of the radio show's portrayal by allowing other cast members as well as the audience to know the Lone Ranger's real identity.

8. From Radio and the Pulps

I DON'T KNOW how many of you sat in front of your radios night after night during the forties with your latest "Captain Midnight Secret Decoder" clenched tightly in your hot little hands, waiting for the end of each adventure when announcer Pierre Andre would come on the air. Andre would give us listeners who formed the home "Secret Squadron" our latest message to decipher. What matter if the message turned out to be "Drink Ovaltine"—it was fun just to work the decoder. It was, therefore, with some relish that I looked forward to seeing one of my favorite heroes on the serial screen when Columbia announced they would release *Captain Midnight* in 1942. But even Dave O'Brien, playing the title role, could not save a script that was so juvenile it insulted the intelligence of children. One chapter ending had the hero trapped in a closet that was slowly filling with water, a reasonable enough peril to accept. But Columbia writers had to embellish the situation: they had a netlike device descend from the ceiling and push O'Brien's head down into the ascending water. The poor devil looked like a pretzel by the final fade-out.

Captain Midnight was only one of the many serials whose leading characters were derived from early pulp magazines and radio favorites. Of all the radio and pulp heroes, perhaps none was more famous than that slinking figure of the night who knew "what evil lurks in the hearts of men"—the Shadow. After nearly a decade of popularity in *Shadow Magazine* and on the airwaves, Columbia brought the character to the serial screen in 1940. Starring Victor Jory in the title role, the film was mediocre. The writers took many liberties with the character, including having Lamont Cranston frequently pose as a ridiculous-looking Oriental called Lin Chang. Audiences looked forward to seeing a man with the incredible ability to "cloud men's minds so they could not see him." Instead there was only a typical masked hero behaving rather like an imbecile. When Monogram Pictures made a brief series of features based on the character, the results were much more satisfactory.

In the early part of this century, Burt L. Standish's fictional hero Frank Merriwell was the idol of every red-blooded American boy. A college hero, Merriwell was an all-around champion athlete and adventurer. Universal brought this prototype of Jack Armstrong to the screen in 1936 in *The Adventures of Frank Merriwell*. Don Briggs played the lead, ably assisted by John King and pert Jean Rogers. Also in the cast were the sons of many favorite character actors of the time, including Wallace Reid, Jr., House Peters, Jr., Allan Hersholt, Edward Arnold, Jr., and Bryant Washburn, Jr. The plot had Frank involved in everything from winning sport contests to working in lumber camps and trying to prevent train crashes. It was what every boy in the audience dreamed *his* later years should be like.

Characters were often embellished in their translation to the screen. An excellent example of this appeared in the serial version of the popular Western radio show, *The Lone Ranger*. The origin of the character on radio was relatively simple: a band of Texas Rangers was ambushed and killed, with the exception of a sole survivor who was discovered and nursed back to health by the Indian Tonto. The survivor, taking the name of the Lone Ranger, avenged the deaths of his comrades and continued to fight for law and order for almost three decades on the radio. The Republic screenplay had the same basic origin, but a unique "mystery" angle was added. The audience was presented with five suspects, who were eliminated one by one until the Lone Ranger was unmasked in the last episode. It was an added bit of creative tampering that audiences did not find offensive.

The sequel, *The Lone Ranger Rides Again*, made a year later, in 1939, gave up the mystery angle altogether, and hero Robert Livingston was shown to be the masked man right from the first episode. Thus he was more like Zorro than radio's "masked rider of the plains."

The Green Hornet was another popular radio personality who was transferred to the screen in two action adventures. Gordon Jones first played the character in *The Green Hornet*, released by Universal in 1940. The routine script had the Hornet battling conventional racketeers. The popular success of the serial was such that Universal released a sequel, *The Green Hornet Strikes Again*, the very same year. This time Warren Hull played the role of the masked avenger. Playing Kato in both versions was Keye Luke.

Gang Busters was one of those serials that really had little to do with its namesake. On the radio, *Gang Busters* was a weekly show depicting various criminals receiving their ultimate just deserts from law enforcement officials. The screenplay for the 1942 Universal release was a typically serial-oriented thriller which had hero Kent Taylor battling the League of Murdered Men. Heading this criminal combine was Ralph Morgan, who ultimately met his end in a subway tunnel. The script was more reminiscent of something that might have been done on *The Shadow* or *The Green Hornet*.

Two more popular radio shows of the forties were brought to the screen by Columbia with only average success. John Hart appeared too old to play the "hero of Hudson High" in 1947's *Jack Armstrong*, although Pierre Watkin was ideal as Uncle Jim Fairfield. A little more acceptable to youthful audiences was William Bakewell as the flying ace, *Hop Harrigan*, released in 1946. Both serials reflected cheap production and weak scripts.

Almost as popular in the early pulps as the Shadow was the Spider, "Master of Men." Wearing a huge cape and mask, the Spider was one of the more colorful adventure heroes dealing out his own brand of justice to the underworld. Warren Hull, one of the more personable and talented serial leads, starred as the Spider in two Columbia productions, *The Spider's Web* in 1938 and *The Spider Returns* in 1941. Both serials had the benefit of mystery men, the Octopus in the first and the Gargoyle in the second. To show how ineffectual director James V. Horne was, in one scene of *The Spider Returns* he actually had two of the villain's henchmen playing "patty-cake" in the background. Knox Manning, a popular newscaster, was the narrator whose voice was heard at the end of each chapter of Columbia serials as previews of next week's episode were shown. Over a scene of two of the Gargoyle's henchmen boarding a train to commit mayhem, Manning was required to ask, "Why are these men boarding the train? Do they have their *tickets?*"

Perhaps the Shadow, the Green Hornet, the Spider, Jack Armstrong, the Lone Ranger, and all the others should have stayed where the imagination could conjure up its own mental portraits of them. They really didn't receive fair treatment on the screen.

Radio's *Hop Harrigan* (Columbia 1946) was brought to the screen with William Bakewell in the title role. In this scene, Hop (*second from right*) is assisted by Sumner Getchell ("Tank Tinker"), Robert "Buzz" Henry, and Jennifer Holt.

Warren Hull was the Green Hornet and Keye Luke was Kato in *The Green Hornet Strikes Again* (Universal 1940). Gas gun and all, this second serial version suffered in comparison with the first because of the amount of stock footage used. Warren Hull was superior, however, to Gordon Jones in the title role.

73

Of all the pulp heroes perhaps none was more famous than Burt L. Standish's Frank Merriwell. Don Briggs was an excellent choice to play the young hero in *The Adventures of Frank Merriwell* (Universal 1936).

above: Gordon Jones brought radio's famous Green Hornet to the screen in 1940. The film remained generally faithful to the character presented on the air. *The Green Hornet* (Universal 1940) has not been reissued since its original presentation, even to capitalize on the fame of the television series done in 1967 at the height of the "camp" craze. *below:* Dave O'Brien was a popular actor-stunt man and brought a degree of professionalism to the title role of *Captain Midnight* (Columbia 1942) based on the popular radio serial. However, the writing was ludicrous, and the serial was far from satisfying.

above: In the first serial version of the radio show *The Lone Ranger* (Republic 1938), the hero was a mystery man who turned out to be one of the suspects pictured here: Lane Chandler, Lee Powell, Herman Brix (later Bruce Bennett), George Letz (later George Montgomery) and Hal Taliaferro (formerly Wally Wales). That's Chief Thundercloud playing Tonto.

left: Deadwood Dick (Columbia 1940) was another popular pulp folk-hero. Don Douglas, a relatively unlikely choice for a serial hero, was surprisingly good in the title role. Assisting him in this scene was Lorna Gray, who shortly after moved to Republic and portrayed a wide variety of evil women under that screen name before changing it to Adrian Booth in the late forties.

right: Of all the radio and pulp heroes brought to the screen, the most famous was *The Shadow* (Columbia 1940). The popular Western villain, Victor Jory, was chosen for the title role. However, this serial, like many Columbia serials, took many liberties with the character by adding elements not contained in the radio series. James Horne, who excelled in directing comedy shorts, directed his serials as though they were being aimed at a market of childish idiots, and his serials contained little merit. *below:* The "All-American Boy" came to the screen from radio with John Hart in the title role of *Jack Armstrong* (Columbia 1947). In this scene, Pierre Watkin as Uncle Jim and Hart are unaware of the villainous John Merton lurking in the background.

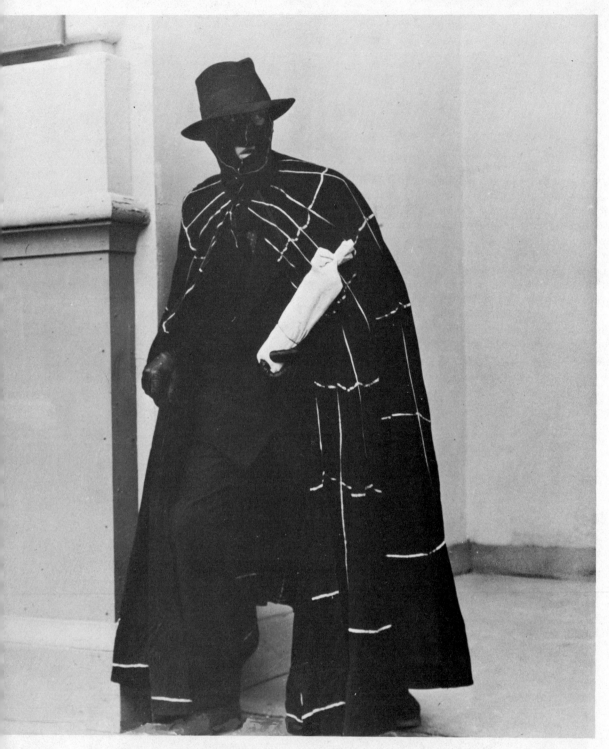

Warren Hull brought the famous pulp hero the Spider to the screen in two serials, *The Spider's Web* (Columbia 1938), from which the above scene is taken, and *The Spider Returns* (Columbia 1941).

Gang Busters (Universal 1942) was an above-average crime serial very loosely based on the popular radio series. In this scene from the film, villain Ralph Morgan thinks he is about to escape safely from the law.

Roy Barcroft was the perfect serial villain. His own favorite role was that of the mysterious reincarnated pirate, Captain Mephisto, in *Manhunt of Mystery Island* (Republic 1945).

9. A Stock Company of Villains

I HAVE DEDICATED THIS BOOK to the memory of the popular serial villain, Roy Barcroft (1902–69), the epitome of the stereotyped badman. Usually wearing a moustache, Barcroft could be equally satisfactory playing either the "brains" or "action" heavy. He schemed and fought his way through hundreds of B-Westerns and over twenty-five serials. He frankly admits modeling his screen characterizations after those of that popular Western villain of the thirties, Harry Woods, and he was able to surpass Woods in popularity during the forties. He made his first serial appearance in *Dick Tracy* in 1937 and free-lanced at various studios until 1943, when he signed a ten-year exclusive contract with Republic. Whatever amount of money he received was well-earned, for in those pre-union days contract players were forced to work back-breaking sixteen-hour days.

It seems rather incongruous that, off-screen, the king of villainy was one of the most beloved and respected members of the Republic acting roster, while many of the heroes turned out to be much less than the gentlemen they appeared to be on the screen. I recall spending a wonderful afternoon in early 1966 with Barcroft discussing serials, and I found that he, unlike so many of the people with whom he worked, loved doing them. He attributed this directly to the Republic stock company of players, who somehow made the tedious job of motion picture acting *fun*—men like Bud Geary, LeRoy Mason, George J. Lewis, and Kenne Duncan. The heroes came for their two or three weeks of work, but those villains were there every day throughout the year, and for Roy Barcroft that made his work a pleasure.

Barcroft's favorite serial role was that of Captain Mephisto in *Manhunt of Mystery Island*, a 1945 Republic action-thriller, but he enjoyed *The Purple Monster Strikes* and *Haunted Harbor* almost as much.

Charles Middleton's film career spanned many years and hundreds of roles, yet he is best remembered for one serial role. As Ming the Merciless in *Flash Gordon*, *Flash Gordon's Trip to Mars*, and *Flash Gordon Conquers the Universe*, he brought new dimension to screen villainy. How many serial fans could ever forget Buster Crabbe's repeated warnings to Middleton to "keep his slimy hands off" Jean Rogers (as Dale Arden)? The role of the despotic emperor was perfectly cast, and Middleton overacted to perfection. Though these Universal films may have been the main course, his superb portrayals of Pa Stark in *Dick Tracy Returns* and 39013 in *Daredevils of the Red Circle* were additional morsels of screen chicanery serial-watchers could relish.

Anthony Warde very likely holds the record

for appearing in more screen fights than any other "action" heavy save only Roy Barcroft. Allan Lane belted him around in *King of the Mounties,* Tom Steele really mauled him in *The Masked Marvel,* Larry Thompson pummeled him in *King of the Forest Rangers,* Bruce Edwards tried to teach him the error of his ways in *The Black Widow,* Kirk Alyn gave him a great going-over in *Radar Patrol vs. Spy King,* and Jim Bannon knocked him clear across the border in *Dangers of the Canadian Mounted.* Could any villain ask for more? And that was just at Republic. Over at Universal he was also Killer Kane, Buck Rogers' number-one adversary.

I have mentioned "brains" and "action" heavy several times. I really should clarify these terms before we proceed any further. The "brains" heavy was the man (or, on occasion, woman) who issued the orders to his henchmen. He usually had little to do until the last chapter except talk, snarl, or grimace. The "action" heavy or heavies went from one chapter to the next trying desperately to kill the hero with fists, knives, guns, bombs or whatever else happened to be handy at the time.

George J. Lewis was an expert at playing both types of roles. As Lionel Atwill's chief henchman, Matson, in *Captain America,* he had the unique distinction of being killed in chapter eleven and brought "back to life" by a miraculous machine, only to be killed again a few chapters later. In *G-Men vs. The Black Dragon* he looked like a fugitive from a tong war as he tried desperately to deprive the United States of the services of Rod Cameron, and in *Federal Operator 99* he tried to convince viewers that he was a gentle "brains" heavy by periodically playing the "Moonlight Sonata" on the piano while he sent Hal Taliaferro out to do his dirty work. Republic did try to convert George, though, by allowing him to assist lovely Linda Stirling in *Zorro's Black Whip.* It was the first time he had played a serial hero since the early days of Mascot when he had starred in *The Wolf Dog* with Rin-Tin-Tin.

In silent serials there was a particular fascination for Oriental villains. The "Yellow Peril" was constantly menacing "our American Way of Life." Warner Oland played this Asian stereo-

type to perfection. When the sound serial thrived in the thirties, the task of portraying non-Caucasian menaces usually fell to Frank Lackteen. But of all his many and varied roles, the one fans most prefer is his portrayal of Shamba, the evil witch doctor in *Jungle Girl.* What a going-over he gave poor Frances Gifford: poison-gas-filled rooms, sacrificial altars, spear-traps, a room in which the floor slid back to reveal an apparently bottomless black abyss, and other assorted nastinesses that would have caused a lesser heroine to collapse from pure fatigue. Years later Republic was to make a feature called *Daughter of the Jungle,* utilizing stock footage from this serial. Lackteen was brought back to shoot additional scenes, and he seemingly hadn't aged at all.

And, of course, mention must be made of at least two ladies who could dish out their own brand of alluring devilment: Lorna Gray and Carol Forman. As the evil Vultura, Lorna actually stole the acting honors from serial queen Kay Aldridge in *Perils of Nyoka.* However, it must be noted that she had the help of Satan, the wildest gorilla since King Kong, while all Kay had was Clayton Moore. In later years Lorna Gray changed her name to Adrian Booth, and became Monte Hale's favorite leading lady. She could have remained malicious for a few more serials, if only to give Roy Barcroft a rest from overwork. A few years later, however, Carol Forman arrived on the scene and began to weave her evil webs as the Spider Lady in Columbia's first *Superman* serial, and over at Republic as *The Black Widow.* She was superb—and she was sexy. What more could one ask for?

And there were so many others! Especially Charles King, the rotund star of so many Westerns and serials; and Kenne Duncan, who, after faithfully serving Roy Barcroft for fifteen action-packed episodes of *Haunted Harbor,* was rewarded with a bullet simply because he knew Roy's real identity; and LeRoy Mason, Bud Geary, Hal Taliaferro, Ted Adams, George Cheseboro, Tom London, Stanley Price, William Haade, Robert Frazer, and Tristram Coffin. They deserve our thanks for making so many heroes look so much better than they really were.

left: LeRoy Mason was equally villainous in Westerns and non-Westerns such as *Daughter of Don Q* (Republic 1946). *below:* Kenne Duncan made hundreds of Westerns and serials, almost always as the villain. In this portrait from *The Adventures of Captain Marvel* (Republic 1941), he was the Scorpion's right-hand man.

left: John Merton departed from his usual Western villainy from time to time to portray mad scientists such as Dr. Tymak in *Brick Bradford* (Columbia 1947). *below, left:* The most famous of all serial villains, character-wise, was Ming the Merciless, portrayed by Charles Middleton in the three Flash Gordon serials. This portrait is from the first of the triology, *Flash Gordon* (Universal 1936). *below, right:* George J. Lewis could play heroes (*Zorro's Black Whip* [Republic 1944] assisting Linda Stirling), but was much better cast as the heavy in serials such as, here, *Federal Operator* 99 (Republic 1945).

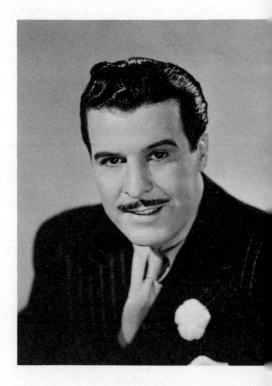

right: Charles King was everybody's favorite villain in serials and Westerns during the thirties and forties. This portrait is from the Tom Mix serial, *The Miracle Rider* (Mascot 1935). *below, left:* Anthony Warde was often used as the main "action" heavy at Republic, but he is probably best remembered for playing Killer Kane in *Buck Rogers* (Universal 1939). This portrait is from *The Masked Marvel* (Republic 1943). *below, right:* Bud Geary, here in *Haunted Harbor* (Republic 1944), usually played "action" heavies superbly.

Frank Lackteen's broad foreign accent made him a natural serial villain. In *Jungle Girl* (Republic 1941) he portrayed Shamba, the evil witch doctor who menaced Frances Gifford.

above: Here in another still from *The Miracle Rider* (Mascot 1935) is Tom London, whose career of portraying good guys and bad guys spanned virtually the entire range of serial production, silent and sound. *left:* John Davidson delighted serial fans as the villainous Lucifer in *Dick Tracy vs. Crime Inc.* (Republic 1941) and Gruber in *Captain America* (Republic 1943), but he could play sympathetic roles with equal skill, such as Tal Chotali in *Adventures of Captain Marvel* (Republic 1941). *below:* Carleton Young specialized in superb character roles, many of them villainous. In *Dick Tracy* (Republic 1937) Young portrayed Ralph Byrd's brother after the mysterious Lame One had performed one of his "operations" to convert him from good guy to bad guy.

Tristram Coffin was usually the "brains" heavy who sent out a parcel of henchmen to attack the hero. Although he did portray one serial hero, Jeff King in *King of the Rocket Men* (Republic 1949), he was much more successful in villainous roles.

Hal Taliaferro changed his name from Wally Wales, which had been his name tag as a Western hero, and became one of the screen's better Western and non-Western villains. In *Federal Operator* 99 (Republic 1945) he was George J. Lewis' right-hand man.

above: John Piccori specialized in portraying demented associates of the lead villain in serials like *Dick Tracy* (Republic 1937), *above,* and *Fighting Devil Dogs* (Republic 1938). *left:* Bob Kortman was another Western and Indian specialist in screen villainy. In *The Miracle Rider* (Mascot 1935) he opposed Tom Mix.

Naturally, there were screen villainesses too. Carol Forman was among the
best of these distaff devils, here portraying the title role in *The Black
Widow* (Republic 1947).

Buster Crabbe in *Tarzan, the Fearless* (Principal 1933), the first of his nine starring serials.

10. The Serial Heroes

In DON SHAY's recently published book of film personality interviews, *Conversations*, Buster Crabbe is quoted as saying: "Actually I think I was kind of an uninteresting person. There was never any glamour for me in the picture business. There *is* a certain amount of satisfaction in having people recognize you, but I've never had anybody pass me in the lobby—you can hear people talk; some of them are extra loud—and say: 'There goes Buster Crabbe, the actor.' Nine times out of ten: 'There goes Buster Crabbe, the swimmer.'"

Most serial filmgoers would disagree. For them he was Flash Gordon, Buck Rogers, Red Barry, Tarzan, Captain Silver, the Mighty Thunda. He was all of these and more. As Pearl White was the chief performer linked with silent serials, so was Buster Crabbe the name most closely associated with the sound serial. There is no question that he was the most popular serial star of the golden age of sound serials, starring in nine episodic delights: *Tarzan, the Fearless, Flash Gordon, Flash Gordon's Trip to Mars, Red Barry, Buck Rogers, Flash Gordon Conquers the Universe, The Sea Hound, Pirates of the High Seas,* and *King of the Congo.* The reason for his serial success was obvious: he was handsome, with a good build, spoke dialogue with a reasonable amount of conviction, and could perform most of the routine action demanded of a perfect hero. What more was needed?

If Republic personnel had been asked what their requirements for a serial hero would be, one would most likely hear: "that the lead very closely resemble one of the stunt men on the studio payroll." That no doubt accounted for some of the rather routine leads they frequently used. But there were a number of actors who did their serial duty in a most creditable fashion.

Tom Tyler, mostly remembered as a Western player, was an excellent choice to play leads in a variety of serials, including *Phantom of the West, Jungle Mystery, Clancy of the Mounted,* and *The Phantom.* Tyler, like Crabbe, was a superb athlete and a physically perfect choice to play super heroes. A minor handicap, however, was his voice, which many found not on a par with his other attributes. It seems a rather strange coincidence that in his most famous serial, *The Adventures of Captain Marvel,* he spoke the equivalent of only one full page of dialogue in the entire twelve chapters. His one long speech, delivered at the end of the serial, seemed almost beyond his capabilities. Despite that flaw, he was one of the all-time serial favorites.

Once cast as Dick Tracy, Ralph Byrd was to remain Dick Tracy for the remainder of his screen career. A very personable leading man, he was excellent in serials like *S.O.S. Coast Guard* and *Blake of Scotland Yard,* but when Republic cast him as the famous comic-strip detective in the 1937 production of *Dick Tracy* his acting fate was sealed. He made three very successful sequels, *Dick Tracy Returns* in 1938, *Dick Tracy's G-Men* in 1939, and *Dick Tracy vs. Crime, Inc.* in 1941. They were all excellent; with many enjoying best his bout with the Spider in the first, while others favored the last, which had him battling the invisible Ghost.

Clayton Moore had one of those strange up and down careers that found him playing both leading man and chief villain with equal success. His first starring role was as Kay Aldridge's defender through fifteen episodes of *Perils of Nyoka.* His future seemed secure at Republic, but World War II intervened, and he, like so many others, went into uniform. When he returned to the studio and serial work in 1946's *The Crimson Ghost,* it was as the "action" heavy opposing Charles Quigley and Linda Stirling. The next year he once again emerged as a leading hero in *Jesse James Rides Again* and followed that with *G-Men Never Forget, Adventures of Frank and Jesse James,* and *Ghost of Zorro*—before once again turning villainous in *Radar Men from the Moon.* In between these Republic parts, he had become television's Lone Ranger (a role he still plays today in personal appearances) and went to Columbia to appear in *Son of Geronimo* (billed as Clay Moore) and *Gunfighters of the Northwest.*

Kane Richmond, a leading man in a number of B-films, appeared to give more dimension to routine roles than the scripts demanded. Playing a dual role in *Spy Smasher,* he delivered an amazingly good portrayal of the comic-strip character in a thrill-packed action serial that had David Sharpe, doubling for Richmond, performing exceptional stunts. In *Haunted Harbor,* Kane had the able assistance of Kay Aldridge as he battled Roy Barcroft for fifteen episodes. Over at Columbia, the results were far less satisfactory. In *Brenda Starr, Reporter* he assisted Joan Woodbury through ridiculous Columbia contrivances; in *Jungle Raiders* the script was self-

defeating, and *Brick Bradford* was a weak and uninspired production. Unfortunately, Kane retired from films much too early to satisfy the appetites of serial fans.

Kirk Alyn gained his reputation playing Superman in two serials at Columbia, but he was much better as a straight actor in favorites like *Daughter of Don Q, Radar Patrol vs. Spy King, Blackhawk,* and *Federal Agents vs. Underworld, Inc.*

Another popular action favorite was Allan Lane. Long before he became the Rocky Lane of Western fame (and the voice of television's famous horse, Mr. Ed) he had starred in four action-packed Republic adventures: *King of the Royal Mounted, King of the Mounties, Daredevils of the West,* and *The Tiger Woman* (Linda Stirling's first serial).

Lee Powell, who achieved star status in *The Lone Ranger* and *Fighting Devil Dogs,* might have become one of the most popular of leading men in serials if fate had not taken a hand—he was killed overseas during World War II when he fell victim to an enemy booby trap.

Few serial leading men ever used their roles as stepping stones to greater film glory, except for John Wayne, who had starred in *Hurricane Express, Shadow of the Eagle,* and *The Three Musketeers* for Mascot, and George Brent, who for the same studio had starred in *Lightning Warrior.* And, of course, Gene Autry became famous after his stint in *Phantom Empire.*

A great many excellent character actors did "lower" themselves from time to time to appear in serial roles, with mixed results. Gilbert Roland wasn't half bad in *The Desert Hawk;* Paul Kelly was successful in combating espionage as the Black Commando in *The Secret Code;* Victor Jory couldn't save *The Shadow* or *The Green Archer* from the ineptness of director, James V. Horne; and Jack Holt, who really looked more like Dick Tracy in the flesh, was *Holt of the Secret Service.*

And then there were the forgotten heroes who made a serial or two and then vanished because they just didn't have the stuff of which serial heroes are made. Among others there were: George Turner, Lewis Wilson, Robert Kellard, Robert Scott, Lee Roberts, Richard Bailey, Marten Lamont, Larry Thompson, and Bruce Edwards.

left: Buster Crabbe, the most famous and durable of all the great serial heroes, in *Flash Gordon's Trip to Mars* (Universal 1938). *below:* Buster Crabbe in a publicity still for *Flash Gordon* (Universal 1936).

right: Buster Crabbe in *Pirates of the High Seas*
(Columbia 1950). *below:* Buster Crabbe in his final
serial, *King of the Congo* (Columbia 1952).

above: The mysterious Scorpion uses George Pembroke as a shield to escape from Tom Tyler in *The Adventures of Captain Marvel* (Republic 1941). Tyler, physically perfect in the role of the superhuman comic-strip character, had only one page of dialogue to deliver in the entire twelve chapters of this serial. *right:* Although more at home in Western garb, Dennis Moore was an effective serial hero in favorites such as *The Purple Monster Strikes* (Republic 1945) and in this scene from the final Universal serial, *Mysterious Mr. M* (Universal 1946).

above: Kirk Alyn, although more famous for his portrayal of Superman in two serials, was much more effective in straight action dramas such as *Daughter of Don Q* (Republic 1946). *left:* For millions of serial-goers, Ralph Byrd *was* Dick Tracy. He played the role in four serials, two features and a television series. He appears above in a portrait from the fourth serial, *Dick Tracy vs. Crime, Inc.* (Republic 1941). *below:* Kane Richmond gets the drop on Kenne Duncan in *Haunted Harbor* (Republic 1944). Richmond was one of the few serial heroes who brought more than average acting ability and talent to his films.

above: Charles Quigley was an ideal type for a serial hero but was used very sparingly. *The Crimson Ghost* (Republic 1946) was his final starring serial. *left, above:* Clayton Moore ranked second to Buster Crabbe in the number of starring serials he appeared in. A very likable hero, he often appeared with equal success as a villain. This publicity still is from one of the best-remembered serials of the forties, *Perils of Nyoka* (Republic 1942). He later went on to much greater fame by becoming television's *Lone Ranger. left, below:* Allan Lane, although more famous as a Western hero in the late forties, was another pleasant and capable serial hero. He appeared in four of Republic's best action serials, the last of which was *The Tiger Woman* (Republic 1944), from which this portrait was taken.

top: Grant Withers, much better known for his note-worthy character work in features, was an excellent serial lead in such favorites as *Radio Patrol* (Universal 1937) and, here with Henry Brandon, *Jungle Jim* (Universal 1937). *above:* Lee Powell in *Fighting Devil Dogs* (Republic 1938). Powell might have been the greatest serial hero of them all if World War II had not come along. He was reported killed in action. *right:* Rod Cameron starred in two wartime action serials and then moved up the ladder to success in feature roles. This scene is one of the chapter endings from *G-Men vs. The Black Dragon* (Republic 1943).

Don Terry, more famous as Don Winslow in two later serials, was excellent in one of Columbia's few good serials, *The Secret of Treasure Island* (Columbia 1938).

Linda Stirling, Republic's most famous serial queen of the forties, in a portrait
drawn by noted artist Gray Morrow.

11. . . . and the Heroines

THE SERIAL HEROINE, who rose to majestic heights of popularity in silent films when stars like Pearl White, Ruth Roland, and Helen Holmes thrilled millions of moviegoers, fell quickly out of favor when the sound serial made its appearance. After all, the serials were now primarily made for young boys, and young boys *knew* that women were too fragile to engage in the strenuous activity demanded of a serial star. A heroine was necessary only as someone to be placed in peril, and as someone to be repeatedly hit over the head so that she would not be in the path of the hero's swinging fists. Her status was dismal, to say the least. However, during the thirties, there was some attempt to once again build a few of the ladies into interesting, if not active, co-stars. Universal tried—but failed—to re-establish the serial queen in a 1934 remake of *Perils of Pauline* starring Evalyn Knapp. Dorothy Gulliver and Lucile Browne made some screen impression over at Mascot, but their appeal was short-lived. The only woman who seemed to make it in the eyes of adventure fans was lovely Jean Rogers. As Dale Arden in *Flash Gordon* and *Flash Gordon's Trip to Mars,* Rogers was a delectable morsel to be pawed again and again by Ming the Merciless. The only problem seemed to be that she screamed and fainted with alarming regularity, and that offset the teasing sensations she imparted to the youthful audience by wearing skimpy costumes. She was, however, an effective aide to John King in *Ace Drummond* and Don Briggs in *Adventures of Frank Merriwell.*

But it was Republic Pictures, as usual, who restored dignity to the weaker sex. In 1941 they acquired the services of beautiful Frances Gifford and presented her with the title role in *Jungle Girl.* She was the dream girl of that serial year as she braved all the perils evil Frank Lackteen and Gerald Mohr could place in her path. She was trapped in a flooded mine, sacrificed on a flaming altar, gassed, precipitated into a burning vat of oil, and in varying ways threatened with death for fifteen thrilling weeks, only to be rescued by her own ingenuity or the skill of hero Tom Neal at the appropriate last moment. She was scheduled, and announced, to play her *Jungle Girl* character Nyoka again in *Perils of Nyoka* the following year, but personal problems intervened and another casting choice was made.

Kay Aldridge had an accent you could cut with a knife, looked terrible in a poorly designed costume (whereas Gifford's outfit was ideal), and couldn't act well enough to deliver more than an adequate performance. Yet she became one of Republic's best-exploited and most-liked serial heroines, appearing in three of their best serials, *Perils of Nyoka, Daredevils of the West* and *Haunted Harbor*. True to the standard heroine's role, Kay received her full share of blows on the head and holds the dubious distinction of being knocked unconscious *twice* in a single episode of *Haunted Harbor*.

And then came Linda Stirling. In its continuing effort to re-establish the idea of the serial queen, Republic tested Linda for the leading role in *The Tiger Woman*. Linda recalled that it was Yakima Canutt who directed her audition, which required her to ride a horse full tilt at the camera and rein up suddenly. According to her, "the horse stopped, but I didn't," and the young Linda Stirling practically fell in Canutt's lap. But the studio was happy with the test, and she got the role of the Tiger Woman, and followed it with leading roles in *Zorro's Black Whip, Manhunt of Mystery Island, The Purple Monster Strikes, The Crimson Ghost,* and *Jesse James Rides Again*. In addition to being the most beautiful of the Republic heroines (she had a very successful modeling career before coming to Republic), she could *act!* Those who viewed the serials when they were originally released looked at them with a certain amount of respect and admiration, but cared little for the effort that went into making them. Today movie buffs regard the serials with considerably more reverence than the people who made them. For example, Linda can only recall that they were a lot of work, great fun, and occasionally quite dangerous. While she was doubled in many instances, she did nearly drown in a sequence for *The Purple Monster Strikes* and narrowly escaped a dangerous fall—she was saved by stunt man Tom Steele—in *Manhunt of Mystery Island*. In filming serials there is always a certain element of risk. Fortunately, Linda Stirling and most of the others survived the perils of making films filled with perils.

There were other females who assisted their male companions with some degree of skill and enthusiasm. Peggy Stewart was excellent in Westerns like *The Phantom Rider* and *Son of Zorro*. Noel Neill of the childlike voice and appearance was ideal as Lois Lane in the two Superman serials, but she seemed miscast as a frontier heroine in *Adventures of Frank and Jesse James*. Helen Talbot was effective in *Federal Operator 99* and *King of the Forest Rangers*. Lorna Gray, when she wasn't playing a villainess in vehicles like *Perils of Nyoka* and *Federal Operator 99*, did take a fling at good-girl roles in *Captain America, Flying G-Men, Deadwood Dick,* and, under the name of Adrian Booth, *Daughter of Don Q*. Iris Meredith was a favorite over at Columbia in *The Spider's Web, Overland with Kit Carson,* and *The Green Archer*.

Most of the girls made one or two serials and then vanished from the screen forever. Few remember Ella Neal, Lita Conway, Vivian Coe, Luana Walters, Sheila Darcy, and dozens of others who had one brief moment of screen glory and then departed for the safety of marriage and private life. Not many serial heroines ever gained more than casual notice from the A-film producers. Carole Landis did rise from *Daredevils of the Red Circle* to minor prominence in lesser Twentieth Century-Fox films, and Jinx Falken of *The Lone Ranger Rides Again* became more famous by adding a "berg" to her last name, but the only one to really gain the top was young Phylis Isley of *Dick Tracy's G-Men;* she was discovered by David O. Selznick and changed her name to Jennifer Jones. There were, however, quite a number of B-film greats who took time off from busy schedules to make an occasional chapter play: Joan Woodbury, Adele Jergens, Veda Ann Borg, Anne Nagel, Phyllis Coates, Jane Adams, Evelyn Brent, Joyce Bryant, Ramsay Ames, Jennifer Holt, and Elyse Knox, to name only a few.

At the time, perhaps all of these gals seemed more a hindrance than a help to the serials' action, but it was still nice to have them around.

After many years of male domination in the serial field, Republic tried to bring back the serial queen in the exciting *Jungle Girl* (Republic 1941), starring the beautiful, and talented, Frances Gifford.

Adrian Booth was famous for playing outstanding villainess roles such as Vultura in *Perils of Nyoka* (Republic 1942) under her screen name of Lorna Gray. Under her new name she became a favorite Republic heroine in Westerns and serials such as *Daughter of Don Q* (Republic 1946), in which she appears here with Roy Barcroft and George Chesebro.

right: Linda Stirling had first-rate assistance from Allan Lane in *The Tiger Woman* (Republic 1944), the first of her six starring serials. *below:* Joan Woodbury was *Brenda Starr, Reporter* (Columbia 1945), a serial based on the famous comic strip. That's Wheeler Oakman, a popular serial villain in the '30s, with the gun.

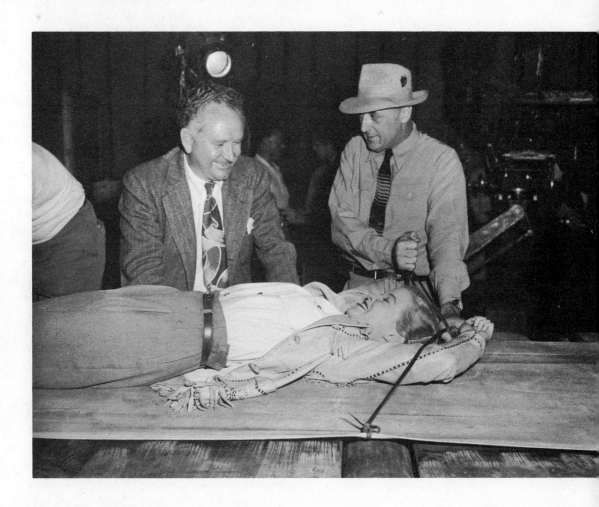

above: Spencer Gordon Bennet, the king of serial directors, shows fellow director Frank Borzage how serial heroine Helen Talbot should be bound in this production shot from *King of the Forest Rangers* (Republic 1946). *left:* Iris Meredith made a career out of screaming in Columbia serials. This time it's in *The Green Archer* (Columbia 1940).

Joyce Bryant almost became the victim of the grotesque villain in *The Iron Claw* (Columbia 1941).

left: Linda Stirling is about to learn the penalty for defying Roy Barcroft (as Captain Mephisto) and Kenne Duncan in the popular *Manhunt of Mystery Island* (Republic 1945). *below:* Pretty Peggy Stewart is being rescued by the masked hero, *The Phantom Rider* (Republic 1945).

Evalyn Knapp tried to bring back "poor Pauline" in the remake of *The Perils of Pauline* (Universal 1934). Hero Robert Allen rescues her, again, in this scene.

Second only to Linda Stirling in popularity among serial fans was Kay Aldridge, here facing one of the many *Perils of Nyoka* (Republic 1942).

Universal's claim to the serial-queen title was beautiful Jean Rogers, here seen as Dale Arden, with Buster Crabbe in *Flash Gordon* (Universal 1936).

Ruth Roman gives directions to Eddie Quillan and Edward Norris in *Jungle Queen* (Universal 1945).

12. Jungle Jeopardy

IT SEEMED RATHER a strange coincidence that both Republic and Columbia started off their serial production schedules with jungle films. *Darkest Africa*, Republic's first serial, released in early 1936, had Clyde Beatty, the famous animal trainer, as its star. Beatty had starred two years before in *The Lost Jungle* for Mascot, and he had proved to be a good box-office draw. Republic's serial was a wildly creative one, with Beatty fighting his way through the jungle to a lost city inhabited by, among many other things, a race of flying Bat Men. Accompanying Beatty, who could hardly be called an actor with any real skill, was Manuel King, a grotesque-looking young boy billed as the "World's Youngest Animal Trainer." There was plenty of stock from the earlier serial, and the film really achieved its only success in the extensive use of Howard Lydecker miniatures, including an erupting volcano at the film's climax. The flying sequences, done both with miniatures and with life-size dummies, were an excellent sampling of the superb effects later used in *The Adventures of Captain Marvel* and *King of the Rocket Men*.

Columbia, not to be outdone by Republic with their use of Beatty, obtained the services of a personality equally as important for their first serial, *Jungle Menace*, released in 1937. Frank Buck had already achieved considerable fame with his film documentary, *Bring 'Em Back Alive*, based on his own best-selling book detailing his capturing of animals for zoos all over the world. Buck, like Beatty, could hardly act his way out of a monkey cage, so what thrills there were in *Jungle Menace*, and there were very few "original" ones, were based mainly on antique stock jungle footage from the Columbia vaults. At least the supporting cast (Reginald Denny, Esther Ralston, LeRoy Mason, Charlotte Henry, and Duncan Renaldo, among others) gave more professional acting performances than Lucien Prival and his companions had delivered in *Darkest Africa*.

Most jungle serials were nothing more than glorified Westerns, usually shot on the same outdoor locations for much of their action, with close-ups being made on cheap studio sets decorated with imitation foliage. In order to spice up the proceedings, animal shots were inserted from stock libraries of various animals fighting each other or slinking around. Whenever the hero was required to fight an animal, he usually wound up with an obvious pet or a stuffed skin. There were exceptions, but they were rare. Herman Brix starred in *The New Adventures of Tarzan*, which actually was shot in Guatemala. Two of Republic's most famous jungle serials were almost entirely shot on the studio's back lot and Iverson's Ranch, the latter location being

111

one of the most-used locations in Western films and easily recognizable because of its rock formation resembling an Indian head.

Jungle Girl, which starred Frances Gifford as Nyoka, attempted to revive the serial-queen image absent from the screen for so many years. The plot was an interesting one. Nyoka's father is slain by his twin brother (both played by Trevor Bardette), who replaces him as a doctor serving the jungle tribes. Spurred on by the machinations of Slick Latimer (Gerald Mohr at his menacing best), the bogus doctor is trying to obtain a cache of diamonds hidden in the Caves of Nakros. With the treasure guarded by the evil witch doctor Shamba (played superbly by Frank Lackteen), it took fifteen thrill-packed episodes for Gifford, Tom Neal, and Eddie Acuff to dispose of all the opposition and rescue the diamonds. The ending of chapter one found Nyoka and Tom Neal trapped in one of the caves and Shamba flooding it, plunging them both to certain death out the opening in the side of a sheer cliff. Who wouldn't come back next week to see how they escaped—as of course they had?

Perils of Nyoka, starring Kay Aldridge as Nyoka (in a role originally intended for Gifford), had a group of scientists, assisted by Clayton Moore and the jungle girl, seeking the legendary Tablets of Hippocrates. These scriptures held the "medical secrets of the ancients," including a cure for cancer. The evil Vultura, played by Lorna Gray, kept sending her henchmen, including Charles "Ming the Merciless" Middleton, out to retrieve the Tablets and the accompanying treasure for herself. The only hint of a jungle in this serial was Satan, an incredibly designed ape who was Vultura's pet.

Although Linda Stirling was beautifully costumed as *The Tiger Woman* and was, supposedly, head of a jungle tribe, there was no sign of anything even faintly resembling a jungle in the entire serial. LeRoy Mason, the villain of the piece, was trying to acquire Linda's oil lands and a mysterious urn containing the secret of her real background, unknown even to her. On her side was dashing Allan Lane, who defended her against the repeated advances of George J. Lewis and others.

Call of the Savage, which had young Noah Beery, Jr., playing Jan of the Jungle, started out as a routine trek through the woods when suddenly in chapter ten a hidden city was revealed, and Beery, aided by others in the cast, had a marvelous time being trapped in such elaborate devices as a room with descending spikes and a similar room whose floor slid back precipitating its occupants into a flaming abyss. Great fun for all!

More than ten years after *Perils of Nyoka*, Republic churned out an incredible cheapie called *Panther Girl of the Kongo*, which had Phyllis Coates, dressed exactly like Frances Gifford's *Jungle Girl* (for the purpose of matching shots), battling an army of so-called claw monsters who were terrorizing the jungle tribes. The monsters were nothing more than simple crayfish filmed against miniature sets created by Howard Lydecker and his special-effects department.

Ruth Roman, who delivered some quality performances in later years, was the mysterious *Jungle Queen* in Universal's 1945 wartime thriller. The plot of this creaking vehicle revolved around Nazis sending their agents into the (back lot) jungle to stir up the tribes to revolt against the Allies. Helping to keep the villains, led by Douglass Dumbrille, in check were Edward Norris and Eddie Quillan.

Lost City of the Jungle, topcasting Russell Hayden and Keye Luke, had Lionel Atwill playing the lead villain. Atwill died during the production of the film, and in order to complete the serial, shots of a very obvious double were used, photographing the replacement from behind. Then reaction shots of Atwill were spliced in at the appropriate time. Thus a cast member would be seen addressing Atwill in, say, a bar room, and his reaction shot would have Atwill standing in a completely different location. Also embarrassingly hilarious to watch was the matching of Hayden's and Luke's new footage with that of Jon Hall and Sabu from scenes taken from the earlier feature, *White Savage*. Footage from this earlier feature was utilized as chapter endings for at least three episodes. Universal certainly got their money's worth!

There were several other jungle serials of varying degrees of importance. Buster Crabbe was effective as the Lord of the Jungle in *Tarzan, the Fearless*, and not so potent as the Mighty Thunda in *King of the Congo*; Clayton Moore was seen completely at a disadvantage in *Jungle Drums of Africa*, which, almost everyone agrees, was the weakest of the sixty-six serials turned out by Republic; William Tracy and

Granville Owen tried valiantly to uncover the secrets of a lost civilization in *Terry and the Pirates* but only succeeded in finding viewers' funny bones; and Tom Tyler roamed his jungle kingdom in *The Phantom* with much less interest and enthusiasm than he had done many years before when he had helped to solve the *Jungle Mystery*.

On the whole, audiences were thankful that the studios' forays into the jungle were of brief duration.

right: Kay Aldridge represented Republic's second attempt (Frances Gifford was the first) to bring back the image of the serial queen. Her most famous role was that of Nyoka in *Perils of Nyoka* (Republic 1942). *below:* Phyllis Coates (wearing an exact duplicate of Frances Gifford's costume in *Jungle Girl* [Republic 1941] for the matching of stock shots) looks amazingly calm under the circumstances in *Panther Girl of the Kongo* (Republic 1955).

above: Clyde Beatty, Cecilia Parker and Syd Saylor are interrupted by something, or someone, in *The Lost Jungle* (Mascot 1934).
left: Popular "Bring 'Em Back Alive" hunter Frank Buck was the star of Columbia's first serial, *Jungle Menace* (Columbia 1937).
below: Noah Berry, Jr., was Jan of the Jungle in *Call of the Savage* (Universal 1935). Harry Woods, usually a villain but this time cast as Jan's aide, seems to be having a bit of trouble with the snake.

right: Republic, like Columbia, also had a jungle serial as its initial serial offering. Clyde Beatty, here protecting Elaine Shepard, was the star of *Darkest Africa* (Republic 1936). *below:* Clayton Moore was the star of the dullest of all sixty-six Republic serials, *Jungle Drums of Africa* (Republic 1953).

above: Frances Gifford is about to be sacrificed on an elaborate altar which would propel her into a blazing inferno by witch doctor Shamba, played by Frank Lackteen in *Jungle Girl* (Republic 1941). *below:* Cecilia Parker is about to be saved from an unpleasant fate by Tom Tyler, Frank Lackteen, and Noah Berry, Jr., in *Jungle Mystery* (Universal 1932).

Herman Brix (later Bruce Bennett) was one of the best screen Tarzans in
The New Adventures of Tarzan (Burroughs-Tarzan 1935).

Richard Talmadge, one of the greatest of all stunt men, in a spectacular leap in
his starring serial, *Pirate's Treasure* (Universal 1934).

13. The Stunt Men

THE MEN WHO *really* provided the major thrills and excitement in the serials were a small group of professional daredevils called stunt men, whose (planned) recklessness often left the viewing audience gasping in amazement.

During the days of the silent serial, many of the stars' reputations were based on the fact that they performed their own hazardous stunts. Joe Bonomo, Walter Miller, and Pearl White, among many others, seemed to flirt with death in every conceivable fashion as they went from one peril to another. However, as production costs rose, it became more apparent to producers that they could not risk injury to their star properties which might cause the shutdown of production on their films. Thus, a few select men who were willing to risk their lives for surprisingly little money began to travel from studio to studio doing yeoman service for countless leading men and women. Richard Talmadge, Cliff Lyons, and Yakima Canutt, in addition to Bonomo and Miller, formed the nucleus of the original stunt group.

Richard Talmadge was perhaps the most reckless of the group, and those who have seen some of his starring films like *The Speed Reporter, Never Too Late,* and his only starring serial, *Pirate's Treasure,* can only gasp in awe at some of the fantastic leaps he made time after time.

Cliff Lyons was an expert horseman and usually confined himself to doubling for cowboy stars like Buck Jones and Ken Maynard in their many features and serials. Rather heavy-set, Cliff was usually easy to spot when he was doing his action work. Talmadge, Lyons, and Yakima Canutt were all to become excellent second-unit directors in later years.

Yakima Canutt! During his heyday period of the twenties and thirties he doubled for so many people that he probably can't remember them all. A remarkable innovator, it was primarily Yakima who found safe ways to train animals to fall so that they wouldn't be injured, whereas formerly they were often brutally maimed and killed to please producers and directors who wanted thrills at any cost. He also helped bring the well-staged screen fight into being, teaching such Western stalwarts as John Wayne and Johnny Mack Brown how to throw a punch and make it look real. And all real action fans recall with admiration Yakima's specialty of jumping from a stagecoach to the lead horses, falling to the ground, letting the horses and coach pass over him and then catching on to the rear of the coach and climbing aboard again. A quite remarkable man!

As the serials grew in popularity in the thirties and forties, a new crop of eager young men entered the field. Tom Steele had a career which covered duty at Mascot, Universal, Columbia, and Republic, spanning almost the entire serial-producing years. Tom, who could handle almost all stunt specialties, was the head of the Republic staff for close to ten years and doubled almost all of the serial leads, as well as the B-Western leads, during those exciting years of the forties. Still active (he drove one of the cars in that amazing chase sequence in *Bullitt*), Tom looks about twenty years younger than he really is. Constantly on the lookout for new ways to bring honor and distinction to his field, he was one of the founders of the Stunt Men's Association. Tom has the unique distinction of having starred in a film almost as long as *Gone with the Wind* in running time and having received *no* screen credit whatsoever. When Republic made their action classic *The Masked Marvel*, Tom played the hero behind the mask, as well as a villain in a later chapter, and doubled in numerous fight sequences for the other leads, and yet his name never appeared on the screen. It seemed a little unfair, especially since the script was written specifically for him. Such are the ways of Hollywood.

Ask any stunt man who *his* favorite stunt man is and chances are that nine out of ten of them will answer David Sharpe. Sharpe, a superb athlete who specialized in tumbling, has also had a career almost equal in duration to that of Steele. Even though he was relatively short, he was often required to double tall leads like Tom Tyler, Allan Lane, and Kane Richmond. His work at Republic always included spectacular leaps from balconies and acrobatically staged fights in which he would do backflips and assorted other tricks that would have us all standing up and shouting in the aisles. In *The Adventures of Captain Marvel,* in which he doubled for Tom Tyler as the comic-strip hero, Sharpe's flying leaps were so superb that after a while you began to think that the Captain really *could* fly. On a panel show Sharpe was once asked if he had ever done any really dangerous stunts. His reply was no. He continued, "I would never do any stunt that I felt I was not physically capable of performing safely." But even Sharpe could miscalculate once in a great while. For a scene in *Spy Smasher* he was required to stage a spectacular forty-foot leap from a building, which was to blow up in miniature on the screen, to a parked truck. However,

he had not calculated on a heavy wind the day the scene was shot, and, because he was required to wear a cape in the role, which acted as a sail, he almost missed his target. Sharpe, like Steele, is still very active today, and you can find him still leaping off balconies (doubling for Tony Curtis in *The Great Race*) or, dressed like a little old lady, doing somersaults on the *Red Skelton* television show.

Dale Van Sickel was another popular favorite at Republic in the forties. His spectacular fight sequences with Tom Steele are classics. Van Sickel, a little heavier set than Steele, was an All-American football player prior to his film chores. Fast-paced action was routine when Van Sickel played the lead in *Captain America,* doubling for Dick Purcell, or *The Crimson Ghost,* in which he so closely resembled Charles Quigley, who was the star. One of Van Sickel's specialties is stunt driving, and his acrobatic car work for films like *On the Beach* is truly remarkable. Dale had a little stronger acting voice than many of his co-workers, so he is often seen playing character roles in Westerns and serials as well as performing stunt duty.

Eddie Parker was a veritable work-horse at Universal and was kept busy on all phases of their film production. It was Parker and Alan Pomeroy who doubled for Randolph Scott and John Wayne in that spectacular fight sequence in *The Spoilers*. At Republic, Parker could be found in at least one fight sequence per serial released during the forties. It seemed rather sad that, after all the incredible stunt work he had done in films, he was to succumb to a heart attack after working with Ken Terrell on a short fight routine for a Jack Benny television show.

Another tragedy was the accidental death of young Jimmy Fawcett, killed when he was struck by an automobile driven by actor Ralf Harolde. He resembled Sharpe physically, and many feel he would have been one of the top in the field, but his career lasted only a few short years in the late thirties and early forties.

And there are so many more who deserve mention: Duke Green, known affectionately as "Crazy Duke" because of his apparently reckless leaps from desk tops or whatever else happened to be available at the time; Ken Terrell, with his acrobatically staged fights; Fred Graham, who frequently took time off from doubling John Wayne in order to be battered around Republic sets; and, among others, Johnny Dahiem, Harvey Parry, Joe Yrigoyen, Carey Loftin, Ted Mapes, Reed Howes, and Duke Taylor.

These men deserve thanks for every one of those thousands of Days of Thrills and Adventure.

The hardest-working of all serial stunt men was probably Tom Steele. Appearing in Mascot, Universal, and Columbia serials, his most famous work was over at Republic, where he appeared in virtually every serial (and hundreds of Westerns and features) made from the early forties to Republic's demise in 1955. Usually doubling for the lead, Tom made frequent appearances in various episodes of each serial and also as the main villain's henchman. His fight sequences with fellow stunt man Dale Van Sickel are action classics. Here Tom doubles for Richard Powers in *Desperadoes of the West* (Republic 1950).

Tom Steele doubling for Rod Cameron in *Secret Service in Darkest Africa* (Republic 1943).

Dale Van Sickel

Another versatile action double was the talented Dale Van Sickel. Equally adept at fights, motorcycle work, and car chases, Dale helped give Republic its distinctive action style in the forties. In this scene from *The Crimson Ghost* (Republic 1946), Dale, doubling for Charles Quigley, runs up the wall in a spectacular fight sequence with Tom Steele doubling for Clayton Moore. Quite often the stunt men themselves devised these gags to provide variety.

Dale Van Sickel, doubling for Dick Purcell in *Captain America* (Republic 1943), delivers quite a punch to Ken Terrell. Note the band around Ken's neck holding his hat on.

David Sharpe

David Sharpe was an all-around athlete and specialized in tumbling, and his stunt work was filled with elaborate leaps and somersaults. Although he was relatively short, he doubled tall leads such as Tom Tyler and Kane Richmond so well that the youthful serial audience never noticed the difference. In this sequence Sharpe doubles for Don "Red" Barry in *Adventures of Red Ryder* (Republic 1940).

above: After a spectacular fight sequence, Sharpe, doubling for Kane Richmond in *Spy Smqsher* (Republic 1942) does one of his specialties. *below:* David Sharpe doubling for Robert Wilcox as the Copperhead in *Mysterious Dr. Satan* (Republic 1940).

below: David Sharpe doubling for Tom Tyler in *The Adventures of Captain Marvel* (Republic 1941). *opposite page, above:* David Sharpe doubling for Ralph Byrd in *Dick Tracy vs. Crime, Inc.* (Republic 1941). *opposite page, below:* David Sharpe was occasionally called upon to double heroines because of his size. In *Perils of Nyoka* (Republic 1942) he performed many of the action stunts for star Kay Aldridge.

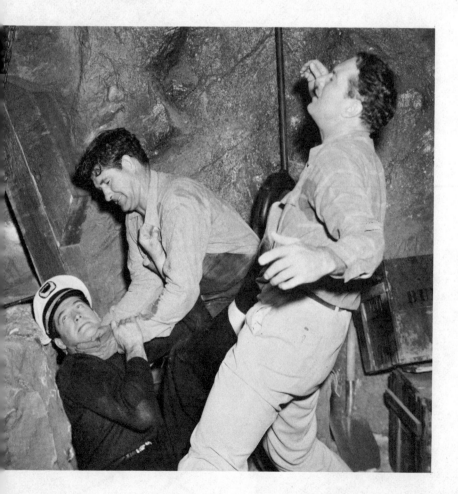

above: When Allan Lane and Lind
Stirling faced Cliff Lyons, Duke Gr
and Eddie Parker in *The Tiger Wo*
(Republic 1944), you knew a trem
dous fight sequence was due any
moment. *left:* In the last chapter of
Haunted Harbor (Republic 1944)
Kane Richmond, doubled in the lo
shots by Dale Van Sickel, battles F
Graham (*center*) and Eddie Parke
doubling for Roy Barcroft.

Yakima Canutt

right: Yakima Canutt is considered the dean of all action stunt men. A tremendous innovator, he went on to become a great second-unit director in later years. In this scene he does a transfer doubling for John Carroll in *Zorro Rides Again* (Republic 1937). *below:* A great deal more adept at stunting than acting, Yakima nevertheless played countless Western villains and minor roles, such as one of the "mole men" menacing Gwen Gaze in *The Secret of Treasure Island* (Columbia 1938).

Most early serial fights were wildly swinging brawls with little technique or form. Yakima helped fashion the well-staged fight which emerged in the late thirties. In this scene from *The Clutching Hand* (Weiss-Mintz 1936), Yakima is about to throw his opponent to the deck. That's Jack Mulhall playing Craig Kennedy, putting a stranglehold on "Bull" Montana.

Joe Bonomo was one of the greatest of the stunt man-stars of the twenties. That's
Ruth Hiatt and James Leong watching Joe's latest feat of strength in *The
Chinatown Mystery* (Syndicate 1928).

Tom Steele, one of the best stunt men in films, portrayed the title role in *The Masked Marvel* (Republic 1943). The Marvel was a mystery man, one of four insurance investigators, who fought the evil Sakima, a Japanese agent bent upon destroying the nation's vital war industries.

14. World War II

REPUBLIC, BEST-EQUIPPED of the serial-producing companies to handle wartime "destruction" scenes on the screen because of their superb special-effects department, devoted five of their seven serials produced during 1942 and 1943 to the subject of fighting the common foe. After that, apparently tiring of the subject, none of the remaining seven serials produced during the war years of 1944 and 1945 had anything to do with the war.

Spy Smasher had hero Kane Richmond, playing twin brothers, opposing a typically hard-faced Nazi, Hans Schumm, called the Mask. Head of a spy ring in America, the Mask was thwarted time and time again as he tried to wreck planes, steal bombsights, and otherwise hinder our campaign against Germany. One particularly exciting chapter climax had Kane Richmond trapped and fleeing through a tunnel on a handcar while flaming oil rushed menacingly behind him. The Mask met a spectacular finish when his escaping submarine hit an Allied mine. One of the requisites of wartime serials was "self-sacrifice," and in *Spy Smasher* both the hero's brother and his closest friend, a Frenchman named Durand, willingly gave up their lives to save that of the spy fighter.

King of the Mounties could claim the distinction of having its hero (Allan Lane playing Sergeant King) battle representatives of all three Axis powers at the same time. Howard Lydecker created a spectacularly effective miniature volcano which the villains entered by means of a miniature "bat plane." For a rousing finale, Sergeant King battled the enemy agents inside the volcano, accidentally knocking some stored bombs into the bubbling lava of the inert monster. Escaping via the "bat plane," he was just able to leave the vicinity of the volcano as the whole mountain erupted in an orgy of destruction. Many years later Republic was to use stock shots of this miniature for the hideout of the *Flying Disc Man from Mars*, and it was laughable to see the mock-up of the spaceship still emblazoned with the "Rising Sun" emblem.

Rod Cameron, playing Rex Bennett, starred in two of the most "explosive" action serials that Republic ever created. Each was filled with complex Lydecker miniatures that erupted in multiple bursts of billowing flame at the end of every episode, or so it seemed. In *G-Men vs. The Black Dragon*, Cameron battled the evil Japanese agent Haruchi, played with appropriate squint-eyed intrigue by Nino Pipitone, who had been smuggled into the United States in a mummy case after he had taken a drug that put him in a state of suspended animation. He too was destroyed when his explosive-laden speedboat crashed into a waiting submarine, sending both man and motorboat to a blazing finale.

Having disposed of the Japanese, Cameron took on the Nazis in another part of the world in *Secret Service in Darkest Africa*. In this action-packed epic, Baron Von Rommler, played by Lionel Royce, captured and took the place of his look-alike, our African ally, Sultan Abou Ben Ali (Royce, again). It took Cameron fifteen episodes and about forty choreographed slugfests to finally uncover the truth and reward the Baron's villainy with death.

The Masked Marvel, an exciting hero, was in reality one of four insurance investigators who were on the trail of the infamous Sakima, a Japanese agent (portrayed by one-time comic-foil Johnny Arthur) bent on destroying our vital war industries. The role had been specifically written to utilize the services of Tom Steele, the head of the Republic serial stunt team. The action sequences were first rate, and once again the special effects dazzled the eye. Sakima met his death in almost a comic fashion. After a gun fight in which the Marvel emptied his gun at the cowering agent, Sakima announced gleefully, "*Your* bullets are all gone, but I still have *one* left." He rose to fire point-blank at the Marvel, only to be felled by another bullet from the masked man's gun. "Did it not occur to your Oriental mind," he proclaimed, "that I might *reload?*" I guess it didn't!

Over at Universal they were fighting the war on a cheaper level. Not possessing a very satisfactory special-effects department, they relied a great deal on integrating newsreel and other stock footage with cheaply done studio interiors. The results were poor, and too many minutes of valuable screen time were wasted. Don Terry was an effective lead in the title role of *Don Winslow of the Navy* and, a year later, *Don Winslow of the Coast Guard*. In both serials he battled a Nazi menace called the Scorpion, who was out to destroy our nation's defenses. A very young Lloyd Bridges also tackled the Nazis in *Secret Agent X-9*, and The Dead End Kids and

The Little Tough Guys took on the enemy in *Sea Raiders* and *Junior G-Men of the Air*. *Adventures of the Flying Cadets* had a bigger budget and managed to be fairly interesting. Combating a mysterious masked villain, the Black Hangman, heroes Johnny Downs and Bobby Jordan portrayed serial protagonists youthful fans could identify with.

Meanwhile, at Columbia they were also carrying on in a somewhat inept fashion, trying to turn out satisfactory serials on a minimal budget and, for the most part, steering clear of war propaganda. The two big exceptions were *The Batman* and *The Secret Code*. *The Batman*, based on the popular comic-strip character, had its masked hero pitted against the evil Japanese agent, Dr. Daka, played for full laugh value by the talented J. Carrol Naish. Its aim sabotage, the laboratory of Dr. Daka was a veritable treasure trove of scientific weapons and devices, including a helmet to convert men into walking zombies and special electrical equipment to bring the dead back to life. On a more pedestrian level, under a trap door the doctor had a carefully prepared pit full of alligators in which he disposed of his unwanted "guests," and, unfortunately, into which he was himself precipitated when chapter fifteen came around.

The Secret Code had versatile performer Paul Kelly playing the masked Black Commando, who was on the trail of an enemy spy ring trying to get possession of a top-secret formula the United States had developed for manufacturing synthetic rubber. After fifteen thrill-packed (for Columbia, they were thrill-packed indeed) episodes, the villains were destroyed by the tried and true method of having their escaping submarine rammed and destroyed. One entertaining gimmick connected with the serial was the inclusion at the end of each chapter of a very short lecture and demonstration on the breaking of secret codes.

opposite page, above: George J. Lewis and Noel Cravat prepare to get Rod Cameron to divulge some defense secrets in *G-Men vs. The Black Dragon* (Republic 1943). This serial contained more of Howard Lydecker's fantastic explosive miniatures than any other Republic serial. *opposite page, below:* Paul Kelly was the Black Commando in the Columbia wartime thriller, *The Secret Code* (Columbia 1942). At the end of each episode the audience was given a short lecture on solving secret messages.

above: Don Terry was *Don Winslow of the Navy* (Universal 1942) and battled the Scorpion, a German bent on Allied destruction. *left:* The *Junior G-Men of the Air* (Universal 1942) fought enemy agents attempting to destroy American air power. In the cast were Frank Albertson, Bernard Punsly, Gabriel Dell, Huntz Hall, and Billy Halop.

right: Lloyd Bridges protects Jan Wiley from Nazi terrorists in *Secret Agent X-9* (Universal 1945). *below:* Allan Lane prepares to tackle Anthony Warde in *King of the Mounties* (Republic 1942). In this rousing epic, the villains were representatives of all three Axis powers: the Nazis, the Italians, and the Japanese. Their stronghold was inside a marvelous Howard Lydecker-constructed volcano, which erupted in a blazing screen finale.

Jack Holt looks as though he has everything well in hand as *Holt of the Secret Service* (Columbia 1941). It was a persistent fault of Columbia serials that they often portrayed a single hero fighting three or more villains at one time—and winning—thus turning the action sequences into comic-strip travesties.

15. They Got Their Men

WHENEVER THE STUDIOS wanted to add variety to their production schedules and still maintain relatively low production costs, they would make a non-Western Western by converting the hero from a fighting cowboy to a gallant Mountie. Aside from the change of costume and a change of location (instead of Iverson's Ranch, the film would probably be shot at Lone Pine, a few hours' drive from the studios), the films remained Western in flavor.

Republic fashioned several excellent screenplays to honor our Canadian neighbors, one of the most enjoyable being *King of the Royal Mounted*, released in 1940. Allan Lane, playing Sergeant King, was an ideal choice to portray the famous Zane Grey character, and the role marked the beginning of a long and rewarding association with the studio. He appeared in three additional serials and scores of Westerns. The action-packed story concerned itself with the discovery of a substance called compound X, which could cure infantile paralysis. Enemy agents found out that the same compound had certain magnetic properties which could make their mines effective against the British Navy. The entire film then dealt with the attempts by the agents to obtain quantities of the rare compound to ship to their government. The film was beautifully photographed, and David Sharpe, doubling in the action scenes for Lane, was in top form.

Two years later Lane starred in a sequel called *King of the Mounties*, which found him battling the Axis powers who were bent on sabotage in North America. Filled with more gimmicks, like a flying "bat plane," the serial was as exciting as the earlier entry.

The only other Mountie films turned out by the studio were 1948's *Dangers of the Canadian Mounted* and 1953's *Canadian Mounties vs. Atomic Invaders*. The former found Jim Bannon playing Christopher Royal on the trail of a gang headed by a mysterious Boss who was trying to locate the treasure of Genghis Khan, which turned out to be "liquid" diamonds which solidified when they were released from their ancient container; the latter found Bill Henry playing Sergeant Dan Roberts as he pursued enemy agents who were trying to establish missile sites from which they could launch an attack against North America. Both serials contained stock footage from the earlier Lane thrillers.

Universal and Columbia had managed to turn out a few serials starring the "Men in Red," but on the whole they were fairly routine actioners.

Tom Tyler was excellent in *Clancy of the Mounted* and Bill Kennedy was adequate in *The Royal Mounted Rides Again*, Universal's two entries in the field, while *Perils of the Royal Mounted*, starring Robert Kellard (billed now as Robert Stevens), *Gunfighters of the Northwest*, with Jack Mahoney (who went through several name changes), and *Perils of the Wilderness*, with Dennis Moore, did very little to cement American–Canadian relationships.

While serial makers were saluting our neighbors to the north, our own law-enforcement officials were helping to stamp out crime on the screen in a number of excellent screenplays. *Federal Operator 99* found Marten Lamont on the trail of the notorious Jim Belmont, a vicious criminal (expertly played by George J. Lewis) who, between various acts of villainy, liked to play the "Moonlight Sonata" on the piano. The finale of this serial was one of the most exciting ever filmed. The studio rented a deserted theatre in Hollywood, and director Spencer Bennet had his actors stage a beautifully photographed chase-and-fight sequence high above the stage in the fly area, from which the evil Belmont plunged to his death.

G-Men Never Forget gave veteran serial villain Roy Barcroft a chance to play a dual role. As the racketeer leader Murkland, Barcroft discovers his close resemblance to Commissioner Cameron. He kidnaps the policeman and assumes his identity to further his reign of terror. Clayton Moore, playing the hero, finally discovers the substitution and rescues the Commissioner. In a wild fight sequence, Barcroft as Cameron killed Barcroft's Murkland.

Our law officers in the South were guarding our security as well. "Slingin' Sammy" Baugh, the famous football star of the late thirties, deserted the gridiron, on film at any rate, to join the Texas Rangers when his Ranger father was mysteriously killed. The villain of the piece was Neil Hamilton, who was working for an unidentified alien power whose representative, referred to as His Excellency, hovered over the Texas plains in a dirigible giving instructions to his earthbound agents to sabotage vital industries. *King of the Texas Rangers*, released in 1941, was filled with spectacular special effects by Howard Lydecker, including a complete oil-field holocaust, the blowing-up of a dam, the wrecking of a tunnel while a train was passing through, and the grand finale which had Baugh's plane plunging into the hovering dirigible, destroying the enemy agents in an exploding ball of flame.

In *Government Agents vs. Phantom Legion*, hero Walter Reed was combating a mystery man known simply as the Voice, who was bent upon disrupting the country's system of highway transportation; and in *Radar Patrol vs. Spy King*, Kirk Alyn had the task of tracking down the head of "the most dangerous ring of saboteurs in the annals of military intelligence," the evil Baroda. Both of these later Republic serials borrowed heavily from *G-Men vs. The Black Dragon* and other vintage material.

Even the United Nations found it needed help when a band of foreign agents began smuggling arms and munitions to subversive native groups in the Asian coastal country of Burmatra, where a revolution was being planned. Dispatched jiffy-quick to dispel these alien dreams of glory was Harry Lauter as *Trader Tom of the China Seas*. Of eleven chapter endings, only two were original for this serial; the remainder were taken from the earlier *Haunted Harbor, S.O.S. Coast Guard*, and *Drums of Fu Manchu*. Economy was indeed the word in those post-1948 serials.

And just to show audiences how important youngsters could be, Universal decided to let the Boy Scouts have their chance to help combat crime. In 1939's *Scouts to the Rescue*, young Jackie Cooper and his pals helped crack a counterfeiting ring operating in a deserted ghost town. Along the way they battled some rather offensive Indians who were trying to conceal a hidden cache of radium in their underground temple. It was excellent fun, and it gave the youthful viewers some heroes with whom they could more closely identify. Universal was to later utilize The Dead End Kids and The Little Tough Guys in future serials, such as *Sea Raiders* and *Junior G-Men of the Air*, for the same reason.

Also on the trail of counterfeiters was Jack Holt as *Holt of the Secret Service*, a Columbia release of 1941 which should have been better made. Unfortunately, Holt was just a little too old to engage in all the action, and kids could not really accept him.

No matter what the challenge may have been to our crime-fighters, the Allies always, somehow, managed to win. Whether it was opposing the Axis powers during World War II (*G-*

Men vs. The Black Dragon, Secret Service in Darkest Africa, etc.) or home-front racketeers *Gang Busters, Secret Agent X-9*, etc.), we sent our best-looking, most-qualified, strongest, and most durable leading men out to fight our battles. And in each and every instance, "they got their man."

right: Tom Tyler uncovers an important clue in *Clancy of the Mounted* (Universal 1933). *below:* In *Federal Agents vs. Underworld, Inc.* (Republic 1949), hero Kirk Alyn frequently tangled with Roy Barcroft and ace stunt man Tom Steele.

above: Allan Lane was a perfect choice to portray Sergeant King in the serial version of the popular comic strip *King of the Royal Mounted* (Republic 1940). This was the first of Lane's four serials for Republic. *below:* George Chesebro gets the drop on Robert Kellard in *Perils of the Royal Mounted* (Columbia 1942).

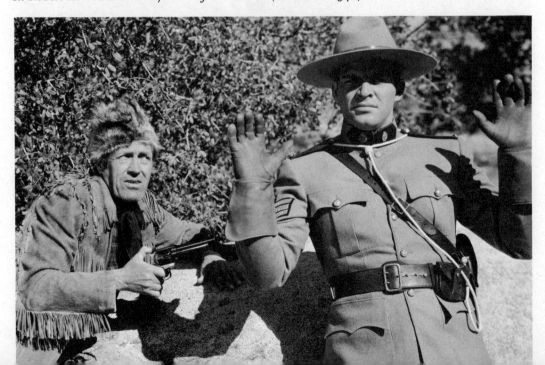

right: Walter Reed delivers a right cross to veteran villain Dick Curtis in *Government Agents vs. Phantom Legion* (Republic 1951). *below:* Harry Lauter, *second from right,* was a United Nations operative in *Trader Tom of the China Seas* (Republic 1954), assisted by Aline Towne as they uncover some villainy being planned by Fred Graham, *left,* and Tom Steele, two of Republic's best stunt men.

above: Jim Bannon thinks he has Anthony Warde under arrest, but stunt man Ken Terrell has other plans in this scene from *Dangers of the Canadian Mounties* (Republic 1948). *right:* Marten Lamont, who possessed a marked English accent, seemed a peculiar choice to play *Federal Operator* 99 (Republic 1945), but he proved quite satisfactory. Ken Terrell gets the handcuff treatment in this scene from the film. *below:* Dale Van Sickel, a superb fight stunt man, takes one on the chin from Bill Henry in *Canadian Mounties vs. Atomic Invaders* (Republic 1953).

above: In *G-Men Never Forget* (Republic 1948) long-time villain Roy Barcroft, *left,* had a chance to play a dual role and ended the serial by killing his villainous counterpart. Aiding in discovering the deception were Clayton Moore and Ramsay Ames. *right:* Jack Mahoney, a first-rate stunt man, provided most of his own thrills in *Gunfighters of the Northwest* (Columbia 1954). *below:* Clayton Moore, this time on the wrong side of the law, tries to get information on the mysterious "cyclotrode" from Charles Quigley in *The Crimson Ghost* (Republic 1946).

The Scorpion was out to gain world domination by controlling the "golden scorpion
atom-smasher" in *The Adventures of Captain Marvel* (Republic 1941).

16. Behind the Mask

THE SCORPION, the Ghost, the Octopus, the Wasp, the Lame One, the Spider, the Rattler, the Black Ace, the Dragon, the Mask, the Crimson Ghost, the Tiger Shark, Captain Mephisto, the Voice, the Eagle, Dr. Vulcan, and the Whispering Shadow . . .

What a magnificent collection, and only partial at that, of marvelous screen monstrosities!

If it was vitally important to the serial fan that the hero be the epitome of the "true-blue" good guy, it was no less important that the principal villain be depicted as evil incarnate. The appearance of a masked menace or mystery man, rather than the routine villain, was a time-tested hook for grabbing the interest of the youthful fan and bringing him back to the theatre week after week.

The concept of the mystery man was a simple theme with variations played over and over again. Usually there were three, four, or five men comprising a board of directors, or group of scientists, or staff of university professors, etc., one of whom led a villainous double life. Trying to guess which of the group was the guilty party was really a waste of time, for logical clues were seldom given to help you in making your decision. Your odds did increase, however, as the suspects in each particular group were gradually eliminated, usually by means of sudden and violent death, until only

two remained in the last chapter. And when the final denouement came, it was often a traumatic experience to find that, after fifteen weeks, you had guessed—*wrong!*

When it comes right down to picking a favorite among all these masters of menace, the choice usually narrows to two: the Lightning from the 1938 *Fighting Devil Dogs* and the Scorpion from the highly successful *The Adventures of Captain Marvel*, released in 1941.

The Lightning was indeed an imposing menace with his glistening black helmet and flowing cape. Possessing a deadly "electronic thunderbolt," he was systematically terrorizing the world by destroying ships, dirigibles, and entire communities. The assorted suspects included electronics specialists, a gardener, and a shifty-eyed butler. Quite naturally, the villain turned out to be the least obvious—or did he? The special effects of the Lightning's deadly attacks were spectacularly effective in helping to establish an aura of supreme evil.

But, as spectacular as the Lightning was, most serial aficionados are prone to accept the Scorpion as the more interesting villain. Perhaps the plot of *The Adventures of Captain Marvel* had more to do with this choice than the villain himself. A group of archaeologists travel to a remote region in Siam and there discover a tomb containing a mysterious "golden scorpion" containing five lenses which, when focused together, can create gold from ordinary rocks or, when placed in another position, can become one of the most deadly weapons known to man. The lenses are divided among the members of the expedition. That night the Scorpion, cloaked in a black mask and robe emblazoned with the emblem of the Scorpion dynasty, makes off with the skeleton of the deadly device, and the serial then moves into high gear as the sinister figure goes after the four lenses held by the remaining members of the party. When the final chapter unreels, all but one of the suspects has been violently disposed of. Captain Marvel exposes the Scorpion just in time to save the world, and the hooded figure is destroyed in the ray of the deadly machine, which is then, in turn, destroyed for all time.

A great factor in the success of the Scorpion's characterization was the use of Gerald Mohr's dubbed-in voice. This was a favorite cheat of the serial-makers. Since most of the suspects' voices would be readily identifiable, other voices were frequently used to the dismay of the attentive viewer. How boldly they cheated was best evidenced in *The Crimson Ghost*, in which they used I. Stanford Jolley's voice for the Crimson Ghost and, at the same time, included him in a scene in one of the later chapters in which he was quickly killed. Of course, there are always exceptions to the general rule: in *Dick Tracy vs. Crime, Inc.* the Ghost's voice actually belonged to the suspect involved.

Captain Mephisto in *Manhunt of Mystery Island* was one of the most intriguing of all serial mystery men. In this action-packed epic the hero (Richard Bailey) and heroine (Linda Stirling) travel to Mystery Island in search of the latter's father, the inventor of a "radiatomic transmitter"—another potentially "world-dominating" device. Of the four owner-suspects on the island, one is capable of placing himsel[f] a strangely constructed chair and by turning great electrical power is able to rearrange molecular structure so that he emerges from chair as a completely different personality— reincarnation of an early pirate, Cap[t] Mephisto (superbly played by Roy Barcroft his favorite serial role). The bold pirate is h[old]ing the girl's father prisoner and is forcing [him] to build a more powerful and deadly machi[ne] Before Mephisto meets his well-deserved e[nd] the hero is almost put through the transform[a]tion in the hope that he will be mistaken for [the] pirate and killed.

The Ghost in *Dick Tracy vs. Crime, Inc.*, b[e]sides wearing a mask, had the additional a[d]vantage of having the ability to become invisib[le] through the aid of a machine developed by h[is] chief henchman, Lucifer. This gave the specia[l] effects people at Republic a chance to utilize a[ll] kinds of visual tricks, and the final fight sequence in chapter fifteen is a masterpiece. In order to make the Ghost visible, Dick Tracy makes use of a special lamp bulb which, when turned on, emits infra red beams which reverse the polarity of the entire room and everything in it, exposing the arch-villain. This tremendous effect was achieved simply by printing the entire sequence in negative. The Ghost's demise was equally spectacular. Fleeing from Tracy, and still invisible, he attempts to escape by crossing high-tension wires. When the power switch is suddenly thrown on, the Ghost bursts into flame and plunges to the ground.

On and on they came. Dr. Vulcan with his "decimator" in *King of the Rocket Men, The Crimson Ghost* with his "cyclotrode," and all the others. They were evil, monstrous, power-mad devils, and they all met well-deserved ends —and audiences *loved* every one of them!

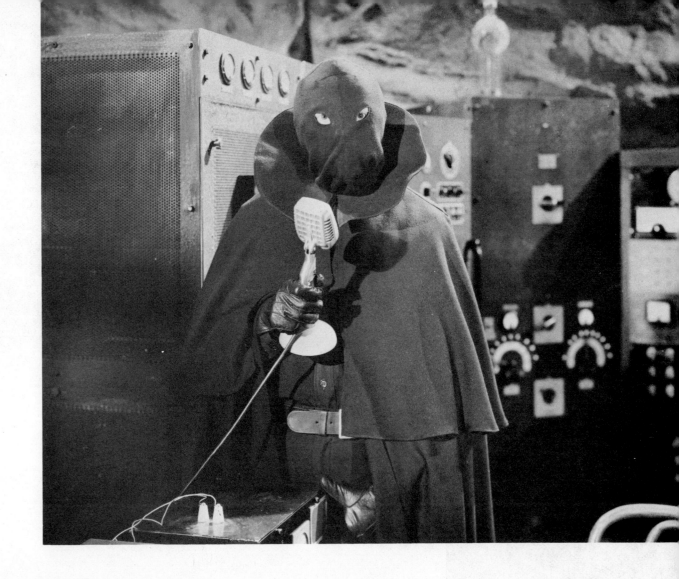

above: Batman and Robin (Columbia 1949) were out to discover who the Wizard was. *left:* Reed Hadley as Zorro and Paul Marian think they are about to unmask the mysterious Don Del Oro in *Zorro's Fighting Legion* (Republic 1939).

149

above: The Wasp finally meets Warren Hull as Mandrake face to face in *Mandrake the Magician* (Columbia 1939). *left: Dick Tracy* (Republic 1937) had to contend with this fellow, who went under the name of the Spider and the Lame One. *below:* Bob Steele is about to unmask the Black Ace in *Mystery Squadron* (Mascot 1933).

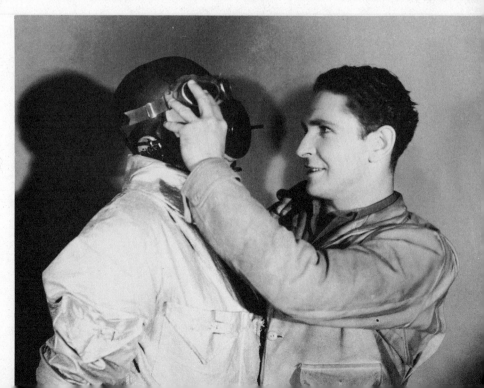

The villainous El Shaitan delivers orders to his men in *The Three Musketeers* (Mascot 1933).

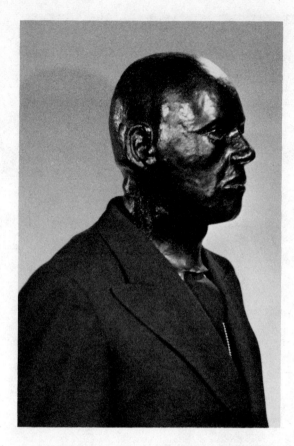

above, left: The Gargoyle was often more laughable than menacing in *The Spider Returns* (Columbia 1941). *above, right:* The Ghost in *Dick Tracy vs. Crime, Inc.* (Republic 1941) also had the power to become invisible. *left:* *The Crimson Ghost* (Republic 1946) was a menacing antagonist with his deadly "cyclotrode."

above: The Black Hangman appears to have the advantage over Charles Trowbridge in *Adventures of the Flying Cadets* (Universal 1943). *below:* The Lightning, chief opponent of the *Fighting Devil Dogs* (Republic 1938), orders his men to fire an "electrical fire bolt."

Dennis Moore, Gregg Barton, and Lee Roberts were the stars of Columbia's final serial, *Blazing the Overland Trail* (Columbia 1956).

17. The Final Episode

HAVING ALREADY WITNESSED the death throes of pulp fiction and the glorious days of radio adventure, it was another minor traumatic experience to watch the serial fade into obscurity. After more than forty years of continuous production, no longer would anxious youths run to their favorite theatres to watch bigger-than-life heroes tackle supreme apostles of evil.

There were several important reasons for the death of the serials. Chief among these, of course, was the problem of economics. In the early days serials could be turned out relatively inexpensively, most of them being primarily shot outdoors. However, as the years progressed and production costs rose, the serial format began to look less and less appealing to the cost-conscious producer. And serials, on the whole, never really created that much revenue. The average episode was rented to a theatre for only a few dollars as an incentive to take additional features from the producing company. Those few dollars did mount up eventually, but as the years progressed the number of theatres running serials dwindled from thousands to a matter of hundreds.

When serials had reached a new peak of popularity in the early forties, it was thought that there would always be a market for the weekly adventures. Unfortunately, the people who believed this had not reckoned on televi-sion. With the growth of that all-seeing eye, youngsters could now watch complete action adventures right at home. Adventure series like *Dick Tracy, Sky King, Sergeant Preston of the Yukon, The Cisco Kid, Hopalong Cassidy, The Gene Autry Show, The Roy Rogers Show, The Lone Ranger*, etc., provided the young viewers with all the action material necessary to keep them satisfied.

There was an additional problem that confronted the serial-makers. Serials had always been filled with assorted violence and mayhem. Now the mothers and professional psychologists were beginning to attack the Saturday cliff-hangers on a rather broad front, claiming they were inducing every conceivable form of nervous ailment from extreme trauma to ringworm. The same rather vague reasons proffered by the same rather vague people caused serials to be canceled when they were shown on television in later years. All this, of course, was despite the fact that the serials provided a basic moral truth: "good always triumphs over evil." There were never any delicate shadings of purpose in the serials. The villains were *all* bad and deserved the violent fates decreed them, and the heroes were *all* good and deserved the right to mete out justice. Now, of course, we are told that life is not all good or all bad but spans the complete range between the two. I think I

155

would have hated to believe, many years ago when I sat in my favorite theatre watching *The Adventures of Captain Marvel*, that the Scorpion was a victim of a deprived childhood and that he wore his mask as an act of visual hostility towards a society which found no place in its overall scheme for him and his kind. Now *that* would have really given me a trauma.

Universal Pictures, whose serial-production history went back into the earliest days of silent films, was the first studio to realize the chapter plays had had it. The studio which had turned out such superior action fare as *Flash Gordon, Ace Drummond, Buck Rogers*, and so many favorites of the late thirties now found its market too limited for the costs involved and canceled further production after 1946. It was, perhaps, just as well, for the quality of their productions had slipped to the point where there was so little action and excitement that it was more of a chore than a pleasure to watch them. Universal had always stressed in their serials plot rather than action, and some of their serials were so talky that you simply couldn't follow what was going on half the time. When *Mysterious Mr. M* brought the Universal serial line to a close, fans viewed the demise with mixed emotions. The plot of *Mysterious Mr. M* found federal agent Grant Farrell (Dennis Moore) assisting a local plainclothesman (Richard Martin) in solving the disappearance of a famous inventor specializing in undersea devices. After thirteen dull episodes the mystery man turned out to be exactly who viewers thought it was in chapter one.

Feeling was more pronounced when Republic finally threw in the towel with *King of the Carnival* in 1955. Even at the end, though economy was all too evident, there was still enough interest (this final serial did have a mystery man) and excitement to satisfy the viewer who was not spoiled by those earlier action classics. Republic, unlike Universal and Columbia, had stockpiled nearly fifteen years of wonderful special effects built especially for their serials and features by Howard Lydecker and his special-effects department. Unlike the cheap newsreel footage constantly integrated in serials at Universal, these spectacular miniatures seemed as thrilling in 1955 as they had in 1945 or earlier. Spliced into new footage, admittedly slower and more routine, the chapter endings were still appealing and continued to bring audiences back week after week. In the great days of the studio as many as seven writers were involved in writing the fast-moving screenplay for a single serial (*Captain America*), and chapters ran up to sixteen or seventeen minutes each, with first episodes running as long as thirty minutes. The final thirteen serials turned out by the studio were written entirely by one writer, Ronald Davidson, and the running time per episode had been reduced to a standard thirteen minutes with a twenty-minute first chapter. The great days of free-swinging fights in which complete sets were demolished were a thing of the past. Fights were now done in small, cramped sets with the stunt men moving at a pace considerably slower than in years gone by. *King of the Carnival* found high-wire acrobats Harry Lauter and Fran Bennett on the trail of a counterfeiting ring operating in the circus in which they were employed. The mystery man was either seen roaming around in a clown costume or heard giving instructions to his henchmen via a two-way radio. Again, there was only one likely suspect for the mystery man. In an exciting finale, the villain is unmasked and plunges to his death after a thrilling chase, thus ending his reign of terror and bringing to a close the serial output of Republic Pictures Corporation.

Columbia decided to ring down their final curtain with the customary cheapness expected from them; they chose a Western, *Blazing the Overland Trail*, and a very routine one at that. The pedestrian plot found evil Rance Devlin (Don C. Harvey) planning to create a private army to take over the territory. Opposing him were Lee Roberts and Dennis Moore (Moore had the dubious distinction of appearing in the final serials of both Universal and Columbia). The film was so full of stock from earlier serials and features that it was hard to accept it as a new attraction. Spencer Gordon Bennet, who had directed more sound serials than any other director, including the thrill-packed *Secret Service in Darkest Africa, The Masked Marvel, Haunted Harbor*, and others, for Republic, and over twenty assorted titles for Columbia, seemed a fitting choice to bring the life of the serial, now in its terminal stage, to a peaceful and routine end. Released in 1956, *Blazing the Overland Trail* climaxed an uninterrupted flow of silent and sound serials which totaled more than five hundred titles spanning a period of forty-odd years.

Except for occasional screening on television, or a very rare re-issue to theatres, the younger generation is unable to see and enjoy these wonderful products of a vanished era. It is really a pity, for every child should be allowed to enjoy his own precious Days of Thrills and Adventure while those fleeting days of youthful escapism are still available to him.

right: Pamela Blake and Dennis Moore tried to uncover the *Mysterious Mr. M* (Universal 1946), in Universal's last serial effort. *below:* That's Harry Lauter lying on the tracks in one of the oldest serial endings. Although *King of the Carnival* (Republic 1955) had a mystery man and utilized some good stock endings, it was a poor finale to the serial output of the greatest of the serial-making studios.

A display ad for the revival of *The Adventures of Captain Marvel* (Republic 1941) in 1966 at the Trans-Lux 49th St. Theatre in New York. Notice the misspelling, of "Scorpion" and "villains"!

18. The Great Serial Revival of 1965-66

TRYING TO FORECAST motion picture trends is almost impossible. The public is, and always has been, fickle and unpredictable. Thus it was a complete surprise to all serial fans when the Batman craze burst on the horizon in late 1965. The "camp" mania was in full bloom, old movie-star posters glared out at us from hundreds of store windows, and film festivals were sprouting up all over the place. Some ambitious young entrepreneur in Chicago decided to book all fifteen chapters of the 1943 Columbia serial, *The Batman,* for a single after-midnight screening. The serial, ludicrous in its stereotyped casting of the Japanese villain, portrayed by J. Carrol Naish, and ill-costumed heroes, Lewis Wilson as Batman and Douglas Croft as Robin, the Boy Wonder, was so funny, and received so much notoriety because of the screening, that Columbia decided to reissue the entire fifteen-chapter serial to theatres in a major re-release. New ads proudly proclaimed: "Made in 1943 . . . . Discovered in 1965! Columbia Pictures presents An Evening with Batman and Robin. The greatest serial ever filmed . . . now the In-tertainment scoop of the year." Even *Time* magazine focused on the phenomenon, and the November 26, 1965 issue proclaimed, "Two high-camp folk heroes in a marathon of fist-fights, zombies & Ravenous Alligators!" The nation's response to the reissue was, indeed, phenom-

enal. The grosses were tremendous, and a sequel to the first serial, *Batman and Robin,* had its fifteen episodes split into two sections which were shown in dozens of theatres on succeeding Saturday matinees.

Republic Pictures Corporation, with a vault full of the best action serials, made up new prints of the 1941 *The Adventures of Captain Marvel* and the 1942 *Spy Smasher*. These two serials, both based on comic-strip heroes, were felt to be the most likely to follow the successful pattern of the Columbia reissues. Unfortunately, the release of *The Adventures of Captain Marvel* failed to achieve any notable success at all. Republic was crestfallen. Why had a superior product failed? Well, the answer was just *that* simple. When audiences had packed into the theatres to see Batman in action, they were prepared to laugh at a film that was basically ludicrous in its representation on the screen. When they came to see Captain Marvel, they had expected to do the same, but didn't. *The Adventures of Captain Marvel* was just too well made to laugh at. They did find themselves laughing *with* it, however, and enjoying it as superior screen escapism from another era. Republic chalked up the experiment as a failure, and *Spy Smasher* never saw the light of a carbon arc.

There was also another reason for the success of *The Batman* reissue. Right to this very day,

159

the Batman is still a regularly distributed comic-book character, appearing every month on the newsstands. Captain Marvel was withdrawn from circulation over fifteen years ago when Fawcett Publications, distributor of the character's adventures, lost a multi-million-dollar suit to National Periodicals, who claimed that the Captain Marvel character was a direct steal from their Superman. Thus, a whole generation of younger filmgoers had never heard of Captain Marvel, while they were completely familiar with Batman.

Republic did derive some subsidiary benefits from the serial craze, however. They re-edited twenty-six of their serials into 100-minute feature versions and made them available to television in a package labeled "Century 66." Many stations continue to play the package even today, although many of the versions vary in quality from excellent to ridiculous. The major problem in editing a fifteen-episode serial is to maintain the continuity and retain most of the action sequences. (One of the sillier complications occurs when characters who have been killed off reappear any number of times thereafter. When episodes were spaced weeks apart, memories were slow to recall who had been killed, and who had appeared in earlier episodes. Stunt man Fred Graham gets killed and reappears at least five or six times in *D-Day on Mars*, the feature version of *The Purple Monster Strikes*.)

Based on the success of the "camp" reissue, Twentieth Century-Fox acquired television rights to the Batman character and went into full-scale production after the series was sold to the American Broadcasting Company. Unfortunately, the character was portrayed on a childish, comic-strip level and held little interest for the serial lover who had hoped for a throwback to the great action days of the forties. The only real interest lay in the casting of name actors and actresses as the villains. Burgess Meredith was a superb Penguin and Cesar Romero was equally delightful in portraying the Joker.

The following season, the Green Hornet was brought to the television screen in a somewhat straighter fashion, played for action rather than laughs. It just didn't catch on and was dropped after only one season.

Merchandising on Batman and Green Hornet items was enormously successful, almost to the point of oversaturation. In a way we were glad to see them both go, and go they did at a rather rapid pace. That fickle public again!

One other side effect based on the success of the original reissue was the release of an abridged version of *The Batman* serial in eight-millimeter film for the home market. Sales were tremendous and encouraged Republic to place a number of its condensed serial versions out in the small-size film also.

And how about the birth of *new* serials? Will some creative young genius suddenly "discover" that you can make films that are exciting and which move, rather than films which are static and overly talky? How about a serial made in the ultimate creative process—3-D? Can you visualize a theatre audience watching a blazing car plunge into its midst, or a bursting dam flooding the middle aisles? The very thought causes the pulse to quicken and the mind to boggle.

There is a definite market for the serial, even if it is only in eight millimeter. One enterprising film-maker has actually produced and marketed a new four-chapter serial satirizing the old Republic style. Louis McMahon's *Captain Celluloid vs. The Film Pirates* may be the prototype of a whole new field of home-movie entertainment. The quality of film and cameras has become so excellent in recent years that cinema buffs may soon start a new type of film production aimed directly at the home movie market.

above, left: Young Douglas Croft was Robin, the Boy Wonder in *The Batman* (Columbia 1943). *above, right:* Lewis Wilson as *The Batman* (Columbia 1943).
below: J. Carrol Naish was an incredibly stereotyped agent of the Rising Sun in *The Batman* (Columbia 1943).

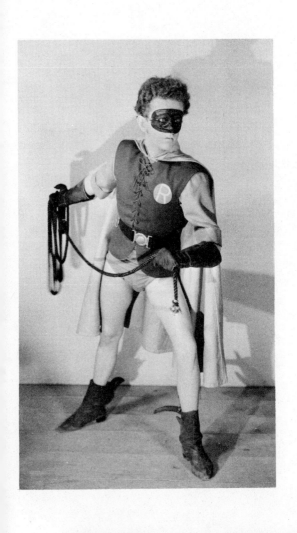

Appendix

COMPLETE LIST OF SOUND SERIALS
(arranged chronologically by studio)

REPUBLIC PICTURES CORPORATION

	TITLE	STAR	NO. OF EPISODES	YEAR
1.	*Darkest Africa*	Clyde Beatty	15	1936
2.	*Undersea Kingdom*	Ray "Crash" Corrigan	12	
3.	*The Vigilantes Are Coming*	Robert Livingston	12	
4.	*Robinson Crusoe of Clipper Island*	Mala	14	
5.	*Dick Tracy*	Ralph Byrd	15	1937
6.	*The Painted Stallion*	Ray Corrigan	12	
7.	*S.O.S. Coast Guard*	Ralph Byrd	12	
8.	*Zorro Rides Again*	John Carroll	12	
9.	*The Lone Ranger*	Lee Powell	15	1938
10.	*Fighting Devil Dogs*	Lee Powell	12	
11.	*Dick Tracy Returns*	Ralph Byrd	15	
12.	*Hawk of the Wilderness*	Herman Brix	12	
13.	*The Lone Ranger Rides Again*	Robert Livingston	15	1939
14.	*Daredevils of the Red Circle*	Charles Quigley	12	
15.	*Dick Tracy's G-Men*	Ralph Byrd	15	
16.	*Zorro's Fighting Legion*	Reed Hadley	12	
17.	*Drums of Fu Manchu*	Henry Brandon	15	1940
18.	*Adventures of Red Ryder*	Don "Red" Barry	12	
19.	*King of the Royal Mounted*	Allan Lane	12	
20.	*Mysterious Dr. Satan*	Eduardo Ciannelli	15	
21.	*The Adventures of Captain Marvel*	Tom Tyler	12	1941
22.	*Jungle Girl*	Frances Gifford	15	
23.	*King of the Texas Rangers*	"Slingin' Sammy" Baugh	12	
24.	*Dick Tracy vs. Crime, Inc.*	Ralph Byrd	15	
25.	*Spy Smasher*	Kane Richmond	12	1942

TITLE	STAR	NO. OF EPISODES	YEAR
26. *Perils of Nyoka*	Kay Aldridge	15	
27. *King of the Mounties*	Allan Lane	12	
28. *G-Men vs. The Black Dragon*	Rod Cameron	15	1943
29. *Daredevils of the West*	Allan Lane	12	
30. *Secret Service in Darkest Africa*	Rod Cameron	15	
31. *The Masked Marvel*	William Forrest	12	
32. *Captain America*	Dick Purcell	15	1944
33. *The Tiger Woman*	Allan Lane	12	
34. *Haunted Harbor*	Kane Richmond	15	
35. *Zorro's Black Whip*	George J. Lewis	12	
36. *Manhunt of Mystery Island*	Richard Bailey	15	1945
37. *Federal Operator 99*	Marten Lamont	12	
38. *The Purple Monster Strikes*	Dennis Moore	15	
39. *The Phantom Rider*	Robert Kent	12	1946
40. *King of the Forest Rangers*	Larry Thompson	12	
41. *Daughter of Don Q*	Adrian Booth	12	
42. *The Crimson Ghost*	Charles Quigley	12	
43. *Son of Zorro*	George Turner	13	1947
44. *Jesse James Rides Again*	Clayton Moore	13	
45. *The Black Widow*	Bruce Edwards	13	
46. *G-Men Never Forget*	Clayton Moore	12	1948
47. *Dangers of the Canadian Mounted*	Jim Bannon	12	
48. *Adventures of Frank and Jesse James*	Clayton Moore	13	
49. *Federal Agents vs. Underworld, Inc.*	Kirk Alyn	12	1949
50. *Ghost of Zorro*	Clayton Moore	12	
51. *King of the Rocket Men*	Tristram Coffin	12	
52. *The James Brothers of Missouri*	Keith Richards	12	1950
53. *Radar Patrol vs. Spy King*	Kirk Alyn	12	
54. *The Invisible Monster*	Richard Webb	12	
55. *Desperadoes of the West*	Richard Powers	12	
56. *Flying Disc Man from Mars*	Walter Reed	12	1951
57. *Don Daredevil Rides Again*	Ken Curtis	12	
58. *Government Agents vs. Phantom Legion*	Walter Reed	12	
59. *Radar Men from the Moon*	George Wallace	12	1952
60. *Zombies of the Stratosphere*	Judd Holdren	12	
61. *Jungle Drums of Africa*	Clay Moore	12	1953
62. *Canadian Mounties vs. Atomic Invaders*	Bill Henry	12	
63. *Trader Tom of the China Seas*	Harry Lauter	12	1954
64. *Man with the Steel Whip*	Richard Simmons	12	
65. *Panther Girl of the Kongo*	Phyllis Coates	12	1955
66. *King of the Carnival*	Harry Lauter	12	

COLUMBIA PICTURES CORPORATION

TITLE	STAR	NO. OF EPISODES	YEAR
1. *Jungle Menace*	Frank Buck	15	1937
2. *The Mysterious Pilot*	Captain Frank Hawks	15	
3. *The Secret of Treasure Island*	Don Terry	15	1938
4. *The Great Adventures of Wild Bill Hickok*	Gordon Elliott	15	
5. *The Spider's Web*	Warren Hull	15	
6. *Flying G-Men*	Robert Paige	15	1939
7. *Mandrake the Magician*	Warren Hull	12	
8. *Overland with Kit Carson*	Bill Elliott	15	
9. *The Shadow*	Victor Jory	15	1940
10. *Terry and the Pirates*	William Tracy	15	
11. *Deadwood Dick*	Don Douglas	15	

TITLE	STAR	NO. OF EPISODES	YEAR
12. *The Green Archer*	Victor Jory	15	
13. *White Eagle*	Buck Jones	15	1941
14. *The Spider Returns*	Warren Hull	15	
15. *The Iron Claw*	Charles Quigley	15	
16. *Holt of the Secret Service*	Jack Holt	15	
17. *Captain Midnight*	Dave O'Brien	15	1942
18. *Perils of the Royal Mounted*	Robert Stevens	15	
19. *The Secret Code*	Paul Kelly	15	
20. *The Valley of Vanishing Men*	Bill Elliott	15	
21. *The Batman*	Lewis Wilson	15	1943
22. *The Phantom*	Tom Tyler	15	
23. *The Desert Hawk*	Gilbert Roland	15	1944
24. *Black Arrow*	Robert Scott	15	
25. *Brenda Starr, Reporter*	Joan Woodbury	13	1945
26. *The Monster and the Ape*	Robert Lowery	15	
27. *Jungle Raiders*	Kane Richmond	15	
28. *Who's Guilty?*	Robert Kent	15	
29. *Hop Harrigan*	William Bakewell	15	1946
30. *Chick Carter, Detective*	Lyle Talbot	15	
31. *Son of the Guardsman*	Robert Shaw	15	
32. *Jack Armstrong*	John Hart	15	1947
33. *The Vigilante*	Ralph Byrd	15	
34. *The Sea Hound*	Buster Crabbe	15	
35. *Brick Bradford*	Kane Richmond	15	
36. *Tex Granger*	Robert Kellard	15	1948
37. *Superman*	Kirk Alyn	15	
38. *Congo Bill*	Don McGuire	15	
39. *Bruce Gentry*	Tom Neal	15	1949
40. *Batman and Robin*	Robert Lowery	15	
41. *Adventures of Sir Galahad*	George Reeves	15	
42. *Cody of the Pony Express*	Jock O'Mahoney	15	1950
43. *Atom Man vs. Superman*	Kirk Alyn	15	
44. *Pirates of the High Seas*	Buster Crabbe	15	
45. *Roar of the Iron Horse*	Jock O'Mahoney	15	1951
46. *Mysterious Island*	Richard Crane	15	
47. *Captain Video*	Judd Holdren	15	
48. *King of the Congo*	Buster Crabbe	15	1952
49. *Blackhawk*	Kirk Alyn	15	
50. *Son of Geronimo*	Clay Moore	15	
51. *The Lost Planet*	Judd Holdren	15	1953
52. *The Great Adventures of Captain Kidd*	Richard Crane	15	
53. *Gunfighters of the Northwest*	Jack Mahoney	15	1954
54. *Riding with Buffalo Bill*	Marshall Reed	15	
55. *Adventures of Captain Africa*	John Hart	15	1955
56. *Perils of the Wilderness*	Dennis Moore	15	1956
57. *Blazing the Overland Trail*	Lee Roberts	15	

UNIVERSAL PICTURES

1. *Ace of Scotland Yard* *silent & part-talkie versions*	Crauford Kent	10	1929
2. *Tarzan, the Tiger* *silent & sound versions*	Frank Merrill	15	
3. *The Jade Box* *silent & sound versions*	Jack Perrin	10	1930
4. *Lightning Express* *silent & sound versions*	Louise Lorraine	10	
5. *Terry of the Times* *silent & sound versions*	Reed Howes	10	

	TITLE	STAR	NO. OF EPISODES	YEAR
6.	*The Indians Are Coming*			
	all-talkie and silent versions	Tim McCoy	12	
7.	*Finger Prints*	Kenneth Harlan	10	1931
8.	*Heroes of the Flames*	Tim McCoy	12	
9.	*Danger Island*	Kenneth Harlan	12	
10.	*Battling with Buffalo Bill*	Tom Tyler	12	
11.	*Spell of the Circus*	Francis X. Bushman, Jr.	10	
12.	*Detective Lloyd*	Jack Lloyd	12	1932
13.	*The Airmail Mystery*	James Flavin	12	
14.	*Heroes of the West*	Noah Beery, Jr.	12	
15.	*Jungle Mystery*	Tom Tyler	12	
16.	*The Lost Special*	Frank Albertson	12	
17.	*Clancy of the Mounted*	Tom Tyler	12	1933
18.	*The Phantom of the Air*	Tom Tyler	12	
19.	*Gordon of Ghost City*	Buck Jones	12	
20.	*The Perils of Pauline*	Evalyn Knapp	12	1934
21.	*Pirate Treasure*	Richard Talmadge	12	
22.	*The Vanishing Shadow*	Onslow Stevens	12	
23.	*The Red Rider*	Buck Jones	15	
24.	*Tailspin Tommy*	Maurice Murphy	12	
25.	*The Rustlers of Red Dog*	John Mack Brown	12	1935
26.	*The Call of the Savage*	Noah Beery, Jr.	12	
27.	*The Roaring West*	Buck Jones	15	
28.	*Tailspin Tommy in the Great Air Mystery*	Clark Williams	12	
29.	*The Adventures of Frank Merriwell*	Don Briggs	12	1936
30.	*Flash Gordon*	Buster Crabbe	13	
31.	*The Phantom Rider*	Buck Jones	15	
32.	*Ace Drummond*	John King	13	
33.	*Jungle Jim*	Grant Withers	12	1937
34.	*Secret Agent X-9*	Scott Kolk	12	
35.	*Wild West Days*	John Mack Brown	13	
36.	*Radio Patrol*	Grant Withers	12	
37.	*Tim Tyler's Luck*	Frankie Thomas	12	
38.	*Flash Gordon's Trip to Mars*	Buster Crabbe	15	1938
39.	*Flaming Frontiers*	John Mack Brown	15	
40.	*Red Barry*	Buster Crabbe	13	
41.	*Scouts to the Rescue*	Jackie Cooper	12	1939
42.	*Buck Rogers*	Buster Crabbe	12	
43.	*The Oregon Trail*	John Mack Brown	15	
44.	*The Phantom Creeps*	Bela Lugosi	12	
45.	*The Green Hornet*	Gordon Jones	13	1940
46.	*Flash Gordon Conquers the Universe*	Buster Crabbe	12	
47.	*Winners of the West*	Dick Foran	13	
48.	*Junior G-Men*	The Dead End Kids	12	
49.	*The Green Hornet Strikes Again*	Warren Hull	15	
50.	*Sky Raiders*	Donald Woods	12	1941
51.	*Riders of Death Valley*	Dick Foran	15	
52.	*Sea Raiders*	The Dead End Kids	12	
53.	*Don Winslow of the Navy*	Don Terry	12	1942
54.	*Gang Busters*	Kent Taylor	13	
55.	*Junior G-Men of the Air*	The Dead End Kids	12	
56.	*Overland Mail*	Lon Chaney, Jr.	15	
57.	*The Adventures of Smilin' Jack*	Tom Brown	13	1943
58.	*Don Winslow of the Coast Guard*	Don Terry	13	

	TITLE	STAR	NO. OF EPISODES	YEAR
59.	*Adventures of the Flying Cadets*	Johnny Downs	13	
60.	*The Great Alaskan Mystery*	Ralph Morgan	13	*1944*
61.	*Raiders of Ghost City*	Dennis Moore	13	
62.	*Mystery of the River Boat*	Robert Lowery	13	
63.	*Jungle Queen*	Lois Collier	13	*1945*
64.	*The Master Key*	Milburn Stone	13	
65.	*Secret Agent X-9*	Lloyd Bridges	13	
66.	*The Royal Mounted Rides Again*	Bill Kennedy	13	
67.	*The Scarlet Horseman*	Peter Cookson	13	*1946*
68.	*Lost City of the Jungle*	Russell Hayden	13	
69.	*The Mysterious Mr. M*	Richard Martin	13	

MASCOT PICTURES

	TITLE	STAR	NO. OF EPISODES	YEAR
1.	*King of the Kongo* *silent & part-talkie versions*	Walter Miller	10	*1929*
2.	*The Lone Defender*	Rin-Tin-Tin	12	*1930*
3.	*Phantom of the West*	Tom Tyler	10	
4.	*King of the Wild*	Walter Miller	12	
5.	*The Vanishing Legion*	Harry Carey	12	*1931*
6.	*The Galloping Ghost*	Harold "Red" Grange	12	
7.	*Lightning Warrior*	Rin-Tin-Tin	12	
8.	*Shadow of the Eagle*	John Wayne	12	*1932*
9.	*The Last of the Mohicans*	Harry Carey	12	
10.	*Hurricane Express*	John Wayne	12	
11.	*The Devil Horse*	Harry Carey	12	
12.	*The Whispering Shadow*	Bela Lugosi	12	*1933*
13.	*The Three Musketeers*	John Wayne	12	
14.	*Fighting with Kit Carson*	John Mack Brown	12	
15.	*Wolf Dog*	Rin-Tin-Tin, Jr.	12	
16.	*Mystery Squadron*	Bob Steele	12	
17.	*The Lost Jungle*	Clyde Beatty	12	*1934*
18.	*Burn 'Em Up Barnes*	Jack Mulhall	12	
19.	*Law of the Wild*	Rin-Tin-Tin, Jr.	12	
20.	*Mystery Mountain*	Ken Maynard	12	
21.	*The Phantom Empire*	Gene Autry	12	*1935*
22.	*The Miracle Rider*	Tom Mix	15	
23.	*Adventures of Rex and Rinty*	Rin-Tin-Tin, Jr.	12	
24.	*The Fighting Marines*	Grant Withers	12	

INDEPENDENT SERIALS

	TITLE	STAR	NO. OF EPISODES	YEAR
1.	*Voice from the Sky* (Ben Wilson release)	Wally Wales	10	*1930*
2.	*Mystery Trooper* (Syndicate Pictures Corp. release)	Robert Frazer	10	*1931*
3.	*Sign of the Wolf* (Metropolitan release)	Rex Lease	10	
4.	*The Last Frontier* (RKO-Radio release)	Lon Chaney, Jr.	12	*1932*
5.	*Tarzan, the Fearless* (Principal release)	Buster Crabbe	12	*1933*

TITLE	STAR	NO. OF EPISODES	YEAR
6. *Return of Chandu (Principal release)*	Bela Lugosi	12	*1934*
7. *Young Eagles (First Division)*	Jim Vance	12	
8. *Queen of the Jungle*			
(Screen Attractions Corp. release)	Reed Howes	12	*1935*
9. *The Lost City (Krellberg release)*	Kane Richmond	12	
10. *The New Adventures of Tarzan*			
(Burroughs-Tarzan release)	Herman Brix	12	
11. *Custer's Last Stand*			
(Stage and Screen release)	Rex Lease	15	*1936*
12. *The Clutching Hand*			
(Stage and Screen release)	Jack Mulhall	15	
13. *The Black Coin (Stage and Screen release)*	Ralph Graves	15	
14. *Shadow of Chinatown (Victory release)*	Bela Lugosi	15	
15. *Blake of Scotland Yard (Victory release)*	Ralph Byrd	15	*1937*

VOLUME 2

A Thousand and One Delights

Dedicated to my mother,
MILDRED BERNADINE MARRIOTT,
with lasting love and gratitude

ACKNOWLEDGMENTS

The author wishes to express his sincere thanks and appreciation to the individuals and organizations listed below who supplied, through the years, the stills and information which have made this book possible.

The Individuals:
Ernest Burns, John Cocchi, Edward Connor, Henry Kier, Al Kilgore, Ernie Kirkpatrick, Paula Klaw, Louis McMahon, Gray Morrow, James Robert Parish, Mark Ricci, Gene Ringgold, Stephen Sally, Chris Steinbrunner.

The Organizations:
Allied Artists-TV, Banner Films, Burroughs-Tarzan, Inc., Cinemabilia, Columbia Pictures Corp., Eagle-Lion Films, Empire Films, Fawcett Publications, Inc., Four Star International, Janus Films, Kier's, King Features Syndicate, London Films, Marvel Comics Group, MCA-TV, Medallion TV, The Memory Shop, MGM, MGM-TV, Monogram Pictures, Movie Star News, National Periodical Publications, Inc., National Telefilm Associates, Paramount Pictures, Paramount-TV, Premium Products, Inc., PRC, Republic Pictures Corp., RKO-Radio Pictures, Screen Gems, Inc., Street and Smith Publications, Twentieth Century-Fox, United Artists, United Artists Associated, United Features Syndicate, Inc., Universal Pictures Corp., Universal-International, Walter Reade-Sterling, Warner Bros, Warner Bros-Seven Arts, Inc.

With Special Thanks to:
Jean Barbour and Malcolm McPherson

Contents

Preface

Remembering the days of one's moviegoing youth can be a pleasant and, at the same time, painful experience. We can conjure up wonderful images of hundreds of entertainment-laden afternoons spent sharing those worlds of pure escapism on the screen which were limited only by the capacities of our individual imaginations; but we all face an annoying enemy as we grow older called *maturity*, which attacks those very same imaginations and tries to convince us that much of what we saw and enjoyed as children was, like a sand castle before the waves, unable to stand the test of time. Unfortunately, like most film buffs, I have spent a good part of my life watching my two-dimensionally-created cinema world crumble bit by bit as each new screening of a long unseen, treasured childhood film revealed itself to be, for want of a better expression, simply awful!

However, though I may have scratched a great many films from my lists of all-time favorites, there still remain a great number of presentations that I feel have held up amazingly well through the years, and those, really, are what *this* book is all about. It is by no means a "history" of films of the forties, for that is too giant a task to cover in one small volume; rather, it is a kind of personal photographic record of what I like to call the "fun films" of that time—films which were largely escapist in nature, many of which turned out as what we now call B-films. On occasion some big-budget films will appear in these pages, as will films made in the thirties, simply because, through reissues during the next decade, they played an important part in my weekly moviegoing routine.

After my first book of movie nostalgia, *Days of Thrills and Adventure*, was published, one of the nicest things said about it was in the review in *Playboy* magazine: their reviewer stated simply that "the author's enthusiasm is contagious." More than anything else, *that* is what I hope to convey to the readers in this book as well—the *enthusiasm* I had as a youngster each time I made that weekly journey to my favorite theater to see the films you'll discover, perhaps for the first time, in these pages.

Jon Hall discovers that this lady is not his runaway fiancée but the evil
Queen of Cobra Island in *Cobra Woman* (Universal 1944).

I.

The King and Queen
of Technicolor

If I had to name the one series of films that most captured the escapist spirit of the films of the forties, I would unhesitatingly choose the six filmed-in-Technicolor Jon Hall—Maria Montez adventures turned out by Universal between 1942 and 1945. These were all action classics designed to entertain and thrill audiences who wanted to get their minds off the everyday problems of a world that seemed to be exploding around them. Just mentioning the name of Maria Montez can conjure up the most delicious memories of azure pools, eye-dazzling costumes, spellbinding action, and worlds that could only exist and be amplified in the minds of the true cinema addicts of those exciting moviegoing days.

The series got off to an extremely glamorous start with Walter Wanger's opulent production of *Arabian Nights* in late 1942. Very loosely based upon the famous tales, the story found Leif Erickson plotting to steal the throne from his brother, Jon Hall. After a murderous attempt on his life, Hall is rescued by the young Sabu (fresh from his personal triumph in *Jungle Book* earlier the same year) and Montez, who played the dancing girl Scheherazade. Montez, who was scheduled to marry Erickson, quickly lost her heart to Hall not knowing he was the rightful ruler. An important participant in the film's colorful chicanery was Edgar Barrier, who planned to force Montez to poison Erickson and thus gain the throne for himself. Needless to say, such devilment was justly rewarded when Barrier dispatched Erickson and then perished himself in a fiery screen finale. The one sour note in the

entire lavish production was the intrusion of banal comedy routines by Billy Gilbert, sneezing as usual, Shemp Howard, and others. It was interesting to note that Turhan Bey, who was to replace Hall as Montez's love interest in the final film of the series, had only a small role in this production as one of Barrier's treacherous henchmen.

A jewel-studded swimming pool was the central point of contention in *White Savage*. Portly Thomas Gomez, after twenty years of patient waiting, hoped to gain the glittering baubles from the Temple Island water tank by marrying Montez, who, as Princess Tahia, ruled the tiny paradise. Hall, playing a shark-hunter interested in acquiring fishing rights off the island, eventually wins the heart of Montez and discovers the secret cache of wealth—to the dismay of Gomez, who, in turn, kills the Princess's brother, played by Turhan Bey in spirited fashion, and frames Hall. Assisting Hall again was his friend and occasional nuisance, Sabu. The film featured a thrilling finale which found Gomez and his band of cutthroats dynamiting the outside wall of the pool, eventually causing tons of rock to fall upon the evil trespassers digging up the treasure. Unfortunately, most of the island seemed to be destroyed at the same time, but back-lot paradises bounce back quickly. It was all adventure in a grand style. Several years later stock footage from these sequences and others were used to create three chapter endings in the serial *Lost City of the Jungle*.

In *Ali Baba and the Forty Thieves* Hall was at

his dashing best as the grown-up son of the Caliph of Bagdad, whom Frank Puglia betrayed and had killed to ingratiate himself with the Mongol tyrant Hulagu Khan, portrayed beautifully by the leering, accented Kurt Katch. Montez, Puglia's daughter, had pledged her love to Hall in a blood ritual when they were children, but, believing him to have been killed at the time of his father's death, was now slated for marriage to the Mongol despot in order to save her treacherous father's life. Hall, portrayed as a youth by Scotty Beckett, stumbled across the treasure-laden secret cave of the forty thieves and, when discovered, announced he was the son of the slain Caliph and joined their band, eventually assuming leadership and converting them from thieves to avengers out to liberate Bagdad from the Mongols. Turhan Bey had his best role to date as Montez's faithful servant who joined the thieves in their campaign. Along for laughs was Andy Devine, who managed to be unobtrusively funny and had the pleasurable assignment of throwing a sword through the demon heart of Katch just as the devil was about to eliminate Hall at the end of a thrilling duel to the death. A highlight of the film was a breathtaking dance, backed by the exquisite music of Edward Ward, photographed from an overhead crane à la Busby Berkeley. One of the distinctive features of the entire series was the fluid use of the camera, and its capabilities were never more in evidence than here, with numerous travel and dolly shots to delight the viewer. *Ali Baba* is my personal favorite in the series, and most Montez aficionados find themselves frequently quoting lines from this film ("Rubies . . . blood red . . . for the people of Bagdad who stood in my way," uttered by Katch as he placed a necklace around Montez's throat, is a favorite). *Ali Baba* was also the longest of the series in running time, taking eighty-seven minutes to unfold its adventurous tale. With the exception of *Arabian Nights*, which ran eighty-six minutes, the other four films ran less than eighty minutes each. In those wartime days when color film was scarce because of military priorities, most color films were shot with virtually no padding to eat up unnecessary footage.

If one Montez was dazzling, then two had to be sensational, and Universal served us this doubledip of pleasure in *Cobra Woman*. In this tropical adventure Montez was captured on the eve of her wedding to Hall and taken to Cobra Island, where it was hoped that she would take over the throne then occupied by her evil twin sister, who had a singularly unpleasant habit of tossing friendly villagers into a nearby volcano as sacrifices. Hall and Sabu, who was making his final appearance in the series, naturally follow the kidnapped Montez to the island where they are captured by the High Priest, played skillfully by Edgar Barrier, whose villainy reaches its zenith when he fatally stabs the Queen Mother (Mary Nash) while a smoldering volcano erupts to bathe his crime in crimson brilliance. Montez accidentally kills her sister and takes her place, but is discovered by Barrier, who forces her to dance in the Cobra Ritual, something she didn't appear to enjoy too keenly but which we in the audience loved. Just in time, of course, Hall and Sabu are freed, and a terrific battle ensues as the volcano erupts anew causing scattered havoc. Lon Chaney, Jr., playing a friendly killer for a welcome change of pace, hurls Barrier into a pit full of spikes as a just reward for his superior show of master villainy.

The weakest film in the series was undoubtedly *Gypsy Wildcat*, primarily because of various excesses in the acting department. This colorful extravaganza of a band of gypsy performers combating an evil overseer found Douglas Dumbrille and Nigel Bruce, ordinarily two polished professionals, hamming and mugging their roles abominably. Montez was a gypsy dancing girl who in reality—and unbeknownst to her—was the heiress to a kingdom now ruled by despotic Dumbrille. Discovering the secret, Dumbrille captures her and plans a quick wedding in order to legalize his position. Hall was a Royal Emissary sent to prove a murder charge against Dumbrille, but nearly wound up being another of his victims while falling in love with Montez. Once again Edward Ward provided a musical score that enhanced the visual spectacle, and an exciting coach chase over treacherous mountain trails was extremely pleasurable to watch. Giving excellent back-up performances were Gale Sondergaard and Leo Carrillo as Montez's foster parents, while Peter Coe as Hall's rival for Montez's affection was, at best, only adequate.

By the time the last film in the series, *Sudan*, reached the screen, much of the magic was beginning to dissipate. Hall was putting on weight and was not quite as dashing as one would want a hero to be. The love-interest assignment was now turned over to Turhan Bey, who played a rebel leader living in a secret mountain hideout who was trying to free his people from the oppression imposed by George Zucco. Zucco plotted to have Montez, the rightful though misguided ruler, killed, but failed in the attempt when Bey rescued her and took her to his hidden retreat. Hall and pal Andy Devine went along for laughs and some adventure, but their days in the sun seemed over. The finale, one of the most exciting in the series, found Montez leading Zucco and his army up a winding mountain trail toward the hidden encampment. Mounted high above the trail was a series of rock-filled containers held closed by fastened ropes that were cut at the appropriate time, unleashing a torrent of death and destruction down upon the invading enemy. Naturally, Montez was spared and Zucco was rewarded with death for his supreme treachery.

With *Sudan* came the end of an immensely popular series of films which were frequently reissued either in pairs or matched up with other Universal color triumphs (like *The Phantom of the Opera*). No one would ever be bold enough to suggest that either Jon Hall or Maria Montez were first-rate actors, but they did have that certain magic when they appeared together that captured our hearts and imaginations.

Maria Montez in a publicity pose for *Cobra Woman* (Universal 1944).

Above: Jon Hall battles Leif Erickson in the final climactic duel to the death while Maria Montez remains a prisoner in *Arabian Nights* (Universal 1942). *Right:* Jon Hall won Maria Montez's love in *Arabian Nights* (Universal 1942) even though she had no knowledge that he was royalty in disguise. *Below:* Maria Montez in a publicity pose for *Arabian Nights*. (Universal 1942).

Top, left: Jon Hall and Sabu participated in a spectacular battle to escape from a slave gallery in *Arabian Nights* (Universal 1942). *Top, right:* Maria Montez in a publicity pose for *White Savage* (Universal 1943). *Left:* Jon Hall in a fanciful action shot from *Arabian Nights* (Universal 1942).

183

Opposite page, top: Technicians set up their equipment to photograph a scene for *White Savage* (Universal 1943) while Maria Montez and Jon Hall go over their dialogue. *Opposite page, bottom left:* Maria Montez leads Jon Hall to the Sacred Jeweled Pool in *White Savage* (Universal 1943). *Opposite page, bottom right:* Maria Montez is told that her brother has just been slain in *White Savage* (Universal 1943).

Left: Jon Hall and Maria Montez ham it up a little for the benefit of the cameraman in this publicity pose for *Arabian Nights* (Universal 1942). *Below:* Sabu's sudden dive into one of those beautiful azure back-lot pools is rewarded with this little surprise in *Arabian Nights* (Universal 1942).

Above: Turhan Bey has caught Ramsay Ames listening in on a conversation between himself and Maria Montez in *Ali Baba and the Forty Thieves* (Universal 1944). *Left:* Frank Puglia presents Maria Montez to bald-headed Kurt Katch in this scene from *Ali Baba and the Forty Thieves* (Universal 1944). *Below:* Kurt Katch as the Mongol tyrant Hulagu Khan in *Ali Baba and the Forty Thieves* (Universal 1944).

Below: Jon Hall decides to enter the well-guarded palace by placing his men in forty large vases which will supposedly be holding oil as a gift for the Khan's wedding in *Ali Baba and the Forty Thieves* (Universal 1944).
Right: The spectacular overhead shots for *Ali Baba and the Forty Thieves* (Universal 1944) as well as for many other Universal adventures were filmed from this elaborate camera boom.

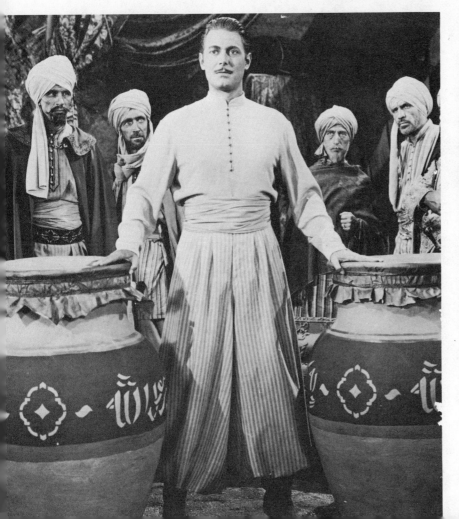

Top: Maria Montez in an exquisite close-up publicity shot for *White Savage* (Universal 1943). *Center:* Maria Montez regains the throne from her evil sister with the help of Lon Chaney, Jr., and Lois Collier in *Cobra Woman* (Universal 1944). *Bottom:* Edgar Barrier met his well-deserved end in *Cobra Woman* (Universal 1944) when Lon Chaney, Jr., threw him into a pit of spikes which was intended for Jon Hall and Sabu. This close-up scene is usually deleted from television screenings by touchy censors.

Left: Maria Montez in a publicity pose for *Gypsy Wildcat* (Universal 1944). *Below:* A little frivolous horseplay between Maria Montez and Jon Hall in *Gypsy Wildcat* (Universal 1944), the weakest of the six films in the series.

Left: Maria Montez in a publicity pose for the last film in the series, *Sudan* (Universal 1945). *Above:* Andy Devine doesn't look too pleased with whatever Jon Hall has in mind to help Maria Montez in *Sudan* (Universal 1945).

Opposite page, top: Maria Montez and Jon Hall in a romantic interlude from *White Savage* (Universal 1943). *Opposite page, bottom:* Edgar Barrier tries to convince Maria Montez that a sacrifice must be made to the Volcano God in *Cobra Woman* (Universal 1944).

Lou Costello and Bud Abbott in their very first movie appearance in
One Night in the Tropics (Universal 1940). They were so successful with
their routines in the film that Universal signed them
to star in their very next film.

2.

Champs of the Chase

While the passing years have proved to me that *the* great comedy team in films was Stan Laurel and Oliver Hardy, during my youthful moviegoing I saw very little of them on the screen. On occasion some theater would book a rerun of *Blockheads* or *Swiss Miss*, but on the whole the rare glimpses I had of the comedic geniuses were in those abominations (which Laurel and Hardy both hated vehemently) turned out by Twentieth-Century-Fox (*Great Guns, Jitterbugs,* etc.). I had to wait over twenty years, until the sixties, to witness what classic comedy, Laurel and Hardy style, was like. However, I and my peer group did have our own comedy team—and on their own merits they were enormously popular and successful. They were, of course, Bud Abbott and Lou Costello.

Both Bud and Lou paid their dues in the Fraternity of Hard Knocks, moving slowly up the ladder of success through clubs, vaudeville, burlesque, radio, motion pictures and, finally, television. While appearing to rave reviews on the Kate Smith radio show in the late thirties, the boys were offered a screen contract to appear as second leads in Allan Jones's starring film, *One Night in the Tropics* (sometimes called *Caribbean Holiday*). Audience response was so good to this initial screen appearance of the boys in 1940 that the studio signed them to star immediately in *Buck Privates*. The rest was history. For over a decade the team worked together (but not without frequent off-screen break-ups, serious illnesses, etc.) to provide a generation of youngsters and adults with outstanding comedy films.

There are many who feel that *Buck Privates* was the pair's best film and all subsequent features merely anticlimactic follow-ups. The point is well taken, for the film certainly had many good things going for it. In addition to featuring two of their funniest routines, the "dice game" and "Army drill" bits, the film also had the advantage of utilizing the services of the popular Andrews Sisters, who sang two of their very best numbers, "I'll Be With You in Apple Blossom Time" and "You're a Lucky Fellow, Mr. Smith." (Most of the team's earlier films featured musical sequences, but these embellishments were left out of many of the later films in favor of straight comedy.) Although the classic routines were delightfully entertaining, I found myself usually laughing at the little throwaway lines (an example: Nat Pendleton as a boxing referee begins to count over a temporarily prostrate Costello, "Two, four, six, eight"; Lou asks anxiously, "What's wrong with one, three, five, seven?"; Pendleton replies, "I don't like them numbers. They're *odd!*") or the quickie bits—Abbott: "Lou, suppose you were forty and you were engaged to a girl who was ten." Costello: "Oh, boy, this is gonna be a pip!" Abbott: "Never mind. Now, you're four times older than that little girl. So you wait five years. You're forty-five and the girl is fifteen. Now you're only three times as old as that little girl. So you wait fifteen more years. The little girl is thirty and you're sixty. Now you're only twice as old as that girl. The question is, how long do you have to wait before you and the little girl are the same age?"

193

It confused Lou, and it confused me, because the logic is mind-boggling.

After having made a filmic mess of the Army, the boys took on the Navy as their next target. In *In the Navy* they had the benefit of the Andrews Sisters again and the considerable talents of Dick Powell as a singing leading man. More classic routines, more engaging songs, and the pattern for success was pretty well established for the next decade or so. As the years rolled by, they delivered their well-aimed barbs in every conceivable format. In *Hold That Ghost*, with Joan Davis as helpmate, they found themselves in a supposedly haunted house where gangsters had hidden some loot; *Keep 'Em Flying* had Martha Raye playing a dual role to confuse Lou, and William Gargan and Dick Foran to verbally fight each other; *Ride 'Em, Cowboy* found the boys out West confusing Dick Foran and cowboy hero Johnny Mack Brown, as well as featuring Ella Fitzgerald singing "A Tisket, A Tasket, I Lost My Yellow Basket" (and the beautiful musical standard, "I'll Remember April," sung by Foran and introduced in a picturesque sequence that is usually the first thing cut out by television stations when they trim the film to fit short time slots); *Pardon My Sarong*, with Robert Paige, featuring the Ink Spots singing "If I Didn't Care," and pitting the boys against the South Sea villainy of Lionel Atwill; *Who Done It?*, a first-rate mystery-comedy that kept you guessing right to the last reel; *The Naughty Nineties*, in which the boys delivered the classic "Who's on first?" routine, and more than twenty-five other film triumphs.

Occasionally Universal Pictures, which had turned out the majority of the Abbott and Costello films, would try to turn Lou into more of a pathos-imbued foil than slapstick comedian in efforts like *It Ain't Hay*, where he accidentally causes the death of a pet horse, *Little Giant*, where he was a salesman put upon continually by an avaricious Abbott, playing a dual role, and *The Time of Their Lives*, in which Lou was a revolutionary Casper Milquetoast falsely accused of being a traitor and who comes back as a ghost in modern times to try to clear his tarnished name. These divertissements never really seemed to pay off. Audiences wanted to laugh at the boys, and the situations in these films did not present enough opportunities for general hilarity. From time to time the two comedians would leave Universal to do duty at MGM or independent studios. These efforts were similarly disappointing,

and there is little people remember from films like *Rio Rita*, *Lost in a Harem*, *Abbott and Costello in Hollywood*, *Africa Screams*, and *Jack and the Beanstalk* with, possibly, the sole exception of the "Slowly I turned" routine (featured in *Harem*).

In 1948 the boys went off on a new kick. Until this time, Universal's stable of captivatingly grotesque monsters (Frankenstein, Dracula, and the Wolf Man) had been relatively sacrosanct. Now the studio decided to have fun with their freakish friends and put Bud and Lou into *Abbott and Costello Meet Frankenstein*. The film was not only an exceedingly hilarious comedy, but a very good horror film to boot. It abounded with all the regular fright-film paraphernalia: misty marshes, a fog-shrouded, island-isolated castle, the standard laboratory replete with all the flashing lights and electrically discharging devices, and an all-star cast featuring Lon Chaney, Jr., as his furry-faced specialty, the Wolf Man, Bela Lugosi as a rather pasty-looking Count Dracula and Glenn Strange as the Frankenstein Monster. The film was full of entertaining little bits of business (such as the Frankenstein Monster recoiling in fear upon seeing a hypnotized Costello), cleverly written sight gags and lines. The one that never fails to break me up is delivered by Lon Chaney, Jr., to Lou over the phone. Chaney is inquiring if Lou, who plays a baggage clerk, has received two large boxes containing the supposed remains of the Frankenstein Monster and Dracula. Lou asks him simply if he has the numbers of the baggage checks, to which Chaney replies, "Never mind that. Tonight the moon will be *full!*" As though that would have *any* meaning at all to a straight-faced Lou Costello.

The pair, as well as the studio, was pleased with the results of that horror-comedy classic and they began to visit the other friendly inhabitants of the Universal crypts in *Abbott and Costello Meet the Invisible Man* and *Abbott and Costello Meet the Mummy*. Neither film even remotely approached the success of their first effort. They were slightly more successful when they appeared with that master of menace, Boris Karloff, in *Abbott and Costello Meet the Killer, Boris Karloff*, and *Abbott and Costello Meet Dr. Jekyll and Mr. Hyde*, although the success was due more to Karloff's work than their own.

Time was taking its toll on the two, however. Abbott was putting on weight, Lou was getting sluggish, and the scripts were becoming increasingly unfunny. The boys had a bad habit of repeating their favorite bits over and over in different films, and then repeating them over again on their live television shows and in their own half-hour filmed television series. People were just becoming oversaturated with Abbott and Costello. Add to those problems the fact that Abbott didn't like to work as often as he had in the past, and that Lou's frequent illnesses were drastically curtailing his effectiveness, and you had the classic picture of two giants risen to the top only to find that the only road left was downhill. Bud and Lou finally called it quits in 1956 after *Dance With Me, Henry* and went their separate ways.

Lou tried to make it on his own as a serious actor and made one feature, *The 30-Foot Bride of Candy Rock*, which was pretty awful, and a couple of television shows (a *General Electric Theater* half-hour and a *Wagon Train* drama). The rotund star who had pleased so many millions during the forties died on March 4, 1959, leaving a legacy of laughter in his films for all of us to continue to share.

Bud Abbott also ran into personal problems which almost threatened to overwhelm him. Before Lou died, Bud was in the process of suing his former partner to obtain money he maintained was due him from the team's television series. On top of that, the Government stepped in and slapped him with a tax-arrears suit that reduced the comic to pleading to all his fans who had enjoyed the team's work in the forties each to send him a dollar to help take care of the debt. Fortunately, he was able to solve his problems and is now retired, contentedly, in California.

The only other comedy team even to make a dent in Abbott and Costello's popularity was that of Dean Martin and Jerry Lewis in the fifties, but their appeal was of considerably shorter duration. Bud and Lou had the luxury, unlike Laurel and Hardy, of enjoying their success and popularity while they were making their films, and we had the good fortune to share their success with them.

Above: Nat Pendleton instructs Bud Abbott to drill Lou Costello and the other men in one of the most famous routines from *Buck Privates* (Universal 1941).

Below: Bud Abbott and Lou Costello meet The Andrew Sisters for the first time on the screen in *Buck Privates.*(Universal 1941).

Right: Lou Costello and Bud Abbott were a couple of Navy misfits in *In the Navy* (Universal 1941). *Below:* Johnny Mack Brown offers Lou Costello and Bud Abbott a job on the ranch, little realizing that they will do more harm than good in *Ride 'Em, Cowboy* (Universal 1942).

Above: Some studio aerial hi-jinks with Bud Abbott and Lou Costello in *Keep 'Em Flying* (Universal 1941). *Below:* Wacky fun in an amusement park involving Lou Costello and his furry friend was a highlight of *Keep 'Em Flying* (Universal 1941). Serial fans will recognize the fake gorilla as the one called Satan in *Perils of Nyoka* (Republic 1942). *Right:* Lou Costello demonstrates to Martha Raye how a torpedo works by accidentally pulling the firing pin, which, of course, leads him into a wild chase sequence in *Keep 'Em Flying* (Universal 1941).

Above: Who Done It? (Universal 1942) was an excellent mystery starring the team. In this scene are Patric Knowles, Lou Costello, Bud Abbott, Ludwig Stossel, and Jerome Cowan. *Left:* A little posed horseplay with Lou Costello, Nan Wynn, and Bud Abbott in this publicity scene for *Pardon My Sarong* (Universal 1942).

Bud Abbott and Lou Costello were crowned at a special dinner at the
Waldorf Astoria in New York when they were "Box Office Team
Number One" in a popularity poll.

Top, left: A gagged-up publicity pose with Bud Abbott and Lou Costello for *In Society* (Universal 1944).
Top, right: Director Charles Barton gives Lou Costello and co-star Marjorie Reynolds some suggestions on the set of *The Time of Their Lives* (Universal 1946). *Left:* A publicity photo from one of the team's MGM films, *Lost in a Harem* (MGM 1944). In this scene are Jimmy Dorsey, Marilyn Maxwell, John Conte, Bud Abbott, and Lou Costello.

Left: The boys did their famous
"Who's on first?" routine in *The Naughty
Nineties* (Universal 1945). This was their
most popular routine, and they did it
thousands of times through the years.
Below: Bud Abbott indulges Lou Costello
while Patsy O'Connor watches in
It Ain't Hay (Universal 1943).

Above: Lou Costello would like to get out of the path of a very unfriendly bull in *Mexican Hayride* (Universal 1948), but Bud Abbott stops him with, "Do you want all these people to think *I'm* a coward?" *Opposite page, bottom:* One of the team's funniest films was *Abbott and Costello Meet Frankenstein* (Universal 1948) with Bela Lugosi as Dracula and Glenn Strange as the Frankenstein Monster.

In another journey away from Universal the boys
starred in an unfunny opus titled
Africa Screams (United Artists 1949).

Top: Lon Chaney, Jr., as the Wolf Man doesn't really seem to bother Lou Costello too much in *Abbott and Costello Meet Frankenstein* (Universal 1948), but the audiences were howling. *Left:* In *Abbott and Costello Meet the Invisible Man* (Universal 1951) the team got involved with an invisible boxer who encouraged Lou to fight with his unseen assistance. *Below:* Lou Costello had a lot of laughs and thrills with Boris Karloff in *Abbott and Costello Meet the Killer, Boris Karloff* (Universal 1949).

By the time Lou Costello and Bud Abbott made *Abbott and Costello Meet the Mummy* (Universal 1955), the team had pretty well reached the end of the comedy trail.

Sabu managed to get to *the* drum in time to warn his friends of a
planned massacre in *Drums* (Korda-United Artists 1938).

3.
Bring Them Back Again
...and Again

One studio called them "Masterpiece Reprints," another "Encore Triumphs," and a third "Classic Re-Presentations." The meaning was the same— old films were coming off the racks and brought back to theaters to garner new audiences and new revenue. During the early forties hundreds of these treasures from the past were presented in local rerun houses, but there were ten films that came back so often (and I saw them *every* time they came back) that they overshadowed all the others. Most of the ten were produced by Alexander Korda in England. As far as I was concerned, and as a reflection of my personal taste, they were all action and adventure classics.

The two films which seemed to pop up endlessly and which I probably saw more than any others in this rerun derby were *Four Feathers* and *Drums* (the original English film title was *The Drum*, but we Americans like more of everything). Both films featured high English adventure in the glorious "For King and Country" tradition. *Four Feathers* was the famous tale of an officer (John Clements) who refused to leave with his regiment on the eve of battle and received a white feather, the traditional symbol of cowardice, from each of his three close comrades and a fourth from his fiancée. In order to make each take his feather back, he performs several extraordinary feats of unquestioned personal bravery. The film was full of lavish color sequences, spectacular battle scenes, and superb performances, especially that of Ralph Richardson who becomes blind from exposure to the sun and is led to safety by Clements (a secret he does not

discover until a most poignant scene at the end of the film in which, now completely and permanently blind, he feels his white feather in a small wallet left by what he thought was a native). And, of course, we mustn't forget the unforgettable scene-stealing performance by that grand old character actor C. Aubrey Smith, in which he recounts the glorious battle-filled days of his youth ("War was *war* in my day, sir!").

Drums was not quite as spectacular as an overall film but still served up a generous portion of excitement and gloriously colorful thrills. The simple plot found Raymond Massey trying to overthrow British rule in India by inviting Roger Livesey and his men to a sumptuous feast where he hoped to massacre them all. Sabu, as a young Prince befriended by Livesey, manages to get to the drum of the film's title and beat out a special predetermined coded message which Livesey recognizes. The effect of the planned attack is softened, and Massey is quickly dispatched. The excellent use of English Technicolor was never more in evidence than in this film full of dashing regimental raiments, exquisitely designed interior settings and scenic splendor.

An American double-bill that never failed to attract capacity crowds was RKO-Radio Pictures' *King Kong* and *Gunga Din*. Although hundreds of "creature" and "pseudo-Kong" films have appeared over the years, none has equalled the particular magic inherent in the original 1933 presentation. The tale of the giant ape transported from his primeval home on Skull Island to New York for exhibition purposes has enthralled several generations of thrill-seeking fans. Fay Wray screamed her way into immortality as the female lead, and Robert Armstrong's Carl Denham was a masterful characterization. The special effects, created by Willis O'Brien at a time when such things were still generally untried and unproved, have seldom until recently even been approached in their creative ingenuity.

Gunga Din is regarded by a great many people as one of the most entertaining and exciting films ever made. Filled with battle sequences spectacular enough to satisfy even the most jaded viewer, the film derives its main virtues from the interplay, physically and verbally, of its three main leads, Cary Grant, Victor McLaglen, and Douglas Fairbanks, Jr. Never was acting chemistry so right with each star filling his role with a gusto and enthusiasm instantly infectious to anyone in the audience caught up in the rhythm of the film. There is one scene in which McLaglen, after having tricked Fairbanks into signing up for a new hitch in the service, flashes an ear-to-ear smile which alone is worth the price of admission. Sam Jaffe's title-role performance as the water boy turned hero is one of finely honed perfection, as is that of Eduardo Ciannelli as the fanatical guru who exhorts his followers to "Rise and kill! Kill lest you be killed yourselves! Kill for the love of killing! Kill for the love of Kali! Kill! Kill! KILL!" And for a touching finale, Montagu Love's reading of Kipling's poem over the body of the slain Din usually had most of us shedding sympathetic tears. (Come to think of it, emotional youth that I was, I'm sure a lump came to my throat also when Kong was shot by the planes off the Empire State Building.) A major source of irritation to *Kong* and *Din* lovers was that on each reissue of the two films more and more footage was edited out to please greedy exhibitors who wanted to squeeze in additional showings. Sometimes the cuts are obvious (as, for example, the delightful scene where McLaglen dips his hands in the punchbowl at the dance in *Din*), but many others were more subtly handled. A few frames here, a closeup there, and before you knew it many minutes from two film classics had disappeared, never again to reappear. Unfortunately, it is these truncated versions that appear on television and in theatrical reissue prints even today.

Another entertaining double-bill from RKO was *She* and *The Last Days of Pompeii*. Though not at the same classic level as *Kong* and *Din*, both films still possessed enough escapist thrills and action to satisfy the vicarious pleasure of younger audiences. In *She* Randolph Scott, Nigel Bruce, and Helen Mack journey to a hidden city in search of a secret force that will prolong life eternally. Facing many perils, including a spectacular ice avalanche, they finally arrive at their destination and meet She-Who-Must-Be-Obeyed (Helen Gahagan), an apparently ageless beauty who has bathed in the mystical Flame of Life and thus gained immortality. Falling immediately in love with Scott, who bore a striking resemblance to a centuries-old ancestor She had killed, Gahagan plots to sacrifice Helen Mack and have Scott enter the Flame of Life and thus share eternity with her. He naturally refuses and rescues Mack just as she is about to be plunged into a sacrificial fiery pit. Gahagan, in order to demonstrate how much she has to offer compared to Mack, once again steps into the flame, but this time finds only death as she crumbles to dust before the amazed eyes of the young lovers. The most outstanding attributes of the film were the enormous eye-dazzling sets and a stirring musical score by Max Steiner (who had also composed the memorable *Kong* music).

The Last Days of Pompeii found Preston Foster rising from humble merchant to supreme gladiator and eventual pseudo-nobleman in the days of early Roman glory. His world crumbles quickly when his son decides upon Christianity and winds up as lion-fodder in the arena. In the film's rousing finale Vesuvius erupts and the city of Pompeii is completely destroyed, but not before Preston heroically dies after allowing his son to escape the clutches of villainous Louis Calhern and flee in the one boat that has escaped destruction.

Another famous Korda package was *Things to Come* (the English title was *The Shape of Things to Come*) and *The Man Who Could Work Miracles*. The latter film was a clever little minor classic which found the gods granting Roland Young, a bumbling little commonplace sort of fellow, the power to perform miracles as a test to judge man's ability to exercise restraint and good judgment. Needless to say, after Young discovers his magical power and performs some elementary feats of magic, his judgment does go awry and he winds up by stopping the sun from setting by causing the earth to cease rotating—which virtually destroys the planet by thrusting everything into space because of the interrupted momentum. As Young himself flies into space he asks that things be as they were before he obtained his miraculous power. This final request is granted, and he and earth return to their drab routine of merely existing.

Things To Come was a marvelously conceived tale of fantasy starring Raymond Massey and Ralph Richardson. The world enters a period of countless wars and is finally nearly totally devastated with only scattered tribes of people surviving. The years pass, and Massey arrives as an emissary from a modernistic city of the future to stun and amaze Richardson (playing a ruthless dictator) and his people who resemble destitute animals more than human beings. Massey, unable to convince them he is friendly, finally has to resort to sending for a squadron of planes which drop bombs filled with a harmless sleeping gas which immobilizes the populace (unfortunately, the whole affair is too much for Richardson, who apparently dies of a heart attack). Back at the modernistic city, a triumph of screen scenic design, a project is under way to send volunteers into space via means of a gigantic space gun. Sir Cedric Hardwicke, as the loyal but misguided opposition, cries out that progress has gone too far. He gathers a huge mob, who march on the gun hoping to destroy it. They are too late; the massive vehicle fires the projectile with its human inhabitants into space, and progress continues to march on.

The two final Korda extravaganzas were sometimes reissued together and, at other times, presented with an assortment of co-features. *Jungle Book* was a colorful picturization of the Kipling tales, and Sabu's performance was probably his most noteworthy. Unlike the other Korda films, *Jungle Book* was filmed entirely in the United States, and most of the film contains sumptuous interior and exterior sets. Filmed in Technicolor, the finale, a spectacularly staged forest fire, is one of the most beautiful sequences ever presented on film. The simple tale of a small boy left in the jungle and raised by wolves, then returned to civilization (which he rejects in favor of returning to his jungle paradise at the film's fadeout) has enthralled children of all ages for almost thirty years.

And last, but certainly by no means least, is my favorite fantasy film of all time, *The Thief of Bagdad*. Easily the most striking film ever done in Technicolor in the opinion of most viewers (Academy Awards went to George Perrinal for his color cinematography, to Vincent Korda for his color art direction, and to Lawrence Butler and Jack Whitney for their special effects), *The Thief of Bagdad* had all the ingredients necessary to provide audiences with unsurpassed excitement and spectacle. The villain of the piece was Conrad Veidt in the role most people remember him for, Jaffar the Magician. No villain ever presented was quite so deliciously evil. John Justin and June Duprez as the young lovers were perfect joys to watch as performers, and Rex Ingram as the Genie left nothing to be desired. The film contained so many pleasurable moments that space does not permit listing them all, but attention should be given to the sequence in which Sabu enters the temple to steal the all-seeing eye of the idol—he climbs to the top via a giant spiderweb and en route does battle with a monstrous spider; and of course the scene where Jaffar tries to escape via a mechanical horse, but is slain by an arrow fired by Sabu. Other pictorial images that remain in the memory are Jaffar, arms outstretched, calling upon his powers to create a giant storm at sea; Sabu when he first frees the Genie from his tiny bottle prison and watches him grow to gigantic proportions; the death of the Sultan by a Jaffar-bewitched statue and the simple beauty of June Duprez in a colorful garden set. If film is indeed an art, then surely *The Thief of Bagdad* must rank as the Rembrandt of film spectacle. Its color, excitement, and overall beauty have never been, nor will very likely ever be, equalled.

Of course, there were other major releases like *Lost Horizon* and *The Count of Monte Cristo*, which played from time to time. I saw them all, but the ten films I've talked about here had a special magical attraction which brought me back to the theater to see them again and again and again. And I *still* see them again and again and again, whenever the opportunity presents itself.

Opposite page, top: In *Four Feathers* (Korda-United Artists 1939)
John Clements redeems one of the symbols of cowardice by pretending
to be a mute native and leading a blinded Ralph Richardson
back to safety after a spectacular battle sequence. *Opposite page,
bottom:* One of the epic battle sequences from *Four Feathers* (Korda-
United Artists 1939). *Below:* Raymond Massey as the treacherous
Prince Ghul invites Roger Livesey, *left*, and Archibald Batty
to a dinner where he plans to massacre them and their men in
Drums (Korda-United Artists 1938).

Preston Foster was the gladiator turned noble who rejected his beliefs when he found his son in the arena about to be slaughtered in *The Last Days of Pompeii* (RKO 1935).

212

Right: The sacrificial procession in *She* (RKO 1935). Gustav von Seyffertitz is leading the parade and Helen Mack is under that white veil. *Below:* Helen Gahagan is in front of the elaborate throne with Randolph Scott and Nigel Bruce standing on the right as another part of the sacrificial ceremony takes place in *She* (RKO 1935).

Above: One of the intricate miniatures in *Things to Come* (Korda-United Artists 1936); the angry mobs attack the Space Gun. *Below:* One of the elaborately decorated and designed sets for *Things to Come* (Korda-United Artists 1936). Raymond Massey, dressed in white, was one of the leaders in this futuristic paradise. *Opposite page:* Raymond Massey as the mysterious visitor who startles a depraved contingent of survivors of a destructive world war in *Things to Come* (Korda-United Artists 1936).

One of the amazing special-effects-created battle scenes in *King Kong* (RKO 1933). That's heroine Fay Wray up there watching her protector do battle.

The spectacular final sequence, touched up a little by studio still artists,
in *King Kong* (RKO 1933).

Above: Sabu challenges the authority of the watchguard serpent guarding a fabulous treasure who seems to be bothering young Patricia O'Rourke in *Jungle Book* (United Artists 1942). *Bottom, left:* Technicians lining up a shot for a sequence in *Jungle Book* (United Artists 1942). *Bottom, right:* Sabu goes to buy a knife and is threatened by Joseph Calleia in *Jungle Book* (United Artists 1942).

Top: John Justin, June Duprez, and Sabu were the stars of the beautifully photographed spectacle, *The Thief of Bagdad* (Korda-United Artists 1940). *Center:* Rex Ingram played the role of the Genie, seen here resting on an intricately conceived miniature, in *The Thief of Bagdad* (Korda-United Artists 1940). *Bottom:* Roland Young demonstrates his newly acquired magical powers with a simple trick to please Sophie Stewart in *The Man Who Could Work Miracles* (Korda-United Artists 1937).

220

Opposite page, top: Victor McLaglen engages in some verbal nonsense with Cary Grant, not realizing he has been brutally beaten by his captors, while Sam Jaffe, in the title role, helps to release him in *Gunga Din* (RKO 1939). *Opposite page, bottom:* Cary Grant, Victor McLaglen, and Douglas Fairbanks, Jr., lead the spectacular charge over the rooftops of a native village in one of the best sequences from the action-packed *Gunga Din* (RKO 1939). *Below:* Eduardo Ciannelli as the fanatical Guru taunts Victor McLaglen and Douglas Fairbanks, Jr., in *Gunga Din* (RKO 1939).

When Lon Chaney, Jr., came towards the camera in close-ups like this
from *The Mummy's Tomb* (Universal 1942), most of us
hid under our seats.

222

4.
And Things That Go Bump in the Night

Can you remember those scenes from the movies of your youth that had you just about hiding under your theater seats, cringing in sheer terror? There are several that I can recall quite vividly. My first memory of fear goes back to the day I saw the evil Queen-turned-Witch in *Snow White and the Seven Dwarfs*. I am sure Walt Disney never intended to terrify the youthful audiences viewing the full-length animated masterpiece, but when that old hag cackled at me in giant close-up from the screen, I am sure my heart dropped clear to my feet. Of course, I was still very young when I saw that film in the late thirties, but even several years later, seeing it in reissue, I was still petrified at the sight. Another scene that absolutely scared the daylights out of me was the classic swimming pool sequence in *Cat People*, that eerie psychological thriller turned out by Val Lewton through RKO in 1942. Jane Randolph, star Simone Simon's rival for the affections of Kent Smith, goes to a deserted swimming pool in a hotel basement. There we find her alone in the dimly illuminated room, with menacing shadows cast on the walls from light reflecting off the water in the pool. We hear the hollow echo of the water slapping against the sides of the pool, and then . . . the menacing purring of a cat! Is it Simon or the escaped black panther we saw gain his freedom earlier in the film? I wasn't sure of anything except that my knees were knocking together. And, finally, there were those damn Mummy films from Universal. I could take most of the creatures they threw at me on the screen. The Frankenstein Monster,

Dracula, the Wolf Man, the Creeper and all the others entertained but hardly frightened me. But when Tom Tyler (as the Mummy in *The Mummy's Hand*) or Lon Chaney, Jr. (as the Mummy in the three remaining films in the series) came at me on the screen with gnarled hand outstretched and the pulse-quickening music of Hans Salter gathering momentum on the soundtrack, that was just too much. I am sure there were other moments of terror that had me running home by the shortest route, but those three sequences to me were the pinnacle of moviegoing horror and suspense.

Almost all the studios tried their hands at turning out some horror material. Republic, whose basic product was Westerns, serials, and short-action programmers, had three pretty good ones that I can readily recall. *Catman of Paris* featured Carl Esmond and Adele Mara in a tale dealing with a strange kind of reincarnation; *The Lady and the Monster* was the first screen version of *Donovan's Brain* and starred Erich von Stroheim as the doctor who inveigles his assistant, Richard Arlen, to help him keep alive the brain of a rich financier who has died in an airplane crash —an act that has terrifying consequences as the brain begins to control Arlen's willpower; *Valley of the Zombies* had Robert Livingston combating Ian Keith, who had apparently become the victim of a strange living-death that could only be continued by drinking blood. All three films were very well done and one might have wished that Republic would have turned out a few more of the bloodcurdlers.

The other minor studios like Monogram and PRC were also turning out some scary items, such as *The Ape Man* with Bela Lugosi, *Return of the Ape Man* with Lugosi and John Carradine, *The Flying Serpent*, and *Fog Island* with George Zucco; once in a great while, the major studios would do a little dabbling in the genre themselves: MGM released *Dr. Jekyll and Mr. Hyde* with Spencer Tracy and *The Picture of Dorian Gray* with Hurd Hatfield, and Warner Bros produced *The Beast with Five Fingers*. This latter film seemed to pop up rather frequently at those great midnight Halloween shows we used to have as kids. The film has always drawn mixed reactions from viewers: some found it quite unacceptable because the audience was allowed to view what supposedly was seen only in Peter Lorre's twisted mind, while others forgot the seeming lack of logic and just relished this gory tale of a dismembered hand that supposedly went around killing people. The photography was subdued, eerie, and full of dark shadows, and Max Steiner's adaptation of music by Bach contributed to the overall mood of the picture.

RKO-Radio Pictures turned out some very interesting, as well as terrifying, horror films in addition to *Cat People*. Boris Karloff had an acting field day in such classic releases as *Isle of the Dead*, *The Body Snatcher*, and *Bedlam*.

But of all the studios turning out this escapist fodder, none was more profusely adept in the art as Universal Pictures. Not only did they continue to turn out features like *Frankenstein Meets the Wolf Man*, *House of Frankenstein*, *House of Dracula*, and the four mummy films, but they also kept in circulation all the great horror classics they had turned out in the thirties like the original *Frankenstein* and *Dracula*, not to mention all the sons and brides and other assorted relatives descended from them. Of all the exciting thrillers that Universal turned out, my personal favorite was the 1943 version of *The Phantom of the Opera*. The film, a remake of the silent Lon Chaney, Sr., classic, really resembled that earlier version very little. Whereas the silent film had great moments of sheer horror, this rehashing of the tale had very little in it to really frighten us except for the very brief unmasking scene at the picture's conclusion. Starring Nelson Eddy, Susanna Foster, and Claude Rains, this version was more a feast for the eye and ear than anything else. Photographed in magnificent Technicolor (it won Academy Awards for color cinematography, color art direction, and interior color decoration), the film included among its other assets beautifully staged operatic sequences (albeit rearranged to suit script demands), enormous sets (especially the underground catacombs and lakes), and excellent performances by its stars, Eddy, Foster, Rains, Edgar Barrier and a plethora of excellent supporting players. Rains's portrayal of the opera violinist who believes his concerto has been stolen and kills the imagined thief, only to be rewarded by having a tray of etching acid thrown into his face, is certainly among his very best. It is only at very rare moments that we feel anything but the very deepest kind of pity for the pathetic man. The film was so popular that the studio seemed always to keep it in circulation via the reissue route, usually paired with another of their great color successes, *Ali Baba and the Forty Thieves*.

Another popular favorite released by Universal in 1943 was *Frankenstein Meets the Wolf Man*. This film, the fifth to feature the Frankenstein Monster and the second to utilize the hairy terror, was great escapist fun which found Lon Chaney, Jr., trying to locate Dr. Frankenstein's notebooks containing the "secrets of life and death." Along the way he met Maria Ouspenskaya in her gypsy garb, lovely Ilona Massey, and Patric Knowles, who hoped to destroy the curse that plagued Chaney every time the moon was full. Under the ruins of the house where the monster supposedly had been destroyed in a raging fire (in *Ghost of Frankenstein* one year earlier), Chaney as Larry Talbot now finds the creature safely frozen in ice. He frees him in hopes that the creature will lead him to the hidden papers. Unfortunately, the creature strikes out and we have to wait for Ilona to get the papers a few reels later. At the end of the film Knowles brings the monster back to full power, Chaney turns into his fuzzy alter-ego, and the two creatures battle each other in a fierce free-for-all that is ultimately decided when a town nut blows up a dam, sending tons of water cascading down the mountainside to inundate the deadly combatants. Fortunately, Ilona and Knowles escape to safety just in time. Chaney's transformation scenes were meticulously done (much more so than in the original *Wolf Man* film), and the film's only sour note was Bela Lugosi as the Frankenstein Monster. He simply looked terrible in the make-up.

In amongst all this superior horror fare turned out by Universal there was one little cheaply-produced PRC release I found entertaining in

1944. Called *The Monster Maker*, the film starred those two grand old acting pros, J. Carrol Naish and Ralph Morgan. Naish, playing a doctor who was experimenting with drugs to cure acromegaly, a serious disorder that causes permanent enlargement of the bones of the head, hands, and feet, injects a drug into the unsuspecting Morgan that produces the symptoms. As the film progresses, Morgan becomes more and more horribly disfigured until the final deadly confrontation in which Naish is destroyed. In the fifties Universal made a film called *Tarantula* starring Leo G. Carroll that also utilized acromegaly as source material.

After all these years, do those classic horror films hold up? A lot depends upon your point of view. They are certainly popular television fare, with almost every city running its own particular type of *Creature Feature* film festival featuring all the old Universal stand-bys. But there is a marked difference: these films were made to be seen in darkened theaters, uninterrupted and uncut. After all, how can you be really frightened by these films when you're sitting in the comfort of a warmly lit living room with parents or friends keeping noisy company with you? No, I think the only way you can recapture the real spirit of these productions is to view them in their original habitats. Even then, in a world full of real-life suffering and horror, I don't quite think that the Wolf Man, Count Dracula, the Frankenstein Monster, the Mummy and all the other delightful monstrosities that peopled those tiny screens in thousands of theaters decades ago carry very much weight anymore. We have matured just too much.

She was one of the dreaded "Cat People"—doomed to slink and prowl by night . . . fearing always that a lover's kiss might change her into a snarling, clawing KILLER!

CAT PEOPLE

with

SIMONE SIMON

KENT SMITH · TOM CONWAY

JANE RANDOLPH · JACK HOLT Re-relea by R K RADI

DON'T BE SURPRISED AT *ANYTHING* YOU SEE !!!

Produced by VAL LEWTON · Directed by JACQUES TOURNEUR

Written by DeWitt Bodeen

J. Carrol Naish turned Ralph Morgan into this grotesque creature
in *The Monster Maker* (PRC 1944).

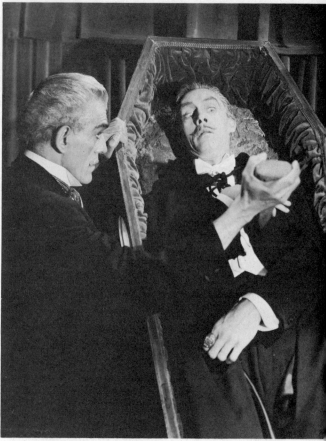

Above: Boris Karloff, who had removed a stake from
skeleton of Dracula and saw John Carradine materialize as the
bloodsucker, now threatens to replace it unless he gets
little cooperation in *House of Frankenstein* (Universal 1945)
Opposite page: Claude Rains leads Susanna Foster to hi
hideaway in the catacombs under the Paris Opera House in
The Phantom of the Opera (Universal 1943).

Right: When opera officials fail to heed his
repeated warnings, Claude Rains as the
horribly disfigured Phantom cuts down the
massive chandelier over the heads of a
packed audience in *The Phantom of the
Opera* (Universal 1943). *Above*: Peter Lorre
feels the deadly pressure of Victor Francen's
piano-playing hand on his throat in
The Beast with Five Fingers (Warner Bros
1946). Supposedly it was this same
dismembered hand that went crawling
around killing assorted victims.

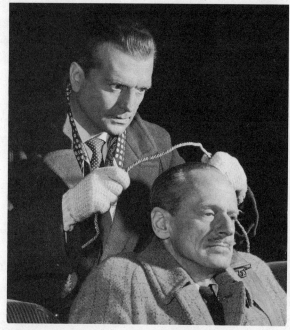

Top, left: A mysterious killer strikes a small town, and the people believe his handiwork to be that of an escaped cat. Margo is the victim in this scene from *The Leopard Man* (RKO 1943). *Top, right*: John Loder was *The Brighton Strangler* (RKO 1945) who dreamed he went about murdering people like Miles Mander in this publicity pose.
Bottom: Una O'Connor doesn't quite know what to make of Claude Rains's bandaged face in *The Invisible Man* (Universal 1933).

Above, left: Lenore Aubert faced this unfriendly fellow (Carl Esmond) in *Catman of Paris* (Republic 1946). *Above, right*: Ian Keith, a really fine actor who bounced around from big-budget features at major studios to B-Westerns at Republic, had an entertaining role as a vampire in *Valley of the Zombies* (Republic 1946). *Right*: Another popular role for Karloff was as Basil Rathbone's court executioner in *Tower of London* (Universal 1939).

Opposite page: Lon Chaney, Jr., was the hairy Wolf Man who attacked Evelyn Ankers in *The Wolf Man* (Universal 1941). *Below*: Bela Lugosi welcomes Dwight Frye to his home in the classic *Dracula* (Universal 1931).

Above: George Zucco planned to give Peggy Moran "eternal life" while Tom Tyler as the mummy watched. The massive set was utilized in *Green Hell* (Universal 1940) as well as in *The Mummy's Hand* (Universal 1940), from which this scene is taken, and other Universal features made during the same period. *Left:* A publicity pose showing how Lon Chaney, Jr., as the Frankenstein Monster was destroyed at the end of *The Ghost of Frankenstein* (Universal 1942).

Below: Kent Smith was the hero and Simone Simon the supposed cat-woman in *Cat People* (RKO 1942).

Above: Boris Karloff and Bela Lugosi have some interesting plans for poor Samuel S. Hinds in *The Raven* (Universal 1935). *Right:* The ever popular Vera Hruba Ralston and Richard Arlen fell under the scientific spell of Erich von Stroheim in *The Lady and the Monster* (Republic 1944), the first film version of *Donovan's Brain*.

Rondo Hatton played the Creeper in several films, including *House of Horrors* (Universal 1946).

Boris Karloff in his most famous role as the Frankenstein Monster in *Frankenstein* (Universal 1931).

Opposite page, bottom: Karloff and Lugosi had the benefit
of Henry Daniell's assistance in *The Body Snatcher*
(RKO 1945). *Above:* Lionel Atwill was the scientist
who turned Lon Chaney, Jr., into a *Man-Made Monster*
(Universal 1941). *Opposite page, top:* Colin Clive, *left*,
and Ernest Thesiger watch as their newest creation,
played by Elsa Lanchester, makes her debut in *The Bride of
Frankenstein* (Universal 1935), which many people
believe to be the best film in the series.

Red Skelton gave Ann Sothern a helping, though apparently missing, hand in this scene from *Maisie Gets Her Man* (MGM 1942), one in a series of excellent comedy films featuring the female cut-up.

5.

The Best Medicine

During times of great national stress, it is usually the entertainment industry that is called upon to help us maintain our sense of humor in the face of adversity. World War II was one of those periods in our history, and the motion picture industry fulfilled its role most nobly by providing us with a wonderful variety of laughter on the screen to help us forget the everyday problems of waging a war for survival. Every studio, large and small, was turning out series comedies, big-budget frolics, musicals, or all-star extravaganzas, and we all found ourselves eagerly caught up in this continuing whirlpool of rib-tickling entertainment.

Family comedies were immensely successful, and the kind you enjoyed most may have reflected your view of your own home situation. For those who believed Dad was a bungler and all-around imbecile, you had the Blondie series. Based on the popular newspaper strip, which is very likely the most widely read in comics history, Arthur Lake as Dagwood and Penny Singleton as Blondie were perfect choices to re-create the inspired lunacy of Chic Young's characters. Indeed, both of them became so identified with these roles that they found their careers as actors virtually destroyed, much the same way Basil Rathbone was type-cast as Sherlock Holmes and Ralph Byrd as Dick Tracy. Although I enjoyed both Lake and Singleton in the number of Blondie films I saw during the time (they did twenty-eight films in all from 1938 to 1951), it was the remarkable performances of Larry Simms (as Baby Dumpling) and Daisy, the dog, that never failed to amaze and delight me.

More idiocy was evident in the popular Henry Aldrich series turned out by Paramount. Jimmy Lydon as Henry and Charles Smith as Homer seemed to get into absolutely incredible situations which seemed almost impossible to resolve. In *Henry Aldrich, Editor*, for example, he ran the school paper. He met a timid little stranger at the scene of a fire who convinced Henry that he could tell the youngster about forthcoming fires in advance. Naturally our young hero started writing about the fires in advance of their happening, and soon the entire town believed he was the one who was really starting them. Before the adventure ended, Henry and his informer, who of course was the real arsonist, were almost trapped in a blazing inferno.

Ann Sothern as Maisie was also around in a number of wacky adventures that found her either helping people out of trouble, or getting into it herself. MGM produced the glossy series, and Red Skelton made an appearance in one of the early adventures. That same studio also turned out the popular Dr. Kildare programmers, which, although not basically funny in premise, did treat its problems with singular lightheartedness. And, of course, MGM also turned out the real giant of the family comedies, the Hardy family films. No matter what problems Mickey Rooney (as Andy Hardy) got into, one good long talk with Judge Hardy (beautifully played by Lewis Stone) usually set everything straight. Probably no other series in screen history so endeared itself to our World War II generation as this.

While Abbott and Costello were the undisputed champions of twin-effort comedy, there were a few other teams that managed to engender sizable laughs from time to time. Olsen and Johnson had brought their inspired zaniness to the screen in the thirties in items like *Fifty Million Frenchmen*, but it was after their record-breaking Broadway success with *Hellzapoppin* that they really captured the public's fancy. They transferred *Hellzapoppin* to the screen in 1941 and followed it with such popular hits as *Crazy House, Ghost Catchers*, and *See My Lawyer*. The films were all full of incredible sight gags, outrageous puns, and a wacky kind of undisciplined mayhem heretofore unknown to moviegoers. Olsen and Johnson would seldom enter a room through a door—they'd just blow a hole in the wall and plow right through.

Wally Brown and Alan Carney were RKO's claim to the twosome title, but I found them usually bland and unfunny. Perhaps it wasn't really their fault but the fault of the writers who were trying to build them into something they really weren't qualified to be. *Zombies on Broadway* was very likely their biggest success, but even that fails to hold up well today.

When Bing Crosby and Bob Hope teamed up it was really big-time humor. Both singer and comedian had large personal followings and had starred in numerous successful musical and comedy films on their own, but when they teamed up the result was a special kind of screen magic that was hard to top. One sure way to start an argument between film buffs is to get them to try and pick their favorite "road" picture. Many like their first efforts, *The Road to Singapore* and *The Road to Zanzibar*, done in 1940 and 1941 respectively. Few tend to like the later ones, *The Road to Bali* (the only one made in color) which appeared in 1952 or *The Road to Hong Kong*, the last of the series to date, made in 1962. It is the middle group which I find most entertaining, and my own favorite has always been *The Road to Morocco*, a 1942 entry that not only had the standard Hope-Crosby humor but also introduced one of my favorite movie songs, "Moonlight Becomes You," sung by Crosby. The other titles, for the record, were *The Road to Utopia* (1945) and *The Road to Rio* (1947).

W. C. Fields had made his most successful and popular films in the thirties for Paramount, but in the forties he turned out four films for Universal that have come to be regarded as comedy gems. *The Bank Dick* was certainly the most memorable, but *You Can't Cheat an Honest Man* (in which favorite radio rivals Edgar Bergen and Charlie McCarthy played co-starring roles), *Never Give a Sucker an Even Break* and *My Little Chickadee* (with Mae West matching him laugh for laugh) were all box-office successes as well.

Because radio played such an important part in our lives in those pre-television days, it was only natural that the studios would bring a great many audio favorites to the movie screen. RKO turned out quite a few that found stars like Kay Kyser (*You'll Find Out*), the Great Gildersleeve (*Gildersleeve's Ghost*), Fibber McGee and Molly (*Heavenly Days*), and others each appearing in his own series of adventures. Sometimes they would use several together (McGee, Molly, Gildersleeve, and Edgar Bergen and Charlie McCarthy appeared jointly in films like *Look Who's Laughing* and *Here We Go Again*) for added box-office appeal. RKO also turned out the popular series of Mexican Spitfire films featuring tempestuous Lupe Valez and her ever suffering co-star, Leon Errol.

Over at Republic they were churning out a very popular series of films starring Judy Canova. Judy was a particular favorite of small-town audiences who loved the hillbilly type of humor she specialized in. Titles like *Sleepy Lagoon* and *Sis Hopkins* usually featured tales about city slickers trying to outfox the country folk but eventually being outwitted themselves. The comedienne also had a very pleasant singing voice, and her songs were always an additional bonus. My favorite film in this series was *Chatterbox* with Joe E. Brown (who was another comedy favorite in a series of Columbia films during these years) playing a radio cowboy, Rex Vane, who suddenly finds he has to prove himself in real life.

Red Skelton began his screen career in a small role in *Having Wonderful Time*, a 1938 film starring Ginger Rogers, and he went on to become a leading box-office draw for MGM in the forties. I particularly enjoyed his three-film series in which he played a radio detective called the Fox who turned his attention to solving real-life mysteries (*Whistling in the Dark, Whistling in Brooklyn*, and *Whistling in Dixie*), but I am sure most of his fans would prefer efforts like *A Southern Yankee, I Dood It* and *DuBarry Was a Lady*, as well as the long string of popular musicals he did with stars like Esther Williams.

Jack Benny turned in some funny work in films like *Charley's Aunt, George Washington Slept Here*, and *The Horn Blows at Midnight* (although Benny has kidded about how badly this film was received, it really is an enjoyable movie). Trying to keep up with Jack was his long-time friend and radio rival, Fred Allen, who had a ball doing little items like *It's in the Bag*.

There seemed to be an endless supply of unimportant musical comedies starring the Andrews Sisters, Allan Jones, Gale Storm, Jane Frazee, and others. Probably the most successful of these minor musicales were those in which Donald O'Connor and Peggy Ryan sang, danced, and mugged their way through every possible backstage plot to the obvious delight of audiences.

The list seems virtually endless as far as laughmakers were concerned, and I haven't even included all those great stars who made those delightful two-reelers that used to be a part of every Saturday matinee: men like Edgar Kennedy, Leon Errol, Andy Clyde, the Three Stooges, etc. And how about those *Pete Smith Specialties* and the popular *Speaking of Animals* series. I wonder how many people remember Lew Lahr, who used to come in for some funny bits at the end of those *Fox Movietone Newsreels* we saw every week? Remember Joe McDoakes (George O'Hanlon), popping up from behind that eight-ball in a popular series of one-reelers?

It may have seemed a frivolous luxury to sit in a theater and laugh while the world was in torment, and I am sure there are those who would say our time should have been spent elsewhere. Perhaps they are right; I don't know. I only know that it seemed right at the time, and I wish we had a little more laughter today to give us a break from the tension of the conflicts we currently face.

Right: W. C. Fields and Leon Errol were up to their usual nonsense in *Never Give a Sucker an Even Break* (Universal 1941). *Below:* Judy Canova and Joe E. Brown were hilarious in *Chatterbox* (Republic 1943), a story that found Brown playing a radio cowboy who was signed to make a real Western film.

Top: Sheldon Leonard, now a successful television producer, played his typical gangster role for the benefit of Wally Brown and Alan Carney in *Zombies on Broadway* (RKO 1945). *Center:* Edgar Bergen and his wooden pal Charlie McCarthy were only two of the radio stars who appeared in *Here We Go Again* (RKO 1942). *Bottom:* Charles Smith and Rita Quigley were almost trapped with Jimmy Lydon, *right,* as Henry in a dangerous fire in *Henry Aldrich, Editor* (Paramount 1942).

Above: Peggy Ryan and Donald O'Connor were audience favorites in a series of musicals like *Patrick the Great* (Universal 1945), from which this scene is taken. *Right:* Lupe Velez clowned with her frequent co-star, Leon Errol, in one of her popular series features, *Mexican Spitfire's Blessed Event* (RKO 1943).

Top: Among the most famous scenes on movie screens during the late thirties and early forties were Mickey Rooney's talks with Lewis Stone such as this one from *The Courtship of Andy Hardy* (MGM 1942). *Bottom:* I wonder if Anthony Quinn suspects some horseplay in this sequence from *The Road to Morocco* (Paramount 1942) with Bing Crosby and Bob Hope.

W. C. Fields was absolutely hilarious
as *The Bank Dick* (Universal 1940).

Left: Ole Olsen, *left,* and Chic Johnson do a bit of clowning with co-star Martha Raye in this publicity pose from *Hellzapoppin* (Universal 1941). *Below:* Willie Best turned in an excellent comic performance along with Bob Hope in *The Ghost Breakers* (Paramount 1940), which was remade in the fifties with Dean Martin and Jerry Lewis, renamed *Scared Stiff* (Paramount 1953).

Arthur Lake as Dagwood and Penny Singleton as Blondie frequently took
second-place acting honors to the performances of the scene-stealing Larry Simms (as
Baby Dumpling) and Daisy (the tiny dog) in films like *Blondie in Society*
(Columbia 1941), from which this scene is taken.

Harold Peary as Gildersleeve and Nicodemus seem to have discovered *Gildersleeve's Ghost* (RKO 1944) in this film from the popular series based on the radio show.

Above: Kay Kyser and his orchestra made several popular features. In *Carolina Blues* (Columbia 1944) he introduced lovely Ann Miller. *Right:* The great Marx Brothers films were made in the thirties, but films like *The Big Store* (MGM 1941) did manage to provide a few laughs. The boys are surrounding Marion Martin in this publicity pose.

Top: Shirley Temple was still captivating audiences in new films and reissues like *The Little Princess* (Twentieth Century-Fox 1939); here she is in a scene with Arthur Treacher. *Bottom:* Margaret O'Brien could melt anyone's heart, including Wallace Beery's, in films like *Bad Bascomb* (MGM 1946).

Jack Benny had a field day in the film version of *Charley's Aunt* (Twentieth Century-Fox 1941). That's Edmund Gwenn looking over the wall, while Richard Haydn, *left*, and James Ellison help Jack dress.

Boris Karloff played the oriental detective Mr. Wong in a popular series of mysteries for Monogram.

6.

The Fun Factory

While my moviegoing elders were extolling the virtues of such quality mystery fare as *The Maltese Falcon, The Big Sleep, Murder, My Sweet, And Then There Were None,* and *Laura,* I was jumping up and down in my matinee seat over a little Monogram cheapie called *The Mystery of the 13th Guest.* A virtual scene-for-scene remake of the 1932 *The Thirteenth Guest* starring Ginger Rogers and Lyle Talbot, this version featured Dick Purcell and Helen Parrish in what many believe is the perfect model for a Saturday afternoon thriller. The film was filled with all the gimmicks the kids loved: a mysterious masked murderer, hidden passageways, an eerie deserted mansion, an electrically wired phone to kill the victims, a motley group of suspects, and three wisecracking detectives (two police, one private). The plot found Helen Parrish returning to a deserted house on her twenty-first birthday to read a letter left by her grandfather thirteen years earlier. Inside the letter is the cryptic message "13-13-13," which turned out to be the number of a safe deposit box. She is quickly disposed of (it later turns out she was an impostor who had had plastic surgery done on her face to resemble the real heir), and more murders occur (the bodies being placed in the identical chairs, of which there were a total of, you guessed it, thirteen, in which all the relatives were seated at the dinner party when the letter was originally presented). The wisecracking private eye was played to perfection by Dick Purcell, and the bumbling police by Tim Ryan, who also had a hand in writing the screenplay, and Frank Faylen.

Two other interesting mysteries turned out by Monogram which were extremely pleasing to watch were *The Phantom Killer* (another remake), in which John Hamilton played a dual role as brothers, one of whom went around murdering people while the other established an alibi, and *The Living Ghost,* a tale that involved turning a man into a walking zombie as the result of a sinister operation. James Dunn gave an excellent performance in the latter film as a sardonic private detective assisted by one of the great ladies of B-films, Joan Woodbury.

No matter what your personal tastes may have been for B-film fodder in the forties, Monogram satisfied you by turning out something in almost every conceivable category. In the Western field they had Johnny Mack Brown, the Range Busters, the Rough Riders, Tex Ritter, and others turning out regular series every year. For action a little further north, they picked up the Renfrew of the Mounted series, which Grand National had started, and turned out some excellent little thrillers starring James Newill. For aerial entertainment, John Trent was Tailspin Tommy in several entertaining programmers. Musicals? They had an endless variety of those, with titles like *Campus Rhythm, Rhythm Parade, Spotlight Scandals,* and *Hot Rhythm,* all full of simply awful numbers filmed against the cheapest sets imaginable. For horror devotees they turned out such pleasant little diverse attractions as *The Ape,* with Boris Karloff jumping around in a furry costume, *The Ape Man* with Bela Lugosi sporting a shaggy face, *Return of the Ape Man,* which found Bela Lugosi taking John Carradine's brain and transplanting it in the head of a Neanderthal man, and *King of the Zombies* and *Revenge of the Zombies*, two grotesque little thrillers that made their black actors look so silly that I am sure we will not quickly see these films shown in public again. Boxing fans were rewarded with the Joe Palooka series, based on the famous comicstrip character, with Joe Kirkwood, Jr., as Joe and Leon Errol as his comical pal, Knobby Walsh.

But of all the material turned out by Monogram's fun factory, probably the three most entertaining and successful series were those which featured Sidney Toler (and later Roland Winters) as Charlie Chan, Kane Richmond as the Shadow, and the seemingly endless parade of East Side Kids adventures.

Although the three Shadow films were entertaining, they were far from being well-made little gems. Instead of mystery and thrills, as one would normally expect, the plots featured more comedy than anything else. Barbara Reed as Margot Lane was always getting in the way of star Kane Richmond with her silly jealous tantrums, causing a boring interruption in the action. The first film of the three, *The Shadow Returns*, was probably the best in the group, and found our hero solving a mystery in which the victims of a mysterious killer were dragged to their deaths from various balconies by means of a bullwhip. In *Behind the Mask*, the masked nemesis of crime solved the murder of a newspaper reporter who was killed in his own office by a killer whose shadow was seen on the glass door of the office but who seemed to disappear from sight almost immediately afterward. (As it turned out, the killer simply climbed out the window to a balcony and re-entered the office to join the crowd rushing to the scene of the murder.) The final effort, *The Missing Lady*, was the weakest film: the Shadow searched out a valuable art piece carved in the shape of a woman, and Miss Reed's antics in this last film were positively nerve-racking as she managed to spend almost three quarters of the film botching things up.

The single most popular mystery series turned out by Monogram was, of course, the Charlie Chan films. Twentieth Century-Fox had thrown in the towel on production of the celebrated detective's exploits in 1942, after having made twenty-eight films starring first Warner Oland and then Sidney Toler. Monogram brought Toler back to do eleven new films beginning in 1944

and wound up their Chan endeavors with six films made in 1947–49 starring Roland Winters after Toler's death. Again, as in the case of the Shadow films, humor was overstressed in the films to the detriment of the action. Admittedly, Mantan Moreland as the comedy relief was infinitely more tolerable to take than Barbara Reed (as a matter of fact, it was Mantan's work that added so much to the general appeal of this particular series), but one might have wished for a little more mystery and a little less nonsense. The Monogram efforts tended to be filled with a great deal more gimmickery than the Fox films: one was amazed at the seemingly infinite variety of fascinating ways to kill people. Probably the most elaborate device was in *The Scarlet Clue*. The killer, wearing a grotesque theatrical mask, sends his intended victims a teletype message instructing them to go to a certain floor in a specific elevator, look out to see if anyone is there and, if not, to go to a higher floor. As the victim reaches his first stop to make his initial observation we see the mysterious killer peeking through a crack in a partially opened door and then pulling an electrical switch. The doors to the elevator close and it starts its ascent, when suddenly the bottom swings open like a trap door and the victim plunges to his death. Great gory fun, of course, but somehow I am sure most of us wondered how such an involved death trap could ever have been installed in the first place. One film had a gun that fired with the aid of an electromagnet, and another had a weapon that fired a bullet made of ice, which of course melted, leaving another baffling challenge to be met by the Oriental sleuth. Toler, who was not Chinese, was excellent in the role of Chan, and the films usually featured an interesting assortment of capable performers as suspects.

Following close on the heels of the Chan films as far as popularity was concerned was the infinite variety of East Side Kids comedies. Although the series continued into the middle fifties (with Huntz Hall outrageously mugging and burlesquing his earlier characterization in unfunny vehicles), it is the films turned out in the early forties that most of us remember and enjoy best. The whole series, quite naturally, had exceptional appeal for children, who, for all practical purposes, saw themselves being pictured on the screen. There seemed to be no end of trouble that the Kids could get themselves into. Usually Bobby Jordan was the scapegoat who got blamed for assorted mayhem (including murder), and

Leo Gorcey, Huntz Hall, "Sunshine" Sammy Morrison (the only regular black member of the gang), and Gabriel Dell (who alternated between being a gang member and being a villain) were called upon to get him out of his current predicament. The most entertaining films in the series for most were probably those that pitted the gang against that perennial screen menace, Bela Lugosi: *Ghosts on the Loose* (which had Ava Gardner playing a small role) and *Spooks Run Wild*. Both had the youngsters running rampant through houses that were supposedly haunted, but which were really being used to cover the illicit activities (counterfeiting, for example) of Lugosi and his gang. My own favorite in the series, and the one which seemed to come back to theaters more often than most, was *Clancy Street Boys*. The plot was relatively simple: rancher Pete Monahan (excellently played by that grand old pro, Noah Beery, Sr.) and his daughter come to New York to visit Muggs (Leo Gorcey) and his mother. Before he died, Muggs's father had told the rancher that he had seven kids (six boys and one girl), and for many years Pete has been sending money to the supposed family as birthday and Christmas gifts. Muggs, in a bold move, has the gang impersonate the family with Glimpy (Huntz Hall) posing as the girl. A gangster gets wind of the scheme and threatens to expose the whole plan, but, when Muggs decides to confess the subterfuge himself, has his gang capture the wealthy rancher in order to extort money. Happily, this film ends, as almost all of them ended, with a pitched battle between the gang of kids and the gangsters.

One would never try to suggest that Monogram turned out quality product (except in rare instances when a *Suspense* or *The Hunted* might pop up), but they certainly turned out a great many films that thrilled and delighted my generation of front-row fanatics. On this score Monogram certainly ranked high, and indeed was a fun factory.

Top: This was the mysterious killer in the Charlie Chan adventure *The Scarlet Clue* (Monogram 1945). *Center:* Pierre Watkin, Joseph Crehan, and Edward Gargan just think they have the Shadow trapped in *Behind the Mask* (Monogram 1946). Kane Richmond is behind the particular mask in this scene. *Bottom:* James Newill and Dave O'Brien were the stars of a number of Renfrew of the Mounted films like *Yukon Flight* (Monogram 1939).

Above: Barbara Reed, *left*, added to Kane Richmond's troubles in *Behind the Mask* (Monogram 1946). *Below*: John Carradine discovered a way to keep Veda Ann Borg, his dead wife, alive in *Revenge of the Zombies* (Monogram 1943).

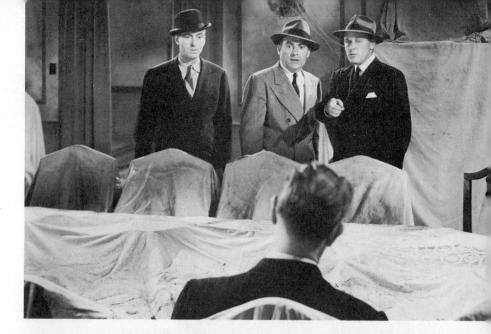

Top: Frank Faylen, Tim Ryan, and Dick Purcell believe that the mysterious killer intends to "line the table with stiffs" in *The Mystery of the 13th Guest* (Monogram 1943). *Center:* The masked killer has Helen Parrish in his clutches in *The Mystery of the 13th Guest* (Monogram 1943). *Bottom:* John Hamilton, playing a dual role, sets up an alibi with Mantan Moreland while his twin commits a murder in *Phantom Killer* (Monogram 1942).

Typical youth-oriented films like *The Gang's All Here* (Monogram 1940) with Frankie Darro, Marcia Mae Jones, Jackie Moran, Keye Luke, and Mantan Moreland were a staple of Monogram in the thirties and forties.

If Mantan Moreland looks a little silly in this scene with Sidney Toler from *The Scarlet Clue* (Monogram 1945) he has good reason: the floor of that elevator opens like a trap door and is the killer's way of eliminating his victims.

Right: Monogram turned out quite a few straight gangster yarns like *Federal Bullets* (Monogram 1937) with, *left,* Milburn Stone, (Doc of TV's *Gunsmoke*) and John Merton. *Below:* A big, lavish musical extravaganza (Monogram style) with Gale Storm, *center,* from *Rhythm Parade* (Monogram 1942).

Left: Guy Kibbee, Leon Errol (as Knobby Walsh), Elyse Knox, and Joe Kirkwood, Jr. (as Joe Palooka) in *Gentleman Joe Palooka* (Monogram 1946), one in a series of films based on the comic strip character created by Ham Fisher. *Below:* Roland Winters as Charlie Chan and Robert Livingston in *The Feathered Serpent* (Monogram 1948).

Top, left: Bobby Jordan, Leo Gorcey and Huntz Hall face another crisis in *Smart Alecks* (Monogram 1942), one of the very popular East Side Kids comedy-adventures. *Top, right*: Irene Rich and Charles Bickford were the stars of *Queen of the Yukon* (Monogram 1940), one of the studio's better outdoor action films. *Bottom*: James Dunn was almost the recipient of that knife in *The Living Ghost* (Monogram 1942). That's Joan Woodbury next to him and Gus Glassmire on the floor.

Top: Irene Ryan, *left*, and strip-tease artist Ann Corio cavorted in *The Sultan's Daughter* (Monogram 1943). Miss Ryan is much better known to today's audiences as "Granny" on TV's popular *Beverly Hillbillies*, and was married to Tim Ryan, who wrote many of the scripts for Monogram films, when they appeared as the popular comedy team of Tim and Irene. *Bottom:* Marjorie Reynolds, Milburn Stone, and John Trent were the stars of four Tailspin Tommy adventures made in 1939 by Monogram.

Tom Tyler as the costumed hero is about to unmask the mysterious Scorpion in *Adventures of Captain Marvel* (Republic 1941).

7.

Saturdays Are for Thrills

In an exhibitor's production guide (a lavishly illustrated brochure put out by the studio to announce its forthcoming product for the year) issued by Republic Pictures in 1942, the following introduction appeared before the pages devoted to new serials: "ACTION speaks louder than WORDS! Every exhibitor knows that a serial depends on its red-blooded action rather than on a barrage of 'talk-talk.' That is why the serial has endured since the inception of the industry, and no doubt it will outlast any other type of motion picture composition. In fact serials become more popular year by year with audiences. Serials must have a staff which is temperamentally suited to this action type product. The personnel must live, breathe and love their work, and they firmly believe that every serial is equally as important to audiences as *Gone with the Wind*. The outstanding success of Republic serials has been largely due to the organization of our incomparable technical staff, who apply themselves diligently and conscientiously to a job that they enjoy. Here's to Action Product! REPUBLIC STUDIOS."

While Republic may have been mistaken concerning the lasting durability of the serials, they certainly were correct, as far as I was concerned, in stressing the action elements of their product.

Oakland, California, in those days of my serial-going youth was a large enough city to have complete coverage of the chapter-plays turned out by the three producing companies. The Central Theater, primarily a rerun house, featured the Universal talk-a-thons; the Rex Theater, an abominably dilapidated scratch house which ran triple features, catered to Columbia devotees; and the Broadway Theater, my home away from home, inherited the Republic material. It had taken only a visit or two to each theater in 1940 and my mind was quickly made up. I craved action, not talk, and only the Republic product seemed to offer action in abundance. I was hooked, and for the next seven years of my life, with very few weekly exceptions, I spent every Saturday afternoon watching twenty-six consecutively produced action-packed thrillers.

I am often asked, because I write so much about Republic serials, which is my personal favorite. I find it an impossible question to answer without a considerable amount of hedging, for I quite honestly loved them all. After all, with few exceptions, they were all cast from the same mold. Each contained a plethora of fights, chases, explosions, and assorted thrills. What emerged after those seven years, then, was a kaleidoscopic tapestry woven into the fabric of my mind that contained the very best elements of all twenty-six films joined together to form, if you will, a montage that I called simply *the* Republic serial. Fortunately, beginning in 1961 I was able to once again view these films which had given me so much pleasure as a child. To my surprise and delight almost all of them were as exciting as I had remembered them to be, and I now find myself able to objectively sort them into general categories.

My favorite plot serial, for example, was *Adventures of Captain Marvel*. This exciting tale of the mysterious black-hooded Scorpion and his quest for the lenses to complete his devilish Golden Scorpion Atom Smasher was a joy to watch. This particular serial didn't have quite as much action in it, primarily due to the leading character's general invulnerability, but it made up for the deficiency by utilizing superb special effects and daredevil stunts by David Sharpe, doubling for lead Tom Tyler.

As all-around action films I would choose *The Masked Marvel* and *Secret Service in Darkest Africa*. Never were fight sequences more numerous or better staged, thanks to the directorial skill of Spencer Gordon Bennet and ace stunt-manship of Tom Steele and the Republic staff. No audience I was ever a part of in those days could ever remain seated after one of the massive set-destroying melees in these films.

My choice for favorite leading man in serials must be evenly divided between Kane Richmond and Allan Lane. Richmond was a perfect choice to play the lead in *Spy Smasher* (I really should say *leads*, because he played a dual role), Republic's smash follow-up in the comic-strip-adaptation vein a year after *Captain Marvel*. One of the best points in his favor was that he could act. This was no small feat, for the serials were full of people who *couldn't* act (look at the four leads in *The Masked Marvel*, for example). Republic brought Richmond back a couple of years later as the lead in *Haunted Harbor*, and he helped make that serial equally enjoyable, teamed up with their current serial queen, Kay Aldridge. Allan Lane was also able to lend his particular brand of he-man appeal successfully to his four serial adventures: *King of the Royal Mounted*, *King of the Mounties*, *Daredevils of the West*, and *The Tiger Woman*. After his serial chores, Lane went on to become one of Republic's most successful Western stars (billed as Allan "Rocky" Lane). Many years later, one of the worst-kept secrets in television history was that Lane did the voice for the famous talking horse, Mr. Ed, in that popular series of the early sixties.

Sometimes I enjoyed a serial simply because I remembered a single chapter ending that was so unusual, as opposed to the routine explosions and car crashes, that it remained in my memory long after I had forgotten the rest of the serial. In *G-Men vs. the Black Dragon*, an action-packed wartime epic starring Rod Cameron, there was an ingenious ending which found leading lady Constance Worth being captured by the villains and tied to a chair. Opposite the chair was a cabinet in which was placed a spear aimed directly at the helpless heroine. By the spear were two tiny Japanese figurines holding miniature spears. These figures slowly rotated towards each other and when the tips of the two spears touched the contact set the full-size missile flying directly towards the wide-eyed prisoner. And, of course, while all of this was going on a monumental fight sequence was in progress as Cameron tried to effect a rescue (which, in the next chapter, he naturally managed).

Another equally elaborate trap was laid by George J. Lewis for hero Marten Lamont in *Federal Operator 99*. Lamont, in disguise, enters an old building and moves down a passageway, at the end of which he spies Lewis sitting behind a desk. Lewis makes a sudden movement and Lamont fires a gun at him—but Lewis has erected a bulletproof glass partition in front of himself. Our hero then turns to make his escape, only to find his way blocked by a barred gate which Lewis closes at the other end of the passageway by remote control. Now completely trapped, Lamont is informed by Lewis that his imprisonment was only part of a surprise, and that now he is "going to get the rest of it." Another switch is thrown and a series of outlet pipes at the base of the passageway begin to emit huge bursts of flame. The scene fades as the jets of searing death move closer and closer to Lamont and the camera lens. How did he escape? Well, I won't hold you in suspense. His female aide, Helen Talbot, enters just in time to open the barred gate from the outside! How else?

Villainy skillfully played can be an entertaining inducement to return week after week. The top contributor in that category was Roy Barcroft. Roy managed to overshadow the acting performances of even the leading men in his two favorite serials, *Manhunt of Mystery Island* and *The Purple Monster Strikes*. In the first serial he played Captain Mephisto, a Mephisto-phelean character created by having one of four suspects sit in a "transformation" chair that altered his appearance to resemble an ancient piratical inhabitant of the island. There is an entertaining scene in which Barcroft explains the process to henchman Kenne Duncan. He speaks of changing the molecular structure of his body. Kenne nods a knowing smile and says, " I understand"—whereupon Barcroft smiles and counters with, "If I thought that you did, I'd kill you." In *The Purple Monster Strikes* Roy was an alien from Mars who came to Earth to steal the plans of a scientist (James Craven) for building a more powerful rocket than the Martians had been able to develop, with the eventual intention of using the new rockets for a later invasion. Roy, who usually weighed over two hundred pounds, had to slim down to a hundred and eighty to wear the tights he was required to don in the role. He often recalled how the crew used to call him "the jerk in tights from Boyle Heights" while he was making the film. He was truly a remarkable villain, with a real-life heart of gold.

The leading lady in the last two serials mentioned (as well as four others: *The Tiger Woman, Zorro's Black Whip, The Crimson Ghost,* and *Jesse James Rides Again*) was Linda Stirling. While Frances Gifford and Kay Aldridge drew an occasional raise of the Barbour eyebrow, I was still too young to fully accept them as anything more than general nuisances in their starring serials (*Jungle Girl* for Gifford and *Perils of Nyoka, Daredevils of the West,* and *Haunted Harbor* for Aldridge); but I was a little more mature when it came to Linda. She was, in point of fact, the first serial heroine I really enjoyed watching on the screen. Even in her earliest efforts she did a most credible, professional job. Unfortunately, the scriptwriters didn't give her too much of a chance to really demonstrate her versatility (how proficient can you be when you keep getting knocked unconscious chapter after chapter?).

One hates to live in the past, but I must frankly confess that on rare occasions I do sometimes wish I were seated back at the Broadway Theater on a Saturday afternoon with those two bags of *freshly* made popcorn (remember *fresh* popcorn, folks?) watching Kane Richmond, Ralph Byrd, Clayton Moore, Allan Lane, and all the others "do their thing."

Eduardo Ciannelli was the evil Dr. Satan who trapped the Copperhead (Robert Wilcox) in a room whose walls came together in *Mysterious Dr. Satan* (Republic 1940).

Kay Aldridge found herself in this perilous trap in *Perils of Nyoka*
(Republic 1942).

Above: John Hamilton, Kenne Duncan, and Dale Van Sickel watch as LeRoy Mason is about to unmask Robert Kent and reveal him as *The Phantom Rider* (Republic 1946). *Below:* "Slingin' Sammy" Baugh and Duncan Renaldo exposed the villainy of Neil Hamilton in *King of the Texas Rangers* (Republic 1941).

Opposite page, top: The mysterious villain of the title captures some heavy water to aid in building his deadly Cyclotrode in *The Crimson Ghost* (Republic 1946). *Opposite page, bottom:* Ace stunt man Tom Steele (as the Marvel) traps fellow stunt man Eddie Parker in *The Masked Marvel* (Republic 1943). *Above:* Marten Lamont (in disguise) found himself in George J. Lewis's intricate trap in *Federal Operator 99* (Republic 1945). *Below:* Allan Lane was *King of the Mounties* (Republic 1942) and helped destroy a nest of enemy agents who were using, among other things, this Bat Plane.

Above: Ralph Byrd as Dick Tracy found himself in a blazing inferno in this chapter ending from *Dick Tracy vs. Crime, Inc.* (Republic 1941). *Right*: Marguerite Chapman and Kane Richmond were the stars of *Spy Smasher* (Republic 1942).

Above: In this cliff-hanger Kane Richmond, rather than the obvious dummy, was supposed to be on that ladder pushed off by Bud Geary in *Haunted Harbor* (Republic 1944). *Right:* Linda Stirling, my favorite serial heroine, and George J. Lewis, playing a hero as a change of pace from his usual villainous roles, in *Zorro's Black Whip* (Republic 1944).

Top: Roy Barcroft instructs stunt man Fred Graham and Bud Geary to destroy an explosive device in *The Purple Monster Strikes* (Republic 1945). *Center:* Hero Rod Cameron was subjected to this deadly device in a chapter ending from *Secret Service in Darkest Africa* (Republic 1943). *Bottom:* One of the perils Frances Gifford and Tom Neal faced in *Jungle Girl* (Republic 1941) was the poison gas filling this room.

Right: George Turner as Zorro saves Peggy Stewart from drowning in a chapter resolution from *Son of Zorro* (Republic 1947). *Below:* Bud Wolfe loads the spear gun while Roy Barcroft describes what will happen to Adrian Booth in *Daughter of Don Q* (Republic 1946) if she doesn't cooperate.

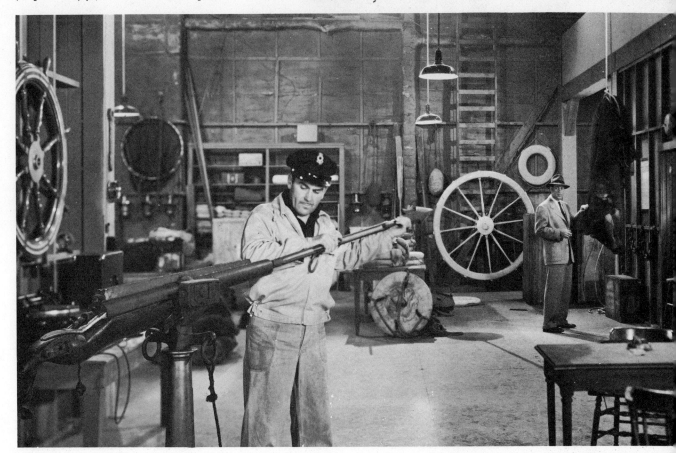

Left: In *Manhunt of Mystery Island* (Republic 1945) Roy Barcroft traps Richard Bailey and Linda Stirling in a sealed-off tunnel and instructs his henchman to open a valve controlling an underground river and "drown the rats!" *Below:* George J. Lewis, *left,* and stunt man Tom Steele are trapped by Dick Purcell as the masked hero in *Captain America* (Republic 1944).

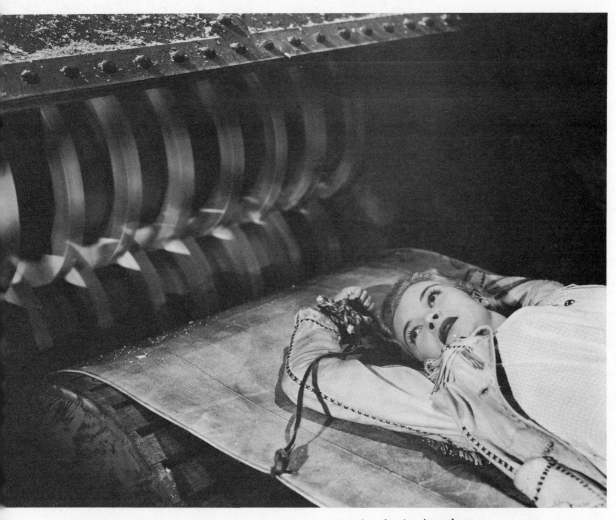

Above: Helen Talbot doesn't appear to enjoy the thought of going into that pulp-shredder in *King of the Forest Rangers* (Republic 1946). *Below*: While Rod Cameron, on the floor, battles Noel Cravat, a deadly spear is set to go off aimed directly at the trapped Constance Worth in this chapter ending from *G-Men vs. The Black Dragon* (Republic 1943).

Above: Carey Loftin, *left*, and Roy Barcroft had Linda Stirling trapped until Clayton Moore came to the rescue in *Jesse James Rides Again* (Republic 1947). *Left:* While Dale Van Sickel, *left*, battles hero Bruce Edwards in *The Black Widow* (Republic 1947), that trunk (with heroine Virginia Lindley in it) is slated for a long drop. *Bottom:* Jack Rockwell and Kay Aldridge have just pulled Allan Lane from a burning death trap in this chapter resolution from *Daredevils of the West* (Republic 1943).

Right: Linda Stirling, Republic's most famous serial queen of the forties, in *The Tiger Woman* (Republic 1944).

Allan Lane saves Duncan Renaldo and Linda Stirling just in time from flaming death in a chapter resolution from *The Tiger Woman* (Republic 1944).

Mike Mazurki was the killer who menaced Anne Jeffreys and
Morgan Conway (as Tracy) in the first of four features based on
Chester Gould's famous strip, *Dick Tracy* (RKO 1945).

8.
Murder for the Masses

Almost everyone loves a good mystery film, and though the major studios produced very few quality big-budget whodunnits in the forties, the minor companies were turning them out quite regularly by the dozens, both in series and as individual thrillers. Many of these sixty-minute programmers were not really mysteries in the true sense of the word, but rather straight action dramas which found the films' heroes tracking down various lawbreakers.

My favorite mystery series was the twelve Sherlock Holmes adventures produced by Universal Pictures between 1942 and 1946, starring Basil Rathbone as Holmes and Nigel Bruce as Dr. Watson. Twentieth Century-Fox had produced two excellent Holmes films, *The Hound of the Baskervilles* and *The Adventures of Sherlock Holmes*, also with Rathbone and Bruce, in 1939, setting both of them in period. The Universal series was moved up in time to the forties, and several of the films found Holmes matching wits with wartime enemy agents. *Spider Woman* was very likely the one film in the series that seemed to play theaters on constant reissue. Gale Sondergaard was the woman of the film's title who very nearly put an end to the detective's career by placing him inside a revolving target at a shooting gallery where he was almost shot to death by poor Dr. Watson. Professor Moriarty nearly finished Holmes in *Sherlock Holmes and the Secret Weapon* by attaching a tube to the detective's arm and draining his blood—and life—away drop by drop. Lionel Atwill was an excellent Moriarty, as was Henry Daniell in the later *The Woman in Green*. The adventure in

the series which really pleased me the most was *Sherlock Holmes Faces Death*, loosely based on "The Musgrave Ritual," one of the original stories by Sir Arthur Conan Doyle. Here Holmes helped solve a mystery by moving real people on a giant chessboard painted on one of the floors of a murder-ridden mansion.

One of the most popular radio shows of the forties was *I Love a Mystery*, which told the continued tales of three devil-may-care adventurers, Jack, Doc, and Reggie. When Columbia brought the characters to the screen they dropped Reggie but featured Jim Bannon as Jack and Barton Yarborough (who had played the same character on radio) as Doc. The series was short (only three titles), but enough chills were delivered in *The Devil's Mask*, with our leads following a trail of shrunken heads, to make up for the deficiency in longevity.

Chester Morris was one of the screen's really fine character actors in the thirties, but his fine performances in films like *The Big House, Five Came Back*, and *Blind Alley* are usually forgotten by most people who remember him only as that dashing detective with a sense of humor, Boston Blackie. In thirteen films he matched wits, insults and intrigue with Richard Lane as Inspector Faraday. Morris was a fine magician in real life, and he often worked routines into the series, which ran from 1941 through 1949 and included such titles as *Boston Blackie Booked on Suspicion, Boston Blackie Goes to Hollywood, Confessions of Boston Blackie*, and *The Phantom Thief*.

Another popular radio show of the time was

The Whistler, which featured a mysterious story-teller who weekly announced, "I know many strange stories, for I walk by night." On the screen the Whistler told some really superb tales that featured Richard Dix in the leading roles. Dix was another excellent actor who had appeared mostly in outdoor action films during the thirties and now found himself relegated to B-film duty. In the first film of the series, *The Whistler*, Dix schemed to have a professional killer murder him and then changed his mind, almost too late. Other titles included *The Power of the Whistler*, *The Mark of the Whistler*, *Voice of the Whistler*, and *The Thirteenth Hour*.

Columbia's Crime Doctor series featured Warner Baxter, another fine actor of the thirties now doing routine programmers, as a leading criminal psychologist. In *Crime Doctor*, the first film in the sequence of ten, it was revealed that Dr. Ordway had originally been a criminal himself, but now, as a result of amnesia, was a successful mental practitioner. *The Millerson Case, Shadows in the Night, The Crime Doctor's Gamble*, and *Crime Doctor's Manhunt* were among the Crime Doctor's more celebrated cases.

The two remaining series turned out by Columbia were also crowd-pleasers. Ralph Bellamy and William Gargan took turns in portraying Ellery Queen in such favorites as *Ellery Queen's Penthouse Mystery* and *A Close Call for Ellery Queen*. Margaret Lindsay was Nikki Porter and Charlie Grapewin played Inspector Queen, with both Bellamy and Gargan in a series that provided considerably more laughs than thrills. Just as Columbia had filled its serials and Westerns with time-consuming, unfunny comic routines, so too did they stress the non-mystery elements in what could have been highly thrilling features. Most of the Lone Wolf films were made in the late thirties, but the studio frequently brought them back to rerun houses in the forties. Warren William was the best of the several actors who portrayed the Michael Lanyard role (others were Melvyn Douglas and Francis Lederer before him, and later Gerald Mohr). Titles included *The Lone Wolf Keeps a Date, The Lone Wolf Spy Hunt, The Lone Wolf Meets a Lady*, and *The Lone Wolf in Mexico*, among others.

RKO was no slouch when it came to series films, either. It had the Saint with Louis Hayward or George Sanders playing the role in most of the films like *The Saint in New York, The Saint in London, The Saint in Palm Springs*, while Sanders and his real-life brother Tom Conway gave screen life to the Falcon in a popular string of adventures that included *The Falcon's Brother* (in which both Sanders and Conway appeared), *The Falcon Takes Over, The Falcon Strikes Back*, and *The Falcon Out West*. Also from RKO came the four Dick Tracy features (there were also four Republic serials based on the character). The first two, *Dick Tracy* and *Dick Tracy vs. Cueball*, featured Morgan Conway as the comic-strip detective, while Ralph Byrd took over in *Dick Tracy's Dilemma* and *Dick Tracy Meets Gruesome*. Recent screenings have shown the films to be generally routine and dull; most people seem to enjoy *Dilemma* best, because of Jack Lambert's portrayal of the villain with a hook for a hand.

Twentieth Century-Fox was still striking paydirt in the forties by reissuing its Charlie Chan and Mr. Moto films made in the thirties. Both series had great production values (usually utilizing the big sets that were built for major Fox films), and Warner Oland and Sidney Toler as Chan and Peter Lorre as Moto always delivered topnotch characterizations. A new series produced by the studio were the Michael Shayne entries featuring Lloyd Nolan as the wisecracking detective in such titles as *The Man Who Wouldn't Die* and *Michael Shayne, Private Detective*. (PRC also had some Shayne adventures a few years later with Hugh Beaumont starring, as well as a short Philo Vance series with Alan Curtis.)

MGM would occasionally come up with another in its popular Thin Man films with William Powell and Myrna Loy again playing Nick and Nora Charles, two sophisticated, debonair, and double-entendre-dropping sleuths in titles like *Song of the Thin Man* and *Shadow of the Thin Man*. All the Thin Man films had excellent production values, although the quality of the mystery content varied.

Paramount contributed its Bulldog Drummond films with John Howard and John Barrymore, and Monogram was turning out its newer Charlie Chans as well as the Shadow and Mr. Wong films (discussed in another chapter).

There were also a great many comedy-mysteries starring such favorites as Milton Berle (*Whispering Ghosts*), Red Skelton (*Whistling in the Dark, Whistling in Brooklyn*, and *Whistling in Dixie*, in which he played a radio detective called the Fox), Olsen and Johnson (*Ghost Catchers*), Abbott and Costello (*Who Done It?*), Fred Allen (*It's in the Bag*), and others.

These generally entertaining short films never

pretended to be material of lasting value and quality. They were made quickly to please an audience who wanted the additional advantage of not only watching a film, but participating in it. It was a challenge to match one's knowledge and abilities against those of the heroes on the screen. What matter if the clues were skimpy, the logic often faulty, and the action sometimes routine, as long as we could watch all those great character actors slinking around to try and throw us off the trail? And if we guessed correctly? Well, the smiles and the "I-knew-who-it-was-all-the-time" lines would flow until we had convinced all our boyhood friends that we were really smarter than Philo Vance, Boston Blackie, the Falcon, the Saint, the Lone Wolf, Bulldog Drummond, Charlie Chan, Mr. Moto, Ellery Queen, and all the others combined. And who could deny, with any degree of authority, that we weren't?

Warren William was the urbane detective-hero in *The Lone Wolf Strikes* (Columbia 1940) who apparently had Montagu Love at a disadvantage in this scene from the film.

Top: Ralph Bellamy was one of several actors who played Ellery Queen for laughs and thrills on the screen. This scene is from *Ellery Queen and the Murder Ring* (Columbia 1941). *Center:* Gerald Mohr was the famous detective in *The Lone Wolf in Mexico* (Columbia 1947), aided by the nonsense of Eric Blore. *Bottom:* In *The Whistler* (Columbia 1944), star Richard Dix involves himself in a situation in which he is almost killed.

Left: George Sanders shows an important clue to Jonathan Hale in *The Saint in Palm Springs* (RKO 1941), one in a long line of Saint films with different stars playing the detective. *Below:* Alan Curtis was one of the screen's portrayers of Philo Vance, here seen with Sheila Ryan in *Philo Vance's Secret Mission* (PRC 1947).

Above: Richard Lane, *left,* and Walter Sande think they have Chester Morris
(as Blackie) trapped again, while Lloyd Corrigan, *right,* watches in *After Midnight with
Boston Blackie* (Columbia 1943). *Below, left:* Barry Nelson, *left,* William Powell,
Sam Levene, and Henry O'Neil help solve an important case in *Shadow of the
Thin Man* (MGM 1941). *Below, right:* William Gargan as Ellery is obviously
being amazed again by Margaret Lindsay (as Nikki Porter) in *A Close Call for Ellery
Queen* (Columbia 1942), another in the popular series.

Right: Ralph Byrd played his Dick Tracy role in four serials, two features, and a television series. This scene is from *Dick Tracy's Dilemma* (RKO 1947). *Below:* Dick Tracy's adversary in *Dick Tracy's Dilemma* (RKO 1947) was Jack Lambert, who met his death when his hook touched high-voltage wires.

Above: Lloyd Nolan, *center,* explains an important discovery to Henry
Wilcoxon while Marjorie Weaver watches in the Michael Shayne mystery
The Man Who Wouldn't Die (Twentieth Century-Fox 1942).
Below: Tom Conway as the Falcon, *right,* spies Robert Armstrong up to no
good in this scene from *The Falcon in San Francisco* (RKO 1945).

Top: Basil Rathbone and Nigel Bruce discover a murdered Halliwell Hobbes in *Sherlock Holmes Faces Death* (Universal 1943). *Bottom:* Alec Craig ushers Basil Rathbone into a waiting trap set by the *Spider Woman* (Universal 1944), played by Gale Sondergaard.

Above: Basil Rathbone, *right*, catches a disguised killer (Gerald Hamer) in the Sherlock Holmes adventure *The Scarlet Claw* (Universal 1944). *Below:* I wonder if the Crime Doctor (Warner Baxter, *left*) can talk his way out of being shot by Steven Geray in *The Crime Doctor's Gamble* (Columbia 1947).

Reginald Denny, *left*, John Howard (as Drummond), E. E. Clive, and John Barrymore were the stars of *Bulldog Drummond's Revenge* (Paramount 1937).

Tom Conway, *left*, and George Sanders were real-life brothers who appeared together in *The Falcon's Brother* (RKO 1942) with Jane Randolph.

John Carradine shows Mr. Moto (Peter Lorre, *left*) an important clue in
Thank You, Mr. Moto (Twentieth Century-Fox 1937).

Above: Wally Vernon looks astonished while Sidney Toler, *right,* looks only interested in a trick by Cesar Romero in *Charlie Chan on Treasure Island* (Twentieth Century-Fox 1939), from which this publicity photo is taken. *Below:* Jim Bannon, *center,* was Jack and Barton Yarborough, *right,* was Doc in the *I Love a Mystery* adventure *The Devil's Mask* (Columbia 1946). That's Paul Burns polishing up a fang or two.

Above: Red Skelton shows co-star
Ann Rutherford a mysterious clue in
Whistling in Dixie (MGM 1942).
Opposite page, top: Ole Olsen and
Chic Johnson were a couple of zany
Ghost Catchers (Universal 1944).
Opposite page, bottom: Brenda Joyce
and Milton Berle bump into
mysterious John Carradine in this
scene from *Whispering Ghosts*
(Twentieth Century-Fox 1942).

William Elliott was Red Ryder and Bobby Blake Little Beaver in a popular
series of action adventures turned out by Republic Pictures in the forties.

298

9.
Dusty Trails to Adventure

To me, one of the most exciting and beautiful sights on the motion picture screen is that of a horse running full tilt photographed against the background of the scenic splendor of the American Southwest. Even in my early days of moviegoing this element of the B-Western films seems to have overshadowed all the usual action embellishments of the genre. Though, as in the case of the serials, I preferred the product turned out by Republic, considering it of higher entertainment value action-wise, I allowed myself to be greedily self-indulgent to the point of enjoying almost all Westerns no matter which studio turned them out.

My first Western idol on the screen was Don "Red" Barry (he had gained the nickname after appearing in the serial *Adventures of Red Ryder*), a short, tough, and thoroughly professional actor who looked excellent in the saddle and performed his dialogue scenes with credible justice. The Barry Westerns were mostly tautly wrought little gems that often stressed the dramatic rather than physical conflicts in the stories. In several of his films Barry played a dual role (usually twin brothers, one bad through circumstances beyond his control, and one good who was invariably a preacher, lawyer, or doctor). He claims to have encouraged Republic to give him these double-duty efforts in order to showcase his acting capabilities. After all, as we all know, the meaty roles in these minor Westerns almost always were plum assignments meted out to the likes of Roy Barcroft, Charles King, Harry

Woods, LeRoy Mason, and similar specialists in the gentle art of chicanery.

Following close on Barry's heels was William "Wild Bill" Elliott (like Barry, he had picked up his middle tag from a character he played in a serial and series of Westerns, Wild Bill Hickok). Elliott had begun his screen career by playing fancy-dressed dudes in scores of minor bit roles in the thirties before finally getting his chance to star in Westerns and serials at Columbia. When he finally moved over to Republic in the early forties, the studio starred him in a series of eight actioners paired with George "Gabby" Hayes (my favorite cowboy sidekick). After that brief series, he was chosen to star in sixteen features based on the exploits of Fred Harmon's famous comic-strip cowboy, Red Ryder, and it is this group of films he is best remembered for. Many of the sixteen films are among the best that the studio ever turned out, each full of thrilling chases, fights, and assorted action all backed by excellent musical scores, mostly composed by Mort Glickman. Remember Red's sidekick, Little Beaver? The role was played by Bobby Blake who, under the name Robert Blake, achieved an outstanding personal success in the film *In Cold Blood* in the middle sixties (his publicity proclaimed him as a *"new"* screen sensation, even though he had appeared in films regularly since the early forties, including such classics as *The Treasure of the Sierra Madre*, in which he sold Bogart the winning lottery ticket that set the film's plot in motion). After the

Ryder series Elliott was bumped upstairs to star in big-budget pictures in which he was never really used effectively. Most of us wished he had remained as Red Ryder, uttering his famous tag line, "I'm a peaceable man, but—"

Picking up the Ryder reins for seven more films was Allan Lane, who had finished his serial duties and his own series of six relatively adventurous efforts. When Republic finally threw in the towel as far as the Ryder character was concerned (after twenty-three features and one serial) Lane tacked on a new nickname and as Allan "Rocky" Lane went on to be a leading Western star until the studio ceased production in 1955.

In the middle forties Sunset Carson made a very impressive entry into the action film sweepstakes, and there are those who claim that he was actually outpulling Roy Rogers in the fan-mail received by the studio from the southern states. I can believe it. Carson was a huge six-foot-four-plus, no-nonsense cowboy whose mainstay was action. No guitar-playing, fancy-dressed drugstore cowboy, he was a rugged ready-made audience-pleaser. Unfortunately, because of personal problems his tenure at Republic was all too brief.

Monogram was turning out some pretty respectable thrillers itself. Johnny Mack Brown was featured in a memorable series which, in almost every case, found him riding into a town (usually using the name Nevada) and bumping into his pal Raymond Hatton (called Sandy Hopkins). Unfortunately, not much money was budgeted for the productions, and the interior sets were usually skimpy and cheap-looking; but once outside, Johnny, expert horseman that he was, made the films a sheer joy to watch. I don't think any cowboy actor was ever able to throw such a realistic-looking punch in a fight sequence as Johnny. Even Yakima Canutt, the king of stunt men, admits that his favorite people to work with were John Wayne and Johnny Mack Brown.

Hatton retained his Sandy Hopkins label when he joined pals Buck Jones and Tim McCoy in the very popular Rough Riders series. The two things I remember most about those films were Buck's chewing a stick of gum whenever he was getting ready for some fast action, and the scene that closed each film where the three comrades rode off in different directions after having completed their latest mission.

Trios seemed to be very popular in those early-

forties days. Republic continued its popular Three Mesquiteers series which had been so successful in the thirties (unfortunately, the original trio of Ray Corrigan, Bob Livingston, and Max Terhune had departed and their replacements, Bob Steele, Tom Tyler, and Rufe Davis didn't seem to possess the same magic), and Monogram brought back Hoot Gibson, Bob Steele, and Ken Maynard as the Trail Blazers. Although Steele was still adept at his work, Ken and Hoot were well past their prime, and it was almost grotesque at times to see them try to recapture the glory they had once possessed as individual stars. The Range Busters were another popular trio who managed to provide occasional thrills. Comprised of Ray Corrigan, Max Terhune, and John King, the Range Busters often seemed to spend a great deal more time clowning around than fighting. One of the films in the series, *Saddle Mountain Roundup*, was really a very exciting little mystery-Western, complete with secret caves and a mysterious murderer. It even was published in one of the popular Big Little Books (remember those, folks?).

And there were numerous other stars who rode the range for our entertainment. Some of them, like Buster Crabbe with his sidekick Al "Fuzzy" St. John, William Boyd as Hopalong Cassidy, and Charles Starrett as the Durango Kid, were excellent, while others such as Jimmy Wakely, Eddie Dean, Whip Wilson, Lash LaRue, and Monte Hale just couldn't quite cut it.

But of all the Western stars of the forties, the two most popular in general appeal were Roy Rogers and Gene Autry. In the thirties Autry was probably *the* biggest B-Western star, and his recordings sold in the millions. While Autry was stashing away a fortune, Rogers was still a member of the Sons of the Pioneers singing group, and he made appearances in several of Autry's early films in singing or bit roles. In the late thirties Rogers had started his own series and was moving up fast on Autry, who was still riding high into the early forties. When war broke out Gene enlisted in the Air Force, and Republic quickly moved Roy in to fill the gap. Within a year Rogers was in fact as well as in title the "King of the Cowboys." Both Autry's and Rogers' features were usually given deluxe theater treatment in Oakland on their initial releases. They seldom appeared at the regular run-of-the-mill "scratch-houses" that fans like myself frequented, but rather as the companion features at the big first-run houses; thus I missed a great many of them (which I fortunately saw many years later when they were all sold to television). The films of both men vary in quality a great deal. Usually the studio would produce a series of eight films per year featuring each star. Four to six of the films would be done on skimpy budgets and would be filmed primarily on the studio's back lot, and the remainder would get the deluxe treatment which included additional songs (with some production value), more picturesque exterior locations, more bit-players, better costumes, higher-caliber villains and about fifteen minutes added running time (most of their films hovered around the sixty-five minute mark, but some of these specials ran as long as eighty-seven minutes). One of the best of the Rogers' "spectaculars" was *Silver Spurs*, made in 1943, which featured John Carradine as the principal heavy. The film was beautifully photographed against the background of the Sierra Nevada Mountains and featured a thrilling wagon chase replete with ace stunt work as an entertaining finale. As the forties moved along, Rogers' films began to lose their tendency to be primarily aimed at juvenile audiences. When men like Sloan Nibley moved in to take over the scripting chores, the films became more rugged, the violence more pronounced (for example, Roy Barcroft's mercilessly dumping oil cans filled with smuggled aliens into a lake in *The Far Frontier*, or Dale Van Sickel and David Sharpe as they gave Roy one helluva working over in *Bells of San Angelo*) and the dialogue more realistic. Other newly acquired assets were the use of Trucolor and the directorial services of William

Witney. Witney was, and continues to be, one of the top action directors around (his handling of the Republic serials in the late thirties and early forties gave them their distinctive action-packed style), and he kept Rogers' films moving along at an audience-pleasing, fast-paced clip.

When Autry returned after his war service, Rogers was now top man at Republic, and rivalry was bound to emerge. Gene made only one short series for the studio, which had made him a star, and then moved over to Columbia Pictures, where he was able not only to star in but produce his own films. Both men retained their enormous popularity into the fifties (each made records, had radio shows, and produced their own television half-hour series) and Roy is still a popular attraction (teamed with his wife and frequent co-star in many of his films, Dale Evans) for even today's audiences.

The B-Western is now a relic of those good old days, seldom seen except on television stations that have the courage to run them for those of us who remember (no New York station has run a Republic B-Western in the eleven years I have lived here), and a few scattered theaters in the southern states that still cater to kids who crave a little action. Station-owners claim that the B-Western has been replaced by the hour-long television show like *Gunsmoke* and *Bonanza*. Surely they must be mistaken. Under *no* circumstances were the B-Westerns *ever* as dull and actionless as those television talk-a-thons. May I suggest to those very same "authorities" on public taste that, if they want to turn out some superior action fare, they hire William Witney—FAST!

Right: In *Thundering Trails* (Republic 1943), Jimmy Dodd, *left,* Bob Steele, and Tom Tyler were the popular Three Mesquiteers who solved a murder mystery. *Below:* Roy Rogers, *left,* had a terrific battle with stunt man David Sharpe at the conclusion of *Bells of San Angelo* (Republic 1947).

Above: Smiley Burnette and Noah Beery, Sr., watched and listened as Gene Autry strummed and sang the title song in *Mexicali Rose* (Republic 1939). *Below:* Roy Rogers, *left*, and Gene Autry, *right*, flank Allen Wilson, a vice-president in charge of production for Republic Pictures, in a rare photo of the two stars together. Immediately behind Roy is one of the top action directors, William Witney.

Above: Eddie Dean delivers a right cross to Eddie Parker in *Shadow Valley*
(PRC 1947). Lying across the desk is veteran Western badman George Chesebro.
Below: The Range Busters, Max "Alibi" Terhune, *left*, Ray "Crash" Corrigan, and
John "Dusty" King listen to Riley Hill disclose some important information in
Texas Trouble Shooters (Monogram 1942).

Above: In *A Missouri Outlaw* (Republic 1941), Don "Red" Barry tracked down four killers who were responsible for a sheriff's death. All four, including John Merton in this scene, wind up destroying themselves.
Right: Tex Ritter was a very popular star in Monogram films and over at Universal where he made some popular features with Johnny Mack Brown.

Left: Sunset Carson was a popular success at Republic in the mid-forties. *Below:* Tim Holt, *right,* ties up Cy Kendall and Ernie Adams in this scene from *The Fargo Kid* (RKO 1940).

Above: Allan Lane as Red Ryder helps Roy Barcroft up after having just given him a beating, while Tom London, *left*, Gene Roth and Trevor Bardette watch in *Marshal of Cripple Creek* (Republic 1947). *Below, left:* Charles Starrett was the Durango Kid in *Challenge of the Range* (Columbia 1949) and dozens of other Western adventures featuring the same character. *Below, right:* Tom Keene, *left*, listens to some advice from LeRoy Mason in *Painted Trail* (Monogram 1938), one of a series of fine films Keene made for RKO and Monogram.

Above: Al "Fuzzy" St. John, *left,* and pal Lash LaRue talk things over in *Cheyenne Takes Over* (PRC 1947). *Below:* Monte Hale mixes it up with stunt ace David Sharpe in *California Firebrand* (Republic 1948).

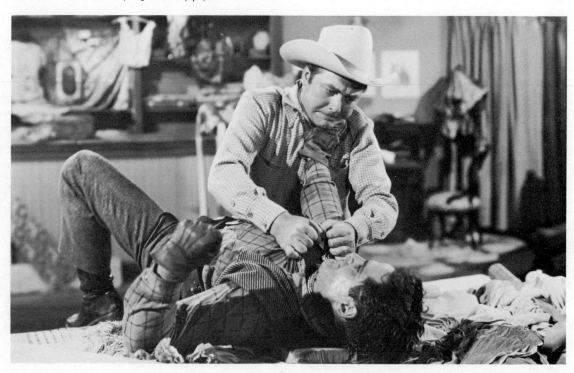

Above: Ghost Town Law (Monogram 1942) featured Buck
Jones, *left*, Tim McCoy, and Raymond Hatton as the
Rough Riders. *Below:* Rod Cameron, *right*, gets tough with
George Eldredge while veteran badman Edmund Cobb watches
in *The Old Texas Trail* (Universal 1944).

Opposite page: Raymond Hatton was Sandy Hopkins to Johnny Mack Brown's Nevada or
Jack McKenzie in a whole series for Monogram. This scene is from *Land of the Lawless*
(Monogram 1947). *Above*: George Houston gets the drop on Glenn Strange in
Lone Rider and the Bandit (PRC 1942). Houston wanted to be an operatic singer
and was making cheap Westerns to get money to form his own company, but he died
a premature death before he could achieve his ambition. *Below*: Eddy Waller,
left, and Allan "Rocky" Lane ask veteran cowboy star Bob Steele some questions
in *Savage Frontier* (Republic 1953).

Douglas Fairbanks, Jr., was the daredevil Irish adventurer in *The Fighting O'Flynn* (Universal 1948), one of the films he produced himself.

10.

New Worlds to Conquer

Who among us hasn't at one time or another in our young lives wished that he or she had lived in another period of history? With razor-sharp rapier we could quickly have dispatched the likes of Basil Rathbone, George Macready, and Henry Daniell, or traveled to an exotic South Sea Island paradise in search of giant pearls and adventure. Movie screens in the early forties were full of exciting escapist films which more than satisfied our cravings for new and thrilling worlds to vicariously conquer.

The king of the great movie swashbucklers was, of course, Errol Flynn, and his dashing presence was available to us in constant reissues of his classic adventures like *Captain Blood, The Sea Hawk,* and *Adventures of Robin Hood.* I had some mixed feelings about the first two films, both of which seemed long and talky except for the thrilling dueling scenes, but I had unabashed enthusiasm for all of *Robin Hood.* Filmed in beautiful Technicolor, who could fail to enjoy this classic tale of Robin and his Merry Men with its fabulous castles, archery tournaments, lavish banquets, and one of the most famous fencing matches in screen history? Who could ever forget Errol and Basil Rathbone as they fought each other on winding staircases, over furniture, and through hallways, with their shadows playing grotesque pantomimes on the columns and walls of the mammoth castle set? And, naturally, as they dueled they threw jeering lines at one another (Rathbone: "You've come to Nottingham once too often, my friend"; Flynn: "After today there'll be no need for me to come again!").

Robin Hood must surely be classified among the top ten entertainment-action films of all time.

Much as I admired Flynn, however, my real hero in those years of the forties was Douglas Fairbanks, Jr. Fairbanks, with that incredibly infectious smile and the animated jauntiness he surely inherited from his famous father, never failed to thrill me in his classic adventures. In *The Corsican Brothers* he had the pleasure of competing with himself as he played the dual role of the Siamese twin brothers who, separated at birth, continue to feel and suffer each other's emotions. Both brothers fought against the tyranny of Akim Tamiroff and his evil henchman, John Emery (as well as fighting each other), until, in the end, one brother sacrifices his life for the other. In *The Exile* Fairbanks was an exiled king who was hounded by a satanically portrayed Henry Daniell, whom Doug dispatched in a spectacular battle with swords in an old windmill. *The Fighting O'Flynn* found our dashing hero fighting with flashing grin and pistols against the oppression being perpetrated by Richard Greene in the Ireland of the 1800s. This film had a rousing battle in a castle parapet with exploding fireworks going off all over the place as its finale. But the best film Fairbanks made in the forties, I still feel, was *Sinbad the Sailor.* Here was glorious color adventure on a grand scale. Fairbanks, as the famed storyteller of the *Arabian Nights,* was in top form as he related this tale of a search for fabulous treasure on a mysterious island. Around to oppose him were Anthony Quinn and Walter Slezak, and the film seemed just chock-full of chases, sea battles, duels, and romantic adventure. I remember my father taking me to San Francisco to see the film, and I could never forget the exciting finale, which found Doug being pursued by Quinn in a furious sea chase. Fairbanks loads a catapulting device with a solid ball of flaming tar and fires it at Quinn's boat, and the screen becomes crimson as we see cross-cutting between the ball of flame coming directly at the camera and the brightening red face of the terrified Quinn until the final dazzling fade-out. Much as I love Fairbanks, however, I do wish he would quit saying on television and elsewhere that he did all his own stunt work. All true aficionados know that many of the spectacular leaps and stunts were, in fact, done by David Sharpe (who actually received second-unit credit on screen for *The Exile*), that great stunt man who enlivened so many serials and features through the years.

Tyrone Power wasn't bad in his few swashbuckling efforts, but his *The Mark of Zorro* I found strangely unappealing, even seeing it as a tolerant child. Whereas Douglas Fairbanks's silent version had been simply full of daredevil stunts and chases, this remake had very little of that sort of thing. The stress was put on the dialogue sequences to the detriment of the action episodes, and the film suffered for it. There was, nevertheless, that memorable duel, perhaps one of the best ever done, between Power and Basil Rathbone. Rathbone loved fencing as a personal hobby, and his enthusiasm is quite evident. Power's other major entry in the action field during this period was *The Black Swan*, a real thriller of a pirate picture that has too seldom been presented on screens and television.

Another popular favorite was Louis Hayward. Having a very likable personality, not unlike that of Flynn and Fairbanks, Hayward entertained us in such pleasant divertissements as *The Black Arrow* and *The Return of Monte Cristo*. His real classics, however, were *The Man in the Iron Mask*, in which he played a delightful dual role as twin brothers vying for a throne, one of whom imprisons the other in a grotesque iron mask so that no one will ever discover the resemblance between the two, and *The Son of Monte Cristo*, in which he led a daredevil bunch of patriots in opposing the rule of a smirking George Sanders. I'll never forget the final action scene where Sanders, slain by Hayward in a duel, falls over a balcony and plunges spectacularly through an ornate glass window to a floor many feet below.

The Son of Monte Cristo used to come back to theaters quite regularly paired with the original *The Count of Monte Cristo*, made in 1934. This early film is quite a classic itself. Although it possesses some good action sequences, the most important attributes of the film are the superb performances of its stars, primarily Robert Donat as the Count. Donat, easily one of the finest actors of all time, had a field day as the sailor who is unjustly sent to prison (by the intrigue of Raymond Walburn, Sidney Blackmer, and Louis Calhern), escapes after nearly twenty years' imprisonment and returns to seek vengeance against the plotters. One might have wished that Donat would have lent his charm and talent to more films of this type.

For jungle devotees, there were, of course, numerous Tarzan adventures. MGM, which had turned out the best films in the series in the thirties, kept bringing back their early adventures in reissues, but it is the RKO entries I recall enjoying the most. This was probably because these later films were full of so many relatively silly gimmicks and situations. In *Tarzan's Desert Mystery*, for example, I remember Boy (Johnny Sheffield) being trapped in a giant spider web, while the web's creator came menacingly close to having a delicious repast until Tarzan arrived in the nick of time. Perhaps all kids are a little sadistic at heart (didn't we all applaud when heroes threw villains off cliffs or destroyed them in other similarly spectacular ways?), and my crowd at the theaters always got a bang out of seeing Tarzan—or his opponents—winding up in quicksand or man-eating plants. Ah, the thrill of it all!

Giant pearls were the ultimate goal of Victor McLaglen and his band of merry cutthroats in the very popular *South of Pago Pago*. They traveled to a remote tropic paradise where Jon Hall tried desperately to convince his people that they shouldn't dive into the extreme depths where the big pearls lay. Needless to say, McLaglen cajoled the natives into diving anyway, and one of the poor devils managed to get his foot caught in the gaping jaws of a giant oyster and was saved just in time by Hall who, after some pressure on his own, convinced his friends to do away with McLaglen and his bunch.

And, finally, there was Cornel Wilde. Wilde has turned into one of the fine actors of our day in the adventure field (no one can ever forget *The Naked Prey*), but in those days he was a yet untrained caricature of the great dashing heroes like Flynn, Hayward, and Fairbanks. *The Bandit of Sherwood Forest* found him playing the son of the famed inhabitant of the greenwood and opposing the villainy of George Macready. There were many excellent riding sequences, and the splendid use of color enhanced the entire production. The ending was a memorable one, which found Macready locking Wilde up as a prisoner and then challenging him to a duel, but depriving him of food and water so that he would be too weak to really be able to fight. Unfortunately, Macready hadn't counted on the cleverness of Anita Louise, who managed to smuggle water and food to Wilde from an adjoining cell, and the battle was thus joined on equal terms with our dashing hero winning duel and fair maiden. *A Thousand and One Nights* was both a pleasure and an annoyance to watch. Another excellent color production, for me the film had far too many laughs (admittedly it was made for laughs) and not enough action. Rex Ingram, who had played the Genie in *The Thief of Bagdad* several years before, was back to do similar duty

in this fantasy which found Wilde constantly being annoyed by a female with magical powers (Evelyn Keyes) and a silly Phil Silvers. The pacing was frenetic as Wilde kept losing and regaining his magical powers to the delight of most of the audience.

Larry Parks, who had scored so well in *The Jolson Story*, tried his hand at becoming a new action hero in *The Swordsman* and *The Gallant Blade*, but in fact he was amazingly bland and uninspiring. By the time he had arrived on the screen, the great days of daring rogues had pretty well vanished. The closest the screen ever got to those great action heroes of the early forties came almost a decade later in the person of Stewart Granger. He alone seemed to inspire that great feeling for adventure we all lusted after in such superior works as *The Prisoner of Zenda* (an almost exact scene-for-scene remake of the famous Ronald Colman version of the thirties) and *Scaramouche* (which featured one of the longest, if not *the* longest, dueling sequence in screen history). Flynn, Fairbanks, Hayward, Wilde, Granger—I wonder if we shall ever see their like upon the screen again.

Tyrone Power was the masked avenger in the sound remake of *The Mark of Zorro* (Twentieth Century-Fox 1940). The film lacked much of the excitement of the silent version, and dialogue sequences became boring after a while to young audiences.

Above: Douglas Fairbanks, Jr., and Joan Bennett in the jungle adventure *Green Hell* (Universal 1940). If that set looks familiar to you, it's because you saw it, slightly altered, in *The Mummy's Hand* (Universal 1940), a scene from which appears in chapter four of this book. *Right:* Errol Flynn and Basil Rathbone fought their first screen duel together in *Captain Blood* (Warner Bros 1935).

Left: Louis Hayward played a dual role in *The Man in the Iron Mask* (Small-United Artists 1939). This is a shot of him as Philippe. *Below:* Warren William, *left,* and Alan Hale fight to free Louis Hayward from his devilish mask in *The Man in the Iron Mask* (Small-United Artists 1939).

Opposite page, above: Jon Hall and Frances Farmer were the young lovers in *South of Pago Pago* (Small-United Artists 1940), an adventure film about men in search of giant pearls. *Opposite page, below:* Clayton Moore, *left,* and Montagu Love assisted masked Louis Hayward in his fight to overthrow evil George Sanders in *The Son of Monte Cristo* (Small-United Artists 1940). *Above:* Basil Rathbone and Errol Flynn in the famous dueling sequence from *Adventures of Robin Hood* (Warner Brothers 1938). *Right:* Douglas Fairbanks, Jr., was the fantastic storyteller who told his most exciting tale in *Sinbad the Sailor* (RKO 1947).

Opposite page, far left: Larry Parks, who had done so well playing the famous singer in *The Jolson Story* (Columbia 1946), was less successful as a swashbuckler in films like *The Swordsman* (Columbia 1948) and as shown here, *The Gallant Blade* (Columbia 1948). *Opposite page, above:* Frances Gifford and Johnny Weissmuller in *Tarzan Triumphs* (RKO 1943), one of a long string of adventures of the famous ape man made in the forties. *Opposite page, below:* Errol Flynn with sword in hand again as the star of *The Sea Hawk* (Warner Brothers 1940). *Above:* Rex Ingram recreated his role of the Genie, which he had played in *The Thief of Bagdad* (Korda-United Artists 1940), for *A Thousand and One Nights* (Columbia 1945). That's star Cornel Wilde in reduced circumstances in this publicity still from the film.

Above: If one Douglas Fairbanks, Jr., was a treat, two were even better. Here they are in a publicity photo with Ruth Warrick for *The Corsican Brothers* (Small-United Artists 1941). *Below:* George Macready, scar and all, greets Barbara Britton in *The Return of Monte Cristo* (Columbia 1946) while a heavily disguised Louis Hayward watches.

Robert Donat brought his considerable acting skill to the role of Edmond Dantes in *The Count of Monte Cristo* (Small-United Artists 1934).

Opposite page, top: Louis Hayward again matched wits and swords with George Macready, *center,* in *The Black Arrow* (Columbia 1948). That's veteran character actor Walter Kingsford looking on. *Opposite page, bottom:* Douglas Fairbanks, Jr., has just finished a duel to the death with Henry Daniell in an old windmill in *The Exile* (Universal 1947). Produced by Fairbanks, the film was one of the few to be made in the forties in Sepia color. *Above:* In *The Bandit of Sherwood Forest* (Columbia 1946), Russell Hicks was the elder Robin Hood and Cornel Wilde his daring son.

THRILL TO THE SPECTACULAR DARING OF THE KING OF *Romance* AND *Adventure!*

...he lived as he loved...

dangerously!

Universal-International In Association With The Fairbanks Company Inc. Presents

MARIA MONTEZ
and Introduces
PAULE CROSET
with **HENRY DANIELL**
NIGEL BRUCE   ROBERT COOTE

and **DOUGLAS FAIRBANKS,** Jr.

in **THE EXILE**

Written and Produced by DOUGLAS FAIRBANKS, Jr.
Directed by MAX OPULS · A UNIVERSAL-INTERNATIONAL RELEASE

Veteran actor Harry Carey and
John Wayne in the excellent
The Shepherd of the Hills
(Paramount 1941).

II.
Man of Action

Few people would disagree that John Wayne is probably the single greatest action star in sound-film history. In his forty years of film-making he has made over one hundred and fifty features, almost all of which were full of thrills and excitement. He has had a fluctuating career that has seen frequent moments of screen glory and dismal moments of quickly forgotten failures. For every *Red River* and *True Grit* there has been a *Tycoon* and *Without Reservations*. A success in *The Big Trail* in 1930, he went on to do quickie B's at Mascot, Warner Bros, Monogram, and Republic. *Stagecoach* brought him back to prominence in 1939 and he never slipped back into the co-feature category again. It is not the Wayne of *She Wore a Yellow Ribbon* and *Rio Grande* that I remember from those affectionate matinee days, however—my visions are of the gun-toting war hero winning World War II in *Back to Bataan, Flying Tigers,* and *The Fighting Seabees,* and the skilled horseman who took great delight in brawling to the finish with such worthy opponents as Ward Bond, Randolph Scott, and Albert Dekker.

Most of those action years of the early forties were spent at Republic, but from time to time Duke would venture off that home range to turn in some smashing portrayals at other studios. At Universal he starred in *Seven Sinners, The Spoilers,* and *Pittsburgh.* The first film found him falling temporarily in love with Marlene Dietrich and having a spectacular fight with Oscar Homolka; the second found him falling in permanent love with Marlene Dietrich and having a classic brawl with Randolph Scott; and the third found him falling out of love with Marlene Dietrich and battling Scott one more time. All three films were very well produced, and by any standards are among the most entertaining action films ever produced.

At RKO Wayne gave credible performances in *A Lady Takes a Chance* with Jean Arthur, in which he played a rodeo cowboy she fell for; *Tall in the Saddle,* in which Ella Raines finally corraled him, but only after many shenanigans and a brutal battle with Ward Bond; and *Back to Bataan,* where, with the help of Anthony Quinn, he helped win a victory in the Philippines.

In *Reap the Wild Wind,* done at Paramount, he was excellent as the skipper who wrecked his own ship on a reef in order to help Raymond Massey and his bunch of salvagers collect a supposed fortune. Filmed in beautiful Technicolor, the film had many spectacular moments, including the famous underwater sequence in which Ray Milland and Wayne battle a giant squid and the latter gives up his life to save his screen rival.

For sheer adventure and excitement, however, it was the work Wayne did at Republic that I really thrived on. In roughly five years Wayne turned out more than a dozen fine action films. Even the ones which were weak in story line, like *Wheel of Fortune, Lady from Louisiana, Lady for a Night,* and *Flame of the Barbary Coast* had many thrilling chase and fight sequences, while the big epics like *Flying Tigers, The Fighting Seabees,* and *In Old Oklahoma* (retitled *War of the Wildcats* in television prints) contained more excitement than the audience really deserved at one time.

Over the years I had often wondered what it was about *Flying Tigers* and *The Fighting Seabees* that made them stand out so prominently as war films. The answer lay not in the excellent performances of Wayne and his supporting cast, but in the superb special effects created by the late Howard Lydecker. I can't recall any war film that had quite so many spectacular effects as these two films. The pyrotechnics were simply dazzling. In *Flying Tigers* Wayne was in command of the famed unit which was fighting the enemy in China before we officially entered World War II. Into the group comes dashing John Carroll, who manages through his own carelessness to make a general mess out of everything, including causing the death of Wayne's closest friend, Paul Kelly. To redeem himself, Carroll takes off on a suicide mission with Wayne to bomb an important bridge. During the attack Carroll is mortally wounded, but he manages to let Wayne get out of the plane in a parachute while he plunges the plane into an enemy train. I can still remember all the close-ups in that film of the grinning Japanese pilots being shot down with blood running from their mouths. We seemed to take sadistic pleasure in watching the enemy bleed a lot. The aerial sequences were the real highlights of this film. Unlike many of the studios who shot their miniatures indoors against painted backdrops, Republic used large-size scale models, meticulously detailed, and photographed them outdoors against actual backgrounds. The difference was like night and day. Next time you see a Universal war film, pay particular attention to the tiny bathtub-like models and you will see the very considerable difference.

In *The Fighting Seabees* it was Wayne's turn to be the pain in the neck who winds up sacrificing his life in a spectacular way. As Wedge Donovan, Wayne was the tough head of a construction company who joins with Dennis O'Keefe, playing a naval officer, to form the Seabees, an advance contingent of engineers and construction men who go in to build airfields and other necessary structures to assist the invasion forces. Because they are untrained and undisciplined, O'Keefe refuses to let them arm themselves, and they are nearly annihilated obeying Wayne's orders. Wedge finally gives in and allows his men to be trained, but the continually aggressive enemy snipers keep popping off his men one by one until he can stand it no longer. The final

blow comes when William Frawley is calmly singing a song as he turns the valve on a just-completed pipeline (you *knew* the minute he started to sing he was bound to get nailed), and an enemy soldier kills him. Wedge again leads his men on a charge and when he leaves camp the enemy decides to attack. The battle is on, and Wayne finally heads back to camp with his men to fight. He decides on a daring plan: to strap a stick of dynamite on the front of a bulldozer and ram it into a tank of oil which will flood the valley with flame and destroy the enemy. He boards the bulldozer (the name "Natasha" was written on it, for those trivia buffs who care!) and aims it at the tank, but an enemy bullet cuts him down and he dies as the inevitable crash and explosion occurs. Lydecker actually filled acres of California real estate with blazing fuel oil to create this spectacular finale. All in all, these are two rousing war films that I find unforgettable.

In *Dark Command* Wayne was a Texas cowboy who came to Kansas and found himself opposing Walter Pidgeon in an important election. Pidgeon, as Will Cantrell, forms a group of terrorists who pillage the area, and is himself finally destroyed in a spectacularly staged gun battle in which almost an entire town goes up in flame. Adding to the excitement was a good performance by Roy Rogers, in one of his few appearances outside of his own starring films, and a thrilling wagon chase ending in a famous stunt sequence in which four stunt men leap from the wagon just as it plunges over a cliff into a lake far below.

In Old Oklahoma had one of the best mass-action chases the screen had seen in a long time. In order to fulfill an oil contract (after many battles, both verbal and physical, with Albert Dekker), Wayne has to deliver a large quantity of the black gold to a distant city. Dekker buys up the only pipeline and forces Wayne to load the volatile fluid in dozens of wagons. The wagons rush across the open plains in a gigantic race against time, with Dekker's henchmen destroying a great many as the deadline approaches. It was a stunt man's delight, with overturning wagons vacated by leaping men showing up all over the place. To add more peril, a giant prairie fire is started and some of the wagons catch aflame (with one plunging spectacularly over a cliff and exploding in mid-air just moments after Wayne's stunt double had unhitched the horses) and are destroyed. But, to no one's real surprise, and with the help of Martha Scott, who keeps Dekker busy, Wayne meets the deadline. Helping the picture to no small extent was a really first-rate musical score by Mort Glickman.

Dakota had action, but it also had Vera Ralston, and I am not sure if even the thrills could overshadow her simply awful performance. *In Old California*, *Lady for a Night*, and *Three Faces West* were interesting but relatively routine, while *Flame of the Barbary Coast* had the considerable benefit of good performances by Ann Dvorak and Joseph Schildkraut and a good (but not as good as Republic should have produced) earthquake sequence.

After five solid years of slam-bang action at Republic, Wayne finally was given an excellent chance to show his versatility in *Angel and the Badman* in 1947. As Quirt Evans, Wayne played the role of a hunted outlaw who was hounded and almost killed until he found help and contentment on the farm of a Quaker family. Gail Russell (who was to star with Wayne in that moody, psychological oddity, *Wake of the Red Witch*, for Republic the following year) was excellent, as was veteran actor, and one of Wayne's closest personal friends, Bruce Cabot.

John Wayne has never claimed to be a great actor and, indeed, he usually plays only himself on the screen. But who ever asked more of him than simply to entertain us with the kind of red-blooded action we craved? I certainly didn't, and most of the kids who sat with me through all those films on their original releases didn't either. John Wayne was the right man at the right time to help make my young moviegoing days so memorable.

Above: The publicity blurb accompanying this shot from *Stagecoach* (United Artists 1939) stated that "Wayne has received Hollywood's 'big break' of 1938." How right that was! *Left:* Wayne and Anna Lee in a quiet moment from *Seven Sinners* (Universal 1940).

329

Top: In one of the most spectacular fights in screen history, Wayne and Randolph Scott went at it in a remake of *The Spoilers* (Universal 1942). Although Wayne and Scott did much of their own work, stunt men Alan Pomeroy and Eddie Parker filled in during the long shots. *Right:* Wayne and Albert Dekker slug it out in *In Old California* (Republic 1942).

330

Right: A gagged-up publicity portrait for *In Old Oklahoma* (Republic 1943) with Wayne and Martha Scott. This film has been retitled recently as *War of the Wildcats*. *Below*: Raymond Massey, Ray Milland, and Wayne were the brawling stars of the Cecil B. DeMille epic sea adventure, *Reap the Wild Wind* (Paramount 1942). Wayne played the villain who sank his own ship on a reef, accidentally killing Susan Hayward.

Above: Wayne and Gordon Jones, *right*, warn daredevil John
Carroll that planes are scarce in *Flying Tigers* (Republic 1942).
Below: Anna Lee and John Carroll talk things over with
Wayne prior to his taking off on a mission in *Flying Tigers*
(Republic 1942). That's Chester Gan in the plane's cockpit.

Above: Wayne gets some friendly advice from Charles Winninger in *A Lady Takes a Chance* (RKO 1943). *Below:* Wayne and Randolph Scott engage in a little clowning around early in *Pittsburgh* (Universal 1942) with Shemp Howard, but they wind up a few reels later having another classic slugfest.

Above: Wayne, Claire Trevor, and Roy Rogers escape from their captors in
Dark Command (Republic 1940). *Below*: It doesn't look as if Wayne is really
frightened by Ward Bond or his gun in *Dakota* (Republic 1945).

Above: Dennis O'Keefe and Wayne seem to be fighting World War II in front of a process screen in *The Fighting Seabees* (Republic 1944). *Right*: Ray Middleton and Wayne in another brawl, this time in *Lady from Louisiana* (Republic 1941).

Opposite page: Wayne leads another heroic charge in *Back to Bataan* (RKO 1945). *Above:* Wayne challenges LeRoy Mason to "make his play" in *Angel and the Badman* (Republic 1947). *Right:* Wayne with Sigrid Gurie in *Three Faces West* (Republic 1940).

Right: Ward Bond and Wayne did most of their
own stunts in *Tall in the Saddle* (RKO 1944).
Below: Wayne and Walter Brennan in *Red River*
(United Artists 1948). This was one of Wayne's
all-time best performances.

Above: Wayne had a few psychological problems in *Wake of the Red Witch* (Republic 1948), besides obvious romantic problems with co-star Gail Russell. As in *Reap the Wild Wind* (Paramount 1942), Wayne went to a watery grave with a sunken ship. *Right:* Wayne was at his best in the remake of *Three Godfathers* (MGM 1948).

12.

The Horn of Plenty

By this time you must think I spent almost my entire moviegoing young life wallowing exclusively in a sea of routine cinema bilge, with only an occasional journey to see those great classic presentations of the forties. Let me put your minds at ease by saying that of course I went to see probably hundreds of other films during this remarkable decade in film history. However, a film book five times this size could not do justice to those great quality products such as *Casablanca*, *Mrs. Miniver*, *Yankee Doodle Dandy*, *Sergeant York*, *This Gun for Hire*, *For Whom the Bell Tolls*, *Spellbound* and so many others. My intention has been to present a picture of what moviegoing was like for an adventurous-minded boy living in the days of World War II and frequenting the small theaters of the time. Escapism, pure and simple, was the name of the game. However, in this final chapter I would like to indulge myself to the point of including some particular highly successful big-budget films that I went out of my way to see and that gave me a great deal of pleasure.

Since we were involved in a massive war effort, it was only natural that we would find the studios turning out dozens of giant wartime spectacles. Warner Bros was producing most of these choice items with their very biggest stars (*Action in the North Atlantic* with Bogart and *Destination Tokyo* with Cary Grant were two of the best), and I found *God Is My Co-Pilot* to be a favorite in a kind of perverse sense. The film was full of all those delightful propagandistic extremes that we now squirm at. Richard Loo,

playing Tokyo Joe, was a classic example of the screen's stereotyped portrayal of the Japanese enemy, and he had a field day delivering such classic trivia lines as "All right, you Yankee Doodle Dandy. Come and get it," and "Here's some of that scrap metal you sent us, Yankee" as he fired a round of bullets at Dennis Morgan—who ultimately dispatched him in flames, delivering the line, "There's your six feet of China. Go fill it!" I guess I was also having a movie love affair with the Flying Tigers themselves, as those P-40s with the painted teeth were featured in both this film and *Flying Tigers* with John Wayne.

Comedies were also big attractions, and I went out of my way to see delightful little gems like *Sitting Pretty* in which Clifton Webb gave his remarkable performance as the genius turned babysitter, Lynn Belvedere, *The Bachelor and the Bobby-Soxer*, featuring Cary Grant in a silly role of a lawbreaker who is sentenced by judge Myrna Loy to an unpleasant task which ultimately finds him behaving like an imbecile with Shirley Temple, and *Mr. Blandings Builds His Dream House*, which found Grant again paired with Myrna Loy and involved this time in building a house in the country complicated by many hilarious obstacles.

Musicals were extremely big in those days and of particular appeal were those lavish Technicolor delights turned out by Twentieth Century-Fox featuring Betty Grable, Alice Faye, and others. Looked at today, a great many of them like *The Dolly Sisters*, *Song of the Islands*, *Diamond Horseshoe*, and *Greenwich Village* simply fail to hold up and are often quite soggy and sentimental bores. But there were several which were quite good, like *Coney Island* and *The Gang's All Here*. *Coney Island* was one of those turn-of-the-century songfests that found rivals Cesar Romero and George Montgomery fighting for the affections of Betty Grable, while Phil Silvers ("Glad to see ya!") was around for laughs. Betty never looked more gorgeous, and she sang some delightful numbers, including "Take It from There." *The Gang's All Here* had some perfectly awful acting from James Ellison, but lavish production numbers staged by Busby Berkeley and an all-star cast headed by Alice Faye, Carmen Miranda, Phil Baker (of the famous $64-dollar-question radio show *Take It or Leave It*), and Charlotte Greenwood with her high-kicking antics. Alice was in top form, also, singing "No Love, No Nothing, Until My Baby Comes Home" and "Journey to a Star." Other musical delights of the time included *Holiday Inn*, in which Bing Crosby sang his famous "White Christmas," *Higher and Higher* with a scrawny Frank Sinatra singing "A Lovely Way to Spend an Evening" and "I Couldn't Sleep a Wink Last Night," and *Hello, Frisco, Hello* with Alice Faye singing the Academy-Award winning "You'll Never Know."

The all-star production was also very much in evidence at the time. Our armed forces needed these star-laden spectaculars as morale boosters, and the studios were quick to oblige. The plots of most of these films were positively dreadful, but the appearance of star after star made up for them. *Hollywood Canteen* was a prime example, in which soldier Robert Hutton mooned over his favorite star, Joan Leslie, and bumped into everyone from Bette Davis and John Garfield (who had actually formed the *real* Hollywood Canteen) to Jack Benny and Roy Rogers. *Thank Your Lucky Stars* was another all-star mess that found Eddy Cantor playing a dual role in a "let's put on a big show" story in which Bogart, Flynn, Sheridan, Davis, and the rest of the Warner Bros' roster either did quick walk-ons or production numbers. Other mélanges included *Star Spangled Rhythm*, *Variety Girl*, and *Duffy's Tavern* from Paramount; *Thousands Cheer* from MGM; *Follow the Boys* from Universal; and *Stage Door Canteen* from United Artists.

Not only were there all-star musicals, but several interesting straight dramas emerged featuring star-filled casts. *Tales of Manhattan* was a fascinating collection of interrelated short tales which were tied together by the movement of a pair of dress tails from person to person. The most mov-

ing performance in the film was given by Charles Laughton as an orchestral conductor who finally gets his big break to lead a concert orchestra and while doing so wears the tails, which start ripping apart at the seams as the concert progresses, turning success into a bitter failure. *Flesh and Fantasy* consisted of three short stories, the most famous of which found Edward G. Robinson having his palm read by Thomas Mitchell and being told that he would commit a murder. The uncertainty of the situation drives Robinson ultimately to killing Mitchell and fulfilling the prophecy. *Follow the Boys* had George Raft and others involved in setting up USO shows, and offered some excellent little bits such as W. C. Fields's classic routines, Jeanette MacDonald's singing, and Orson Welles with his famous magic act. One of the least remembered all-star presentations was a delightful film called *Forever and a Day*, which had seven directors utilizing almost eighty famous stars and character actors to tell the story of a house through the years as it was inhabited by different owners.

There were three crime stories that I found of particular appeal. *T-Men* with Dennis O'Keefe was a taut, gripping little crime meller that had plenty of action and thrills. Wallace Ford, that great character actor, gave an excellent performance as a stool pigeon, and I can never forget the scene where he is eliminated by the mob by being locked in a steam room as they turn the heat up to full strength. *To the Ends of the Earth* had Dick Powell going all the way around the world on the trail of the mysterious head of a dope-smuggling operation, and *The Street with No Name* was another exciting crime-fighting saga, which pitted Mark Stevens against a vicious Richard Widmark, who, at the film's finale, sets up Stevens in an elaborate trap where he is to be killed by his own men, but is thwarted and mowed down by police bullets.

I even went to see such diverse material as *Kings Row*, an excellent drama which was indeed way ahead of its time and which I am sure I never appreciated fully until I saw it again many years later; *Saboteur*, a fine Alfred Hitchcock film with a shattering finale that found Norman Lloyd (who later became a producer and director) falling to his death from the upraised arm of the Statue of Liberty; *Lifeboat* (another Hitchcock vehicle), with its complex collection of all-star castaways headed by Tallulah Bankhead, and the stark drama and tragedy of *The Ox-Bow Incident*.

Even as I write these few last paragraphs the titles keep coming into my mind, and they really seem to be limitless, so I will dispense with the naming of any additional films for fear of overlooking all those obvious entries I probably should have listed.

The horn of plenty really did spill forth an abundance of screen entertainment in the years of the forties. And though we had our *Tahiti Honey, Sweethearts of the U.S.A, Hullabaloo, Pierre of the Plains,* films that few people ever saw or heard of again, there was always a *For Me and My Gal, How Green Was My Valley, Cover Girl,* and similar divertissements to compensate.

I am sure the percentage of hits as far as entertainment value is concerned was considerably greater than the product turned out today.

And for those of you who are just laying in wait out there with questions like "Why didn't you include . . ." and "How come you chose . . ." formed angrily on your lips, let me only paraphrase the statement of the storyteller in *Jungle Book* who, when asked what happened to Mowgli after the forest fire at the film's end, replied, "That is *another* story." Thus I say to all my readers that perhaps their choices may appear in some future collection—but that, my friends, is *another* book.

Left: Betty Grable and June Haver in one of the decade's gaudiest Technicolor musicals, *The Dolly Sisters* (Twentieth Century-Fox 1945). *Below:* In one of the connected stories of *Tales of Manhattan* (Twentieth Century-Fox 1942) Charles Laughton gets a set of dress tails to wear at his concert. They begin to fall apart at the seams as he begins conducting, turning his triumph into moving failure.

In this sequence from *Forever and a Day* (RKO 1943), a film that told a story
of a house through various ownerships, Ian Hunter, Sir Cedric Hardwicke, and Buster
Keaton seem to be having some difficulties.

Above: In *Flesh and Fantasy* (Universal 1943) Thomas Mitchell reads
Edward G. Robinson's future in his palm, and predicts that he will kill
someone. Mitchell turns out to be the victim. *Below:* Alan Hale, *right*, tries
to convince Dennis Morgan that there is a guiding "force" that helps
them in battle in *God Is My Co-Pilot* (Warner Bros 1945).

Above: Bing Crosby and Bob Hope hoked it up in a little golfing routine in the all-star *Variety Girl* (Paramount 1947). *Right:* Barbara Hale and Frank Sinatra were two of the stars in *Higher and Higher* (RKO 1943).

A sequence in the star-laden review *Star Spangled Rhythm* (Paramount 1942)
found Fred MacMurray, Lynn Overman, Ray Milland, and Franchot Tone doing a skit
lampooning women at a card game.

Right: Mark Stevens and Lloyd Nolan look down at the bullet-riddled body of Richard Widmark in *The Street with No Name* (Twentieth Century-Fox 1948). *Above:* One of the sequences in *Follow the Boys* (Universal 1943) had Orson Welles doing his magic act. *Left:* Charlie Grapewin and George Raft were two vaudeville hoofers who formed USO tours in *Follow the Boys* (Universal 1943).

Above: Robert Cummings was the innocent victim
of persecution in *Saboteur* (Universal 1942).
Below: Betty Grable in a production number from
Coney Island (Twentieth Century-Fox 1943).

Left: Gypsy Rose Lee was one of the all-star guests in *Stage Door Canteen* (United Artists 1943). *Above:* Wallace Ford, *left,* was the informer and Dennis O'Keefe an undercover Treasury Department agent in *T-Men* (Eagle-Lion 1947).

351

Above: Alice Faye, Phil Baker, and Carmen Miranda were the stars of *The Gang's All Here* (Twentieth Century-Fox 1943), a glossy Technicolor musical with numbers staged by Busby Berkeley. *Opposite page, top:* Reissues of *The Wizard of Oz* (MGM 1939) with Judy Garland, Jack Haley, and Ray Bolger never failed to attract packed matinee houses. *Opposite page, bottom:* Dick Powell tracked down the mysterious head of a dope-smuggling ring in *To the Ends of the Earth* (Columbia 1948). Here he is with Vladimir Sokoloff, *left,* and Peter Chong.

Above: Bette Davis was one of the real-life founders of, and a guest star in, *Hollywood Canteen* (Warner Brothers 1944). *Opposite page, top:* John Boles and Gene Kelly are two more stars who wanted to form entertainment units for our servicemen, here seen in *Thousands Cheer* (MGM 1943). *Opposite page, bottom:* Bing Crosby and Marjorie Reynolds starred in *Holiday Inn* (Paramount 1941), the film in which Crosby introduced the song "White Christmas."

THE THRILL OF IT ALL

VOLUME 3

Dedicated to my father,
Walter Ernest Barbour,
with all the love and affection a son
can give

ACKNOWLEDGMENTS

The author wishes to express his sincere thanks and appreciation to the individuals and organizations listed below who supplied, through the years, the stills and information which have helped make this book possible.

The Individuals:
Roy Barcroft, Ernest Burns, John Cocchi, Edward Connor, Henry Kier, Ernie Kirkpatrick, Paula Klaw, Louis McMahon, Don Miller, Gray Morrow, Sloan Nibley, James Robert Parish, Marshall Reed, Mark Ricci, Stephen Sally, Jim Shoenberger, Tom Steele, Linda Stirling.

The Organizations:
Allied Artists-TV, Cinemabilia, Columbia Pictures Corp., Eagle-Lion Films, Fawcett Publications, Four Star International, Fox Film Corp., Grand National Pictures, Kier's, King Features Syndicate, Lippert Films, MCA-TV, Medallion-TV, The Memory Shop, MGM-TV, Monogram Pictures, Movie Star News, National General Corp., National Telefilm Associates, NBC-TV, Paramount-TV, Premium Products, Inc., Producers Releasing Corp., Red Ryder Enterprises, Republic Pictures Corp., RKO-Radio Pictures, Screen Gems, Inc., Screen Guild Releasing Corp., Twentieth Century-Fox, United Artists, United Artists Associated, Universal Pictures Corp., Universal-International, Warner Bros, Warner Bros-Seven Arts, Inc., William Boyd Enterprises.

With Special Thanks To:
Jean Barbour and Malcolm McPherson

I would also like to gratefully thank the following three close personal friends. First, William K. Everson, the film historian, who graciously lent me many rare stills from his private collection for use in my survey of the B-Western, and whose own best-selling book, *A Pictorial History of the Western Film* (Citadel Press), furnished invaluable background information; second, Bob Price and Sam Sherman, whose definitive articles on both great and obscure Western stars in magazines like *Wildest Westerns* and *Screen Thrills Illustrated* also provided me with much essential reference material. Almost everyone who writes or studies the Western film genre invariably "borrows," and neglects to credit, factual material from these three men, and I would like to personally take this opportunity to thank them and acknowledge their valuable and extensive contributions.

CONTENTS

PREFACE

One of the most moving and poignant moments I have ever witnessed on the motion picture screen was not in a sequence from a regular theatrical feature but rather in a short filmed prologue made with cowboy great William S. Hart in 1939 to introduce his famous silent epic Western *Tumbleweeds*, which United Artists was reissuing to theatres. In this brief foreword Hart, then in his late sixties, presented the audience with historical information about the opening up of the famed Cherokee Strip, with its famous landrush, on which *Tumbleweeds* was based. Then, in the final moments of this historic film clip, Hart, his voice tremulous and charged with emotion, his body tense with enthusiasm and fists clenched, summed up for the audience not only what he felt, but what every true lover of the B-Western has similarly felt at one time or another in his life:

"My friends, I loved the art of making motion pictures. It is as the breath of life to me. The rush of the wind as it cuts your face. The pounding hoofs of the pursuing posse. Out there in front—a fallen tree trunk that spans a yawning chasm, and an old animal under you that takes it in the same low, ground-eating gallop. The harmless shots of the baffled ones that remained behind and then . . . the clouds of dust through which comes the faint voice of the director: 'Okay, Bill, okay! Glad you made it. Great stuff, Bill, great stuff and say, Bill, give old Fritz [Hart's famous horse] a pat on the nose for me, will ya?' Oh—the thrill of it all!"

I'm with you, Bill, and give old Fritz a pat for me, too.

Alan G. Barbour
1971

Looking at this scene of Tom Mix sitting astride his famous horse, Tony, it is easy to see why millions of movie fans made him the most popular Western screen idol of them all.

1
SILENT HOOFBEATS

The short happy life of the American B-Western very closely paralleled that of a man. It was born, suffered growing pains, matured, reached peaks of outstanding success and sank to valleys of utter failure, and finally grew senile and died prematurely after a lifespan of about fifty years.

The birth of the genre took place in 1903 when, after a few very short experimental films were made featuring scenes of contemporary Western action of brief fictionalized historical incidents, the Edison Company made *The Great Train Robbery*. The film ran for only about ten minutes, but within that time span it told a complete story of a robbery, with chase and final action-packed showdown. It wasn't much, but it was a beginning, and other studios made copies to cash in on the original's success. About 1908 G. M. Anderson, who had played several small parts in *The Great Train Robbery*, made a short Western called *Broncho Billy and the Baby*. It had an interesting plot line which found Anderson playing a "good" badman who sacrifices himself to save a child. The name "Broncho Billy" caught on, and Anderson made hundreds of one- and two-reel Westerns based on the character he had developed and he became the screen's very first Western hero.

The further development of the Western format was enhanced in the 1908-1913 period when pioneer directors like D. W. Griffith and Thomas H. Ince both cranked out one- and two-reelers featuring such notables of the screen as Lillian Gish and Blanche Sweet as female leads.

Unlike *The Great Train Robbery*, which was shot in the "wilds" of New Jersey, Griffith shot most of his films in and around Hollywood, which was still fairly primitive country containing large stretches of uncluttered scenery. Titles came out like *The Goddess of Sagebrush Gulch*, *The Battle of Elderbush Gulch*, and *The Last Drop of Water*. The films were full of action and, at the same time, had moments of striking visual beauty. It was another step in the maturing process.

Two men who were to make enormous contributions in the development of the genre both began their screen careers at approximately the same time, in 1914. William S. Hart had a distinguished background of theatrical experience already behind him when he began appearing in one-reelers. He caught on to the new art quickly and graduated to feature-length work in a very short time. Before long he was already turning out minor classics like *Hell's Hinges* and *The Aryan*, both made in 1916. By the twenties Hart had perfected his role of the "good" badman and went on to do films like *The Testing Block*, *Three Word Brand*, and *Wild Bill Hickok* for Paramount. He made his final film in 1925: the epic *Tumbleweeds*, which Western authority William K. Everson considers worthy of being ranked with *The Covered Wagon* and *The Iron Horse*, two of the best Western films ever made. Hart, in addition to starring in *Tumbleweeds*, also co-directed the film with King Baggott. He then retired from the screen and wrote his autobiography. Many years later, in 1939, *Tumbleweeds* was reissued and Hart made a ten-minute introduction to the film in which he told the audience some facts about the opening of the Cherokee strip, and then concluded with the moving comments mentioned in the preface.

The second man who made an important impact on the development of the Western was director John Ford. He began in films as an actor and stuntman in 1914, and by 1917 Universal had signed him to direct some two-reel Westerns which featured, among other stars, Hoot Gibson and Harry Carey. Unfortunately, almost all of these films have been lost and are unavailable to historians and scholars for study, causing a noticeable gap in the appreciation of Ford's early career. Motion picture companies were, and unfortunately continue to be, fearfully shortsighted. Early films made on nitrate stock were allowed to decompose, or were simply junked, since it was felt that there would be no future use for them after their initial screenings. Rumors persist that Universal, while filming a spectacular fire sequence for a later feature film, used literally hundreds of rare original negatives as fuel, thus forever destroying many of their silent classics. Fortunately, Ford's very first film, *Straight Shooting*, made in 1917 and starring both Carey and Gibson, is one that has survived. In 1924 Ford made his classic *The Iron Horse*, and he has remained the dean of Western directors for over fifty years.

As the Western grew in popularity and men like Hart, Carey, and Gibson prospered, it was only natural that there would be a veritable rush to bring new faces to the screen in outdoor action dramas. Men like William Desmond, Roy Stewart, Dustin Farnum, and William Farnum were box-office favorites, and a great many others have long since been completely forgotten.

The twenties approached rapidly, and the new decade would bring more than a score of new stars into the Western fold. Some, like Buck Jones, Ken Maynard, Tim McCoy, Bob Steele, and Hoot Gibson would continue to be popular for years to come, while others like Ted Wells, Fred Thomson, Jack Hoxie, Fred Humes, and Leo Maloney would either become character actors or fade into complete oblivion.

However, of all the great stars who achieved popularity in the twenties, none was greater than Tom Mix, the most popular Western star who ever appeared on the motion picture screen.

Mix had actually begun his screen career as early as 1911; he made almost a hundred one and two-reelers for Selig, which kept him busy until 1917. At that time Fox Studios offered him a contract, and he went to work for them, appearing in such features as *Fame and Fortune*, *Treat 'Em Rough*, *Ace High*, *Rough Riding Romance*, *Fighting for Gold*, and *Western Blood*.

Between 1920 and 1928 Mix made more than sixty films, all of which helped Fox Studios pay the rent and made Mix a living idol to millions of fans, not only in the United States but around the world. In 1928 he left Fox and signed with FBO to make a brief series. When sound came in in 1929, Mix was one of those stars who couldn't make the transition, and after a brief series for Universal and a serial for Mascot he was washed up in films. His final years were spent touring with his own Tom Mix Circus, and on October 12, 1940 he was killed in an automobile accident in Arizona.

In retrospect it is easy to see why Mix had been so popular with the public. Prior to his screen career he had led an adventure-filled real life that many wished they could emulate. He fought in the Spanish-American War, was a performer in a Wild West show, was a real deputy U.S. Marshal in Oklahoma, and broke horses for the British for the Boer campaign in Africa. When he started making his films, he wanted to be completely opposite in character from William S. Hart. Where Hart stressed character studies and plodding but effective dramatic sequences, Mix wanted to feature action and more action. His films were full of chases filmed at breakneck speed and fight sequences that were models other studios worked from. He also had a tremendous flair for showmanship, and he wore the fancy clothes and frills of a type which was to become famous when worn by Autry, Rogers, and others in years to come. Even his horse, Tony, became a celebrity, often getting fan mail all his own. Small wonder a generation of film fans adored Tom Mix.

The twenties offered more new faces to Western fans than any other decade. In addition to the ones already mentioned there was Wally Wales, who later became a staple in the Western stock company of villains in sound films using the name Hal Taliaferro; Edmund Cobb, who did similar duty; Art Acord, who made many popular serials and features for Universal; Buddy Roosevelt; Buffalo Bill, Jr., whose real name was J. C. Wilsey; Bob Custer; Bill Cody;

Lane Chandler; Jack Perrin; and Jack Luden. Many future stars of greater magnitude had humble beginnings in this period. Gary Cooper made appearances in Paramount features like *Arizona Bound* and *Nevada*. William Boyd, who was to appear in classic Paramount films directed by men like Cecil B. DeMille, made his Western debut in 1926 in Pathé's *The Last Frontier*. Warner Baxter turned up in *Drums of the Desert*, a 1927 Paramount release, and Jack Holt made a long series of exciting adventures for the same studio, many of which were based on Zane Grey stories like *The Mysterious Rider*.

However, even though the decade produced a quantity of new stars, by the beginning of the sound era the genre had lost a considerable amount of general appeal, much the same way as serials lost favor at the same time. It was left to a new breed of heroes to bring fresh excitement to the Saturday afternoon oaters in the early thirties; and very few were able to do just that.

It should also be noted that many of the films made by the stars discussed above should certainly not be classified in the same B-Western category with a typical Johnny Mack Brown or Charles Starrett Western of the thirties or forties. Many of the films of Hart, Carey, Gibson, and Mix had very strong production values, and a good deal of time and money was spent to give them a quality far removed from what is normally considered a B-Western film. Out of necessity these people are grouped together to give some indication of the roots from which the little hour-long action features sprang.

Bob Kortman, with cigar, and Broncho Billy Anderson in *The Golden Trail*, one of the hundreds of two-reel Westerns the first cowboy hero of the screen turned out.

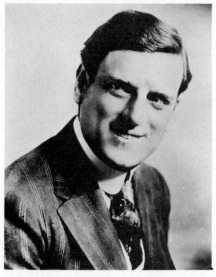

A portrait of G. M. "Broncho Billy" Anderson.

Don Coleman achieved a small degree of success in films like *The Bronc Stomper* (Pathé 1928).

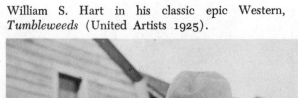

William S. Hart in his classic epic Western, *Tumbleweeds* (United Artists 1925).

William Desmond was a big favorite of silent film audiences, and went on to do excellent character roles in talking features.

Bill Cody met with some degree of fame in silent Westerns, but lost out when sound came in. This is a general advertising poster put out to promote Bill.

Few people can recall Jack Padjan, *left*, but most film lovers fondly recall his opponent in this scene from *Crashing Through* (Pathé 1928): Tom Santschi made hundreds of films, including *The Spoilers* in which he had a classic battle with William Farnum.

Harry Carey, a major star of silent Westerns and in later years one of the screen's most beloved character actors.

Would you like to bet whether or not Leo Maloney will really make that obviously staged leap in this scene from *Border Blackbirds* (Pathé 1927)?

Fred Kohler, *center*, has obvious plans for Sally Blane, but Jack Luden has other thoughts in mind in *Shootin' Irons* (Paramount 1927).

Jack Hoxie and Elinor Field in *Don Quickshot of The Rio Grande* (Universal 1923).

Billy Franey and Bill Cody in *King of the Saddle* (Associated Exhibitors 1926).

Fred Thomson, here seen in *The Pioneer Scout* (Paramount 1928), was one of the few stars who was able to give Tom Mix any real competition at all.

Jack Holt parlayed his pleasing personality and athletic ability into an outstanding early film career. This portrait is from *Man of the Forest* (Paramount 1926).

Jack Holt is behind that serape in *The Mysterious Rider* (Paramount 1927), one of numerous films based on stories by Zane Grey.

373

Buddy Roosevelt, *left*, and Robert Homans, *right*, get the goods on Lafe McKee in *The Bandit Buster* (Pathé 1927).

Harry Woods gets the drop on a furry-clad Buck Jones while Eva Novak gives him a gentle hint in *30 Below Zero* (Fox 1926).

Tom Mix and a fuzzy scene-stealer in *Fighting for Gold* (Fox 1919).

Famous silent hero Tom Mix in a pensive scene from *Do and Dare* (Fox 1922).

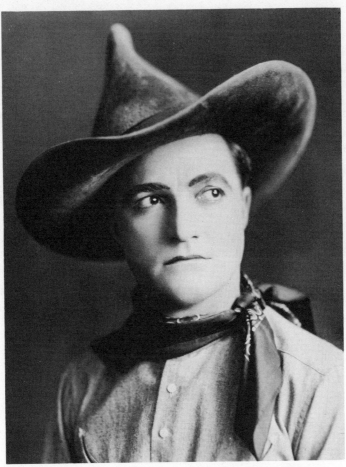

Tom Mix, the most popular of all the great Western heroes of the screen.

Buck Jones delivers his brand of justice to Fred Kohler in *Outlawed Guns* (Universal 1935). Notice Fred's deformed right hand, which he usually concealed from the camera's eye or explained away by saying that some gunman had shot off his fingers.

2

BEST OF
THE BREED

As the third decade of the twentieth century began, the great Western heroes of the silent screen found themselves facing a villain more deadly than any they had opposed on the screen to date: sound! The movies could now speak to their audiences and, unfortunately, a large majority of silent saddleburners sounded simply terrible and found their careers wiped out almost overnight. The mightiest to fall was Tom Mix, who as a silent star had achieved unbelievable popularity with Western fans. He made one series of talkies for Universal that had some good action sequences, and a serial for Mascot, *The Miracle Rider*, which was his last starring film; then he rode off into the second-class world of rodeo, circus, and fair appearances as a once-great movie idol. But there were several stars, six to be exact, who did adapt well to the new sound medium and who became the giant stars of the early thirties: Buck Jones, Tim McCoy, Hoot Gibson, Tom Tyler, Ken Maynard, and Bob Steele.

Buck Jones, whose real name was Charles Gebhart, had had a wide variety of jobs before breaking into films around 1917; he had worked on a ranch as a cowpuncher, worked as a mechanic at the famous Indianapolis racetrack, done army service in the Philippines and trick riding with a wild West show and, eventually, made appearances with the famous Ringling Bros Circus. He entered films by appearing in bit roles in two-reelers and features and as a stuntman extraordinaire. Fox Studios finally gave him his big break in 1920 by starring him in *The Last Straw*. After that he appeared in dozens of features for the studio throughout the twenties. Around 1928 he tried to go into independent production, but failed badly with a film called *The Big Hop*. Another big failure was the Buck Jones Wild West Show, which he put together in 1929. He made his first talkie, *The Lone Rider,* for Columbia in 1930. After a string of further adventures for that studio, he made a series under his own production banner and released them through Universal from 1934 to 1937. On occasion Buck would venture from the Western range to do straight dramas, but those films were generally met with token approval. Jones continued making films and serials, with some lessening of his popularity, right through to 1942, when he was killed in the tragic Coconut Grove fire in Boston.

Hoot Gibson also had real-life experience as a working cowboy before he entered silent pictures as a player and stuntman. He got his first chance to shine in a series of two-reelers produced by Universal in 1919. A year later he made *Action*, his first full-length film under the direction of John Ford. After that film he made a long series of starring films for Universal, and became one of the studio's biggest box-office draws. Unlike most of the cowboy stars, Hoot tried to inject humor into his roles. He was always throwing in wisecracks or clowning around. He seldom wore a regular gun and holster, but rather carried his six-shooter either in his boot or in his belt. Hoot found the going a little rough when sound came in. He made a series in 1931–1932, had a few scattered roles in 1935 (including an excellent part in the all-star Three Mesquiteers film made by RKO, *Powdersmoke Range*), and made another series in 1936. In 1937 he made an appearance in the Republic serial *The Painted Stallion*, but he really had little to do. After that he was to remain off the screen until the early forties, when he popped up again in the Trail Blazers series for Monogram, which was met with mixed feelings.

Tom Tyler, who had changed his name from Vincent Markowski for screen use, wanted to be a performer from his earliest days. He finally worked his way to Hollywood and entered the film industry as a prop man and stunt double. His first Western features were made in 1925, and he continued making outdoor thrillers for FBO Studios until 1928. The following year he made another series for Syndicate Pictures with titles like *The Man from Nevada, The Canyon of Missing Men,* and *Call of the Desert.* His first talking starrer was the serial *Phantom of the West*, made in ten chapters by Mascot. It wasn't a very good film, but Tom came across well, and in 1931 he made his first sound feature Western, *West of Cheyenne.* Throughout the remainder of the thirties he was to do Westerns and serials for Universal, Monogram, Syndicate, and other studios in an apparently endless stream as his popularity continued. In the forties he gained fame as one of the Three Mesquiteers, as the hero of two serials, *Adventures of Captain Marvel* and *The Phantom*, and as a fine character actor in numerous big-budget features. When his health began to deteriorate in the late forties, Tom spent his remaining years doing bit and small featured roles, usually as a villain, for assorted studios. It was a sad finish to a relatively illustrious screen career.

Ken Maynard was a much better rider than actor (and there are those who maintain that his brother was an even greater rider and actor) in a long screen career that began in 1924. Ken, like Buck Jones, had also been featured with the Ringling Bros circus when he was discovered by director Lynn Reynolds and urged to make a screen test. He was successful in the test, and was signed to do a series that included such films as *The Demon Rider, The Grey Vulture,* and *Fighting Courage* for independent producer Charles Davis. Ken was signed by First National and made more than fifteen productions for the studio between 1926 and 1929. In later years, when John Wayne became a star in a short series for Warner Bros, stock footage from many of these early Maynard films was utilized quite extensively. Ken then did a brief series for Universal which was released in silent versions and in a synchronized sound system (done with recordings) that featured mostly music and sound effects. His first real talkies appeared in 1930 when he did a series for Tiffany (*Alias the Bad Man, Pocatello Kid, Hellfire Austin,* and others) which lasted until 1932. Bouncing from studio to studio, Ken made features for World-Wide, Universal, Mascot, and Columbia. Like Hoot Gibson, Ken made a screen comeback in the Monogram Trail Blazers series in six productions and then, after appearing in an Astor-released feature called *Harmony Trail*, retired from the screen. Maynard, who once was one of the biggest Western stars ever, spent all his money and now lives in the humblest of circumstances in a run-down trailer camp in the San Fernando valley.

Tim McCoy was one of the most likable performers of all the great Western stars of the period. An acknowledged authority on Indian folklore, Colonel Tim began his screen career in the MGM production of *War Paint* in 1926, after having served as a technical advisor on such film classics as *The Covered Wagon* and *The Vanishing American.* His MGM films were all well-done little gems filled with good location work, often made on authentic Indian Reservations, and good action sequences. Tim made his entrance into talkies by appearing in the first talking serial, Universal's *The Indians Are Coming.* He did another serial for the same studio a year later, *Heroes of the Flames,* and then moved over to Columbia where he made sixteen films in two years, among them *Texas Cyclone, Rusty Rides Alone, The Western Code,* and *The Riding Tornado.* The following year Columbia put Tim into a series of non-Western features, but McCoy, though he turned in excellent performances, was not cut out to do things like *Police Car 17, Hold the Press,* and *Speed Wings,* and the next year he was back in the saddle for another series of Westerns for the studio. McCoy, following in the footsteps of all the other stars of the time, then bounced from studio to studio doing work for Puritan, Victory, Monogram and, in the forties, PRC. In 1941–1942 Tim joined Buck Jones and Raymond Hat-

Ken Maynard and his horse, Tarzan, in a scene from *Fighting Through* (Tiffany 1930).

ton in Monogram's popular Rough Riders films and then called it quits. He did appear on television with his own show in which he demonstrated his Indian knowledge, and he made brief appearances in films like *Around the World in 80 Days* and *Run of the Arrow* in the fifties, and in Alex Gordon's *Requiem for a Gunfighter* in the sixties he looked a great deal better than the film's much-younger star, Rod Cameron. He now spends his time touring with circus shows.

Rounding out this action sextet was young Bob Steele. Born Robert Bradbury, Jr., he and his twin brother, Bill, broke into films at an extremely early age when their famous director-father photographed them, originally for fun only, in film which was eventually released as a series of two-reelers in the mid-twenties under the overall title of *Adventures of Bill and Bob*. In 1927 Steele made his first starring Western, *The Mojave Kid*, and followed that with thirteen more titles which were all released by FBO. These were followed by seven films made for Syndicate Pictures in 1929–1930. His first talkie was *Near the Rainbow's End*, made in 1930, and was followed by thirteen more titles in 1931–1932. The following year he made another eight features, including *Gallant Fool* and *Trailing North*, and a thrilling serial for Mascot, *Mystery Squadron*, in which he and his pal

Guinn "Big Boy" Williams tracked down the mysterious Black Ace. Following the same pattern as had the other stars, Steele then bounced around doing films for Supreme, Republic, RKO (the famous *Powdersmoke Range* film mentioned earlier), Metropolitan, and, in the forties, PRC and Monogram. In among all these starring Westerns Steele had some fine character roles in features like *Of Mice and Men* and *The Big Sleep*, in which he demonstrated his acting versatility. Even recently, on television, he turned in an extraordinarily touching performance as the star of one of the *Family Affair* television shows, in which he played an old-time star who payed a visit to Brian Keith's on-screen kids who had watched his old films on TV (they actually used some of Bob's old footage); the children were disappointed to find their cowboy idol an elderly has-been, but were eventually won over by his charm and personality. It was an excellent showcase appearance for a fine performer.

It is, of course, hard to capsulize six full-length careers spanning literally hundreds of screen appearances in only a few brief paragraphs, but these men really need no written words to describe their invaluable contributions to Western screen history. Their films speak for them.

Come out from behind that mask, Buck Jones. We
know it's you in *Sunset of Power* (Universal 1936).

Lona Andre was Buck Jones's leading lady in his Northwest Mounted Police adventure
Border Brigands (Universal 1935).

Helen Mack and Buck Jones in *California Trail* (Columbia 1933).

Ward Bond, *left*, and Bob Kortman are about to receive a slight surprise from Buck Jones in *The Crimson Trail* (Universal 1935).

LeRoy Mason looks like he's getting the worst of things from Buck Jones in *When a Man Sees Red* (Universal 1934).

June Gale gives Hoot Gibson a knowing look in *Rainbow's End* (First Division 1935).

Hoot Gibson connects with Roger Williams while Lafe McKee watches in this scene from *Frontier Justice* (First Division 1936).

Rex Lease, in black, gives Hoot Gibson a good wrapping up in *Cavalcade of the West* (Diversion 1936).

Lafe McKee, Hal Taliaferro, Hoot Gibson, and Bob Kortman in one of Hoot's best talking films, *Swifty* (First Division 1936).

In this scene from *Partners of the Trail* (Monogram 1931) Tom Tyler, *right*, gives Reginald Sheffield a helping hand. Sheffield was the father of young Johnny Sheffield, who became Boy in the Tarzan films.

384

I think Tom Tyler wants Slim Whittaker to keep his mouth shut in *The Man from New Mexico* (Monogram 1932).

Bob Kortman, *left*, seems to be encouraging Al Bridge, in the buckskin outfit, to fight with Tom Tyler, *center*, while others try to keep them apart in *The Forty-Niners* (Freuler Films 1932).

Ken Maynard makes one of his more subtle entrances in *Gun Justice* (Universal 1934).

Ken Maynard tries his fist on Fred Kohler's jaw for size in *The Fiddlin' Buckaroo* (Universal 1933).

Ken Maynard gets the drop on Bob Kortman, Lucile Browne, and plane in *King of the Arena* (Universal 1933).

Ken Maynard does some fiddlin' and foolin' with Charles King, *right*, and Frank Yaconelli in *Strawberry Roan* (Universal 1933).

That's Rex Lease lying on the ground after Tim McCoy has taken care of him in *Code of the Rangers* (Monogram 1938).

Charles King, *right*, and Karl Hackett are about to meet Tim McCoy face to face in *Phantom Ranger* (Monogram 1938).

A general ad mat for Tim McCoy's films; different titles would be placed under his name.

A nice portrait of Tim from his Columbia days of the early thirties.

A picturesque shot of Tim McCoy in *Phantom Ranger* (Monogram 1938).

Marion Shilling and Joe Sawyer get a glassy stare from Tim McCoy in *The Westerner* (Columbia 1935).

Harry Strang, Lane Chandler, Tim McCoy, John Merton, and Betty Compson in *Two Gun Justice* (Monogram 1938). Tim frequently used the gimmick of dressing up like a Mexican and using a dialect which didn't always sound totally convincing.

I wonder if Tim McCoy, *right*, is trying to teach Lafe McKee some of his Indian folklore in this scene from *End of the Trail* (Columbia 1933).

A mustache-less Charles King, *left*, gets an unhelping hand from young Bob Steele in *The Fighting Champ* (Monogram 1932).

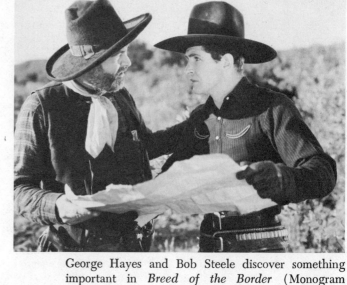

George Hayes and Bob Steele discover something important in *Breed of the Border* (Monogram 1933), directed by Bob's father, Robert Bradbury, Sr.

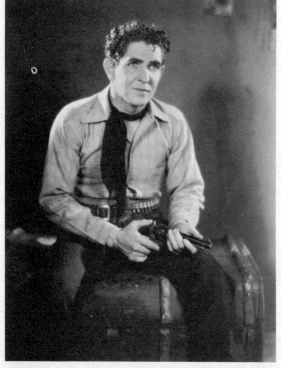

A nice portrait of Bob Steele from *The Ridin' Fool* (Tiffany 1931).

Bob Steele gets the drop on veteran screen badman Earl Dwire in *The Gun Ranger* (Republic 1936).

Bob Steele has bested Charles King again, to the obvious approval of Earl Dwire, *left*, in *The Trusted Outlaw* (Republic 1937).

Doris Hill and George Hayes shared billing with Bob Steele in *Trailing North* (Monogram 1933).

A favorite portrait of John "Duke" Wayne from the thirties.

3
SINGIN' SANDY
MAKES HIS MARK

John Wayne as a *singing* cowboy? Hard as that may be for latter-day Wayne fans to believe, Duke actually did play a songbird of the saddle in several of his starring films of the thirties. Admittedly, he only mouthed the words while pros like Smith Ballew supplied the real vocals, but for the official record he did predate on the screen the eventual number-one sagebrush thrush, Gene Autry. It's a dubious distinction to be sure, but playing a singing cowboy was only one of a large assortment of screen characterizations Wayne was called upon to portray in that first decade of his remarkable screen career.

John Wayne, né Marion Michael Morrison, was an all-American football player for the University of Southern California when he was first noticed by the distinguished director John Ford, who was making a football film on location. Ford didn't make use of the young man at the time, but eventually the two entered into a personal and screen friendship which endures to this day, more than forty years later. Wayne actually credits Tom Mix with getting him a part-time job at Fox, where he wound up as a general prop man. One day, while he was doing a routine job for the John Ford film *Mother Machree,* the noted director singled him out and gave him an unbilled bit part in the film. It was the beginning of the long climb to the peak of screen stardom.

Wayne did a series of bit roles in between 1928 and 1930 before Ford encouraged fellow-director Raoul Walsh to give the young man the lead role in his ambitious production of *The Big Trail.* Walsh heeded the suggestion, had young Marion Morrison officially change his name to John Wayne, and hoped a new star would be born. Unfortunately, it didn't quite work out that way. *The Big Trail* was, on most counts, a true epic Western filled with wonderfully cinematic tableaus filmed in picturesque locations, and pictorially the film still holds up well today; but in acting talent it is sadly lacking. Wayne simply wasn't yet ready for the big push upward. He was young, inexperienced, and awkward, and his delivery of lines was far from satisfactory. Matched up against such notable hams as Tyrone Power, Sr., and Ian Keith, his deficiencies became even more apparent. However, on the plus side was the fact that he did photograph well, and he was able to be convincing in the action sequences. At a time when sound pictures were just beginning to make themselves felt, Wayne certainly should have made enough impression to launch himself in a more than routine way, but the higher-ups at Fox failed to capitalize on the young star's potential. They threw him into a couple of straight dramas as a follow-up to *The Big Trail,* and both Wayne and the studio were disappointed.

Wayne left Fox and went over to Columbia, where he played lesser roles in routine features, including an appearance with Buck Jones in *Range Feud.* In 1932 and 1933 he was bouncing around like a ball, doing screen duty at several studios. At Mascot he appeared in three full-length serials in which he received star billing, *Shadow of the Eagle, Hurricane Express,* and *The Three Musketeers.* All three films were full of the thrilling kind of action sequences that Wayne was to thrive on for most of his career. He also had top billing in a short series of B-Westerns for Warner Bros. Containing mostly stock footage from silent Ken Maynard vehicles, Wayne really had little to do in *Haunted Gold, Ride Him, Cowboy, The Big Stampede, The Telegraph Trail, Somewhere in Sonora,* and *The Man From Monterey* except fill in the gaps joining the older action sequences together. Sandwiched in among these starring roles were additional lower-billed appearances in items like *Central Airport* and *The Life of Jimmy Dolan.*

In the latter part of 1933 Wayne signed up to do a long series of starring B-Westerns produced by Lone Star Productions and released through Monogram Pictures. It was a field day for the young leading man as he rode, fought, laughed and "sang" his way through sixteen adventures with titles like *Riders of Destiny* (the first in the series and the one in which he played Singin' Sandy), *Sagebrush Trail, Blue Steel, Randy Rides Alone, The Star Packer, Rainbow Valley,* and the last in the sequence, *Paradise Canyon.* These films offered viewers more than just a pleasing new leading man. Supporting Wayne was a superb collection of fine character actors who were to form a kind of Western stock company. Heading the list was George Hayes, who alternated between playing good guys, old timers, and scheming villains. He hadn't yet tacked on the "Gabby" nickname, and often was completely cleanshaven. Appearing in almost three-quarters of the titles was stunt ace Yakima Canutt. Although on a rare occasion he might play a sympathetic role (such as Yak, the Indian in *The Star Packer*), he was usually cast as Wayne's chief antagonist. A warm relationship had sprung up between the two men when they had appeared together in earlier vehicles at Warner Bros, and Canutt was to teach Wayne most of the intricate tricks of stunt work. Credit is usually given these two men for developing the polished kind of on-screen fight which is used today. Where formerly fisticuffs were simply wildly swinging affairs with opponents lashing out at each other helter-skelter, now we had those glorious long follow-through right and left crosses and uppercuts. Though many may argue that the earlier

free-for-alls engaged in by stars like Bob Steele and Ken Maynard were more realistic, on screen they usually looked chaotic and generally awful. Other important members of the company were Earl Dwire (like Canutt, he alternated between playing good guys and bad guys), Lafe McKee, George Cleveland and Buffalo Bill, Jr. (Jay Wilsey). It should also be noted that eleven of the films were directed, and many of them written, by Robert N. Bradbury, who was cowboy star Bob Steele's real-life father.

In 1935 Monogram, Mascot, and Consolidated merged to form the new Republic Pictures Corporation. Having hit a small size bonanza with the Gene Autry features, the new company decided to give Wayne a little bigger boost up the ladder of success and spend a little more time, money, and effort on a new series of features. *Westward Ho, New Frontier, Lawless Range, The Lawless Nineties, King of the Pecos, The Oregon Trail, Winds of the Wasteland,* and *The Lonely Trail* were the result. On the whole, all eight films were topnotch Republic productions, and Wayne was maturing enormously as an actor, rapidly becoming a big box-office favorite with Western fans. But Wayne's wanderlust struck again, and he left the increasingly lucrative wide-open spaces of the Republic back lot for the uninteresting sound stages of Universal Pictures, where he starred in a series of six entertaining, non-Western programmers: *Sea Spoilers* was a Coast Guard adventure; *Conflict,* an involved prizefight yarn; *California Straight Ahead,* a race between trucks and a train; *I Cover the War,* a story of newsreel cameramen; *Idol of the Crowds,* a tale about an ice-hockey player; *Adventure's End,* in which Wayne was a pearl diver involved in a ship mutiny.

From Universal Wayne made a very brief journey to Paramount to co-star with Johnny Mack Brown in one of that studio's short (fifty-nine minutes) Zane Grey features. *Born to the West,* often reissued under the title *Hell Town,* was an entertaining feature, but really only noteworthy for the pairing of the two big-name Western heroes.

One of the most popular series of Westerns ever turned out was the long string of adventures starring the fictional Three Mesquiteers. Ray Corrigan, Robert Livingston, and Max Terhune had come together to form a magic combination that spelled box-office success in sixteen titles produced between 1936 and 1938. When they had finished the second series of

Wayne should have become a major star after his appearance in *The Big Trail* (Fox 1930), but he was still too inexperienced. That's Ian Keith and Marguerite Churchill with Wayne in this scene from the film.

eight films (almost all of Republic's film series with its Western stars were scheduled for eight titles per year, with very few exceptions), the studio decided to remove Livingston from the trio and feature him in some of the studio's regular dramatic features. The void left in the group had to be quickly filled, and Wayne was sought out and signed. Generally unhappy with the Universal features, Duke was only too glad to return to the Republic action plant to do one new series of eight films playing the role of Stony Brooke. Beginning with *Pals of the Saddle* in late 1938, he starred in *Overland Stage Raiders* (a thrill-packed tale which involved the hijacking of a plane carrying a valuable gold shipment), *Santa Fe Stampede, Red River Range, The Night Riders, Three Texas Steers, Wyoming Outlaw,* and a remake of the earlier *New Frontier.* By the time this series was filmed Republic had begun to master its filming techniques, and all of the slickness and polish that was to make Republic famous was very much in evidence. After these films were finished, both Wayne and Corrigan were to leave Republic, but for entirely different reasons. Corrigan, tired of second billing and wanting more money (although he was making plenty from the use of his ranch by virtually all the studios) decided to go into production for himself and,

moving to Monogram, formed the Range Busters with John "Dusty" King and his Three Mesquiteer pal, Max "Alibi" Terhune. In its own way the new trio also achieved some success, but it really couldn't compare with its earlier Republic counterpart.

For Wayne real stardom was just a few features ahead. While he was busily churning out the Mesquiteer tales, his friend John Ford was getting ready to film *Stagecoach.* The pivotal role in the basically talky drama was the Ringo Kid, a role Ford wanted only one man to play, John Wayne. A caption on one of the publicity stills of Duke for the picture proudly announced that Wayne had received the "big break" of 1938 by being chosen for the role. That was one piece of advertising copy historic for its understatement, and something rare in the annals of generally exaggerated promotional baloney.

The die was now cast. John Wayne, who wasn't quite ready for stardom when it was first offered him more than eight years earlier, would now find the going a great deal easier. Marlene Dietrich had a classic line to deliver to Wayne in *The Spoilers* a few years later: "Anything you win, you can collect." Big Duke Wayne fought ten years and earned the right to enjoy his next thirty as one of the giants in the industry.

Wayne gets the drop on none other than Buck Jones in *Range Feud* (Columbia 1931).

Wayne with Sheila Terry in *Haunted Gold* (Warner Bros 1932).

A little clowning from Luis Alberni seems to amuse Wayne in *The Man from Monterey* (Warner Bros 1933).

Wayne, Frank Rice, and Billy Franey spot something interesting in *Somewhere in Sonora* (Warner Bros 1933).

Albert J. Smith gives the Duke a little harassment of sorts in *The Telegraph Trail* (Warner Bros 1933).

Wayne in *Sagebrush Trail* (Monogram 1933), the second of his Lone Star Westerns.

George Hayes, *center*, without his "Gabby" tag, was the villain, along with henchman-stunt ace Yakima Canutt, *right*, in *Randy Rides Alone* (Monogram 1934).

Another excellent publicity photo of Wayne in the thirties.

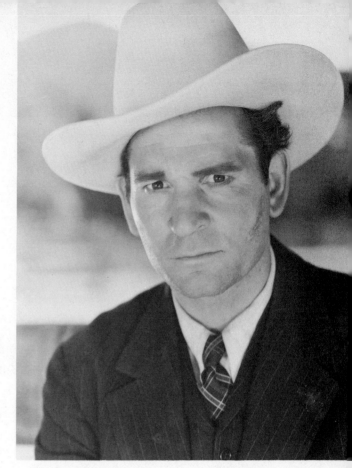

Yakima Canutt, the acknowledged dean of stunt-
men, starred in many of Wayne's Lone Star films.
In this portrait he is made up for his role in
Paradise Canyon (Monogram 1935).

In another scene from *Randy Rides Alone* (Monogram 1934), Wayne and Canutt engage in one of
their frequent screen battles.

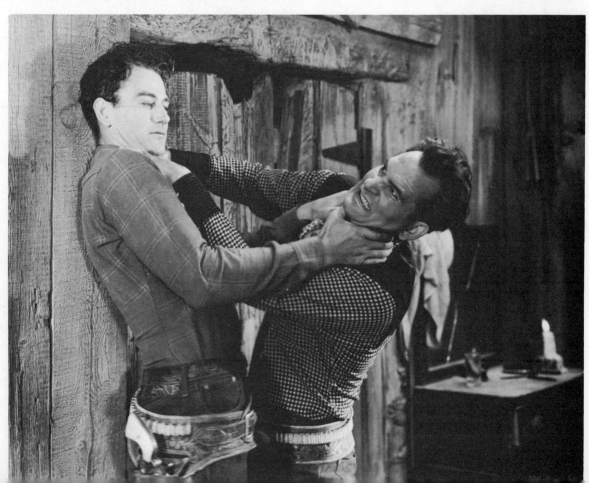

Wayne has just finished giving Edward Parker a lesson in *The Star Packer* (Monogram 1934). In the background, Yakima Canutt, playing a good Indian role, takes care of Earl Dwire.

Director Robert N. Bradbury, the father of star Bob Steele, gives some directions to the cast of *Blue Steel* (Monogram 1934). Wayne is over against the rail, and in the crowd you can spot Eleanor Hunt, Ed Peil, and, right behind Peil, Yakima Canutt.

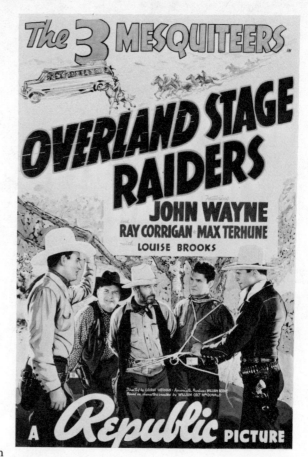

Duke Wayne gets the drop on Yakima Canutt in order to rescue Marion Burns and Earl Hodgins in *Paradise Canyon* (Monogram 1935).

John Wayne and Johnny Mack Brown teamed up in *Born to the West* (Paramount 1938), which has been retitled as *Hell Town*.

Wayne, Ray Corrigan, and Max Terhune, the Three Mesquiteers, give Dick Alexander an unexpected bath in *Santa Fe Stampede* (Republic 1938).

4

NEW TRAILS
TO ADVENTURE

The thirties was a vintage decade for the new breed of Western screen hero who could adapt himself well to the sound era. Films were now beginning to require professional-caliber acting from its cowboy heroes, and those who couldn't measure up soon lost favor with audiences. The "realistic" cowboy gave way rapidly to the polished pro who could deliver dialogue with a flair, and one by one the greats of the silent era were pushed aside. Tom Mix, who was perhaps the most popular of all Western stars during his heyday of the twenties, just couldn't make the grade; after a few routine Universal efforts and a wishy-washy serial for Mascot, *The Miracle Rider,* he gave up. A new decade of Saturday afternoon matinee worshippers found its own bigger-than-life idols.

William Boyd had been a major star at Paramount during the silent film period, but he found his career turning downward rapidly in the early thirties when he appeared in a load of potboilers for studios like RKO. However, his career took a new and prosperous turn in 1935 when he made *Hop-a-Long Cassidy* for Paramount (later retitled *Hopalong Cassidy Enters*). His portrayal won instant approval from audiences and launched Boyd on a series that was to span thirteen years and produce sixty-six titles. Boyd's distinct screen personality was one of the most pleasing ever presented to viewers, and a single flash of his smile and a quick burst of his hearty laughter alone were worth the price of admission to one of his films. Throughout the series he had

the able assistance of capable partners like James Ellison, Russell Hayden, Jay Kirby, Rand Brooks, and others; he rounded out his action trio with comical sidekicks like George Hayes, who was called "Windy" a few years before he got permanently saddled with his "Gabby" nickname, and Andy Clyde as "California Carlson," as well as a few less notable players. The Cassidy films were usually filmed on location in more picturesque areas than the minor studios used, primarily because a good deal more money and time were spent on their production; they had well-written scripts and relatively long running times. During the final year of production the titles of the Cassidy films really shook up some fans who were used to things like *In Old Mexico, Hills of Old Wyoming,* and *Hidden Gold* and suddenly found titles like *The Dead Don't Dream, Sinister Journey,* and *False Paradise* flashing on their screens. Boyd later became a millionaire when he wisely bought up all the rights to his films and then put them on television.

George O'Brien was another big star in silent films, appearing in such classics as *The Iron Horse* and *Sunrise* as well as a long string of excellent Fox films based on stories by Zane Grey. O'Brien had a winning personality not unlike Boyd's, and was at his very best when he was flipping wisecracks to the assorted tough guys in his films. Extremely well-built, George often posed for professional pictures in muscle and body-building magazines and often had the

411

An important ingredient of the Hopalong Cassidy features was the use of picturesque locations like this one in which Russell Hayden, George "Gabby" Hayes, and William Boyd shot *Rustler's Valley* (Paramount 1937).

girls in the audience groaning in appreciation when he bared his expansive chest. Still in superb shape today, George can look back to his fine performances in films like *O'Malley of the Mounted, The Border Patrolman, When a Man's a Man,* and dozens of other excellent screen favorites.

When Gene Autry had made his successful appearance at Republic as a singing cowboy, it was only natural that other studios, expressing their usual lack of creative imagination, would try to cash in on the craze by bringing out some new stars as competitors. Grand National introduced popular Tex Ritter to the screen in *Song of the Gringo* in 1936, and he went on to do work at Monogram, Columbia, Universal, and PRC, appearing either solo or with such popular favorites as Johnny Mack Brown and William Elliott. Monogram also had Jack Randall, the brother of cowboy star Robert Livingston, who sang, wisely but not too well, and fought his way through a number of generally excellent productions into the forties. Randall might have become an even bigger star if he had not succumbed to a heart attack while making a Columbia serial, *The Royal Mounted Rides Again.* Even the prestigious Warner Bros tried to get their share of the matinee dollar by starring Dick Foran in a series in which he was billed as "The Singing Cowboy." Foran was a fine actor and had one of the nicer singing voices, but the series was a short one and he went on to do better work in serials and features as a star and leading character actor. Future Western star William Elliott popped up in the Foran films as a *villain.* At Universal Bob Baker was given quite a build-up as a singing hero, but his career was of short duration. Even pairing him up with Johnny Mack Brown failed to generate much real interest, although he was a pleasant and capable performer. Fred Scott had done a considerable amount of screen work in the early thirties before he turned to the saddle in 1936 to star in *Romance Rides the Range.* As "The Silvery Voiced Buckaroo," Scott appeared in titles like *Moonlight on the Range, Knight of the Plains,* and *Songs and Bullets.* It was in a Scott film called *Melody of the Plains* that comic sidekick Al St. John first acquired the "Fuzzy" nickname he was to be stuck with for the rest of his life. Ray Whitley gained his reputation as a singing sidekick to stars like Tim Holt, but he was talented enough in his own right to do a series of two-reel musical Westerns for RKO. Smith Ballew had a good voice but a very short career, and men like Art Jarret and Tex Fletcher were eliminated from the running almost immediately. The field was really cornered by Autry and, eventually, Roy Rogers over at Republic.

Though Western songbirds of quality were in relative short supply, action fans did have numerous new star favorites to rout for. Tom Keene, also called George Duryea and Richard Powers in films, had a long string of successful films made for various studios. Quick with a quip, like Boyd and O'Brien, he gave a striking image on screen in films like *The Law Commands, Rebellion, Glory Trail,* and others. Rex Bell made over a dozen Westerns in which his youthful, boyish appearance stood him in good stead, but he never really quite caught on. Although he wasn't the big screen hero he would have liked to have been, he did have the consolation prize of being married to silent screen great Clara Bow and eventually becoming Lieutenant Governor of Nevada. Kermit Maynard, Ken's younger brother, made numerous films in which he capably demonstrated his prowess with horses and stunt scenes. Comparing the two brothers, I personally find Kermit the more appealing as an action star, but fans at the time didn't agree, and he was eventually relegated to character roles in which he always turned in a fine job.

Johnny Mack Brown had started his screen career as a romantic leading man in big MGM silent productions, including *Our Dancing Daughters* and *Divine Woman* in 1928, but was discarded from the giant studio, rumor has it, when he began to pay too much attention to Marion Davies, who was then the exclusive property of William Randolph Hearst. Johnny found himself out in the cold and decided to become a Western actor, succeeding admirably in his ambition. He became a tremendous popular favorite at Universal, where he made both serials like *Wild West Days* and *Flaming Frontiers,* and numerous features both singly and on occasion paired with stars like Tex Ritter and Bob Baker. As a Western star he was one of the most convincing of the breed. When he threw a fake punch he gave it everything he had, convincing the audience that he was really connecting.

Warner Baxter, a really first-rate actor, brought two great Latin characters to the screen in the persons of the Cisco Kid and Joaquin Murrieta.

412

A 1942 Paramount publicity portrait of William Boyd as Hopalong Cassidy.

Given the professional polish expected from major studios, the Cisco Kid films from Twentieth Century-Fox and the Murrieta portrayal for MGM were tight little programmers that were a decided cut above the lesser B-Westerns, but which should be included in our survey just for the record.

Other stars who made final top-billed appearances or who were in series that would endure for only moderate runs included Wally Wales, who went on to continued success not as a leading man but as character actor Hal Taliaferro; Rex Lease, who performed similar duty and who can be found appearing in literally hundreds of roles in Westerns during the thirties and forties; Jack Perrin, who was to pop up in bit roles which were a far cry from his starring days; Bob Allen, who was a fine performer and gave many excellent performances, but who just didn't have enough magnetism to survive in the celluloid jungle; Reb Russell, whom I don't want to even think about because he was so awful; Jack Luden, who wasn't much better; Lane Chandler, whom I have always liked and who has lasted until today as an excellent character actor (remember him as one of the suspects for being the masked man in the serial *The Lone Ranger*?); Bill Cody, who, like Perrin, had star billing but not star quality; Yakima Canutt, who eschewed stardom in favor of becoming one of the greatest stuntmen the screen has ever known; and additional once-great favorites like Bob Custer, Guinn "Big

Boy" Williams, Buddy Roosevelt, Art Mix, Jack Hoxie, William Farnum, Jack Holt, Edmund Cobb and probably a dozen or more others that I am sure I have unintentionally overlooked. (Remember John Preston as Morton of the Mounted, folks?) There were even Westerns that featured a female lead, Dorothy Page, in titles like *Water Rustlers* and *The Singing Cowgirl*.

Additional Western favorites who started their illustrious saddle careers in the thirties, some as stars and others as supporting players, were Charles Starrett, who made a long string of successful outdoor films long before he became known only as the popular Durango Kid, wearing the black outfit and mask; Buster Crabbe, who played good guys, bad guys, Indians, and what-have-you; Dave O'Brien, who not only acted but did a good deal of stunt work; William Elliott, who started by playing fancy-dressed dudes and worked his way into becoming a popular favorite in Westerns and serials at Columbia; Donald Barry, who was doing minor roles in preparation for his forthcoming screen stardom; Allen Lane, whose screen career really went back to the beginning of the thirties; and Tim Holt, who started his Western career right at the close of this prolific decade. There were giant stars, minor greats, so-so players, and complete duds. Whatever your particular appetite demanded, this third decade of the B-Western had something or someone who was bound to satisfy you.

William Boyd finds a mortally wounded George Chesebro and is off on another Hopalong Cassidy adventure, this one called *Borderland* (Paramount 1937).

A scene from one of George O'Brien's excellent Fox films, *The Golden West* (Fox 1932). That's Stanley Blystone as a sullen army officer.

Tom London, *left*, and LeRoy Mason give George O'Brien a hard time in this scene from *The Border Patrolman* (Fox 1936).

Another picturesque scene, this time with George O'Brien and Cecilia Parker in *The Rainbow Trail* (Fox 1932).

A publicity shot of Tex Ritter, one of Gene Autry's main competitors in the saddle serenaders' derby in the late thirties.

Tex Ritter and Kenne Duncan in a scene from *Roll, Wagons, Roll* (Monogram 1939).

Dave O'Brien is about to give Jack Randall (Robert Livingston's brother in real life) a bit of a headache in this scene from *Driftin' Westward* (Monogram 1939).

Veteran badman Harry Woods, *left*, seems impressed by Charles Starrett's fancy gunplay in *Gallant Defender* (Columbia 1935). This film is also noteworthy because a young member of the Sons of the Pioneers singing group, which appeared in the film, was the as yet undiscovered Roy Rogers.

Dick Foran, the Singing Cowboy, squares off against Harry Woods in this scene from *Land Beyond the Law* (Warner Bros 1937).

Dick Foran takes on Edmund Cobb in this wrestling match featured in *Cherokee Strip* (Warner Bros 1937).

Fred Scott was another very likable singing cowboy of the thirties.

Bob Baker, *left*, another thrush of the saddle, serenades his comical sidekick Fuzzy Knight in *Border Wolves* (Universal 1938).

Smith Ballew made a few features like *Roll Along, Cowboy* (Twentieth Century-Fox 1937) as another sagebrush troubadour, but was an unsuccessful competitor in the singing sweepstakes.

Kermit Maynard, Ken's younger brother and an excellent rider and stuntman, made a very entertaining string of adventure films in the mid-thirties. *His Fighting Blood* (Ambassador 1935) with Paul Fix, from which this scene is taken, was one of the better entries.

Ray Whitley, *center*, was the sidekick of a number of Western favorites like Tim Holt and Rod Cameron and also made a number of two-reel musical Westerns such as *Cupid Rides the Range* (RKO 1939) with Elvira Rios and Glenn Strange, from which this scene is taken.

Tom Keene (also known in films as George Duryea and Richard Powers at various times) in a striking scene from *Under Strange Flags* (Crescent 1938).

Tom Keene, *left*, does battle with veteran villain and
onetime star Monte Blue in *Desert Gold* (Paramount
1936), a film starring Buster Crabbe.

Rex Bell gives Bud Osborne a good going-over in
The Diamond Trail (Monogram 1933).

Johnny Mack Brown and Frances Robinson in *Desperate Trails* (Universal 1939).

Rex Bell, who eventually became Lieutenant Governor of Nevada and who was married to Clara Bow, here shown with Luana Walters in a scene from *Fighting Texans* (Monogram 1933).

Anthony Warde, *left*, in one of his few Western roles, seen with Johnny Mack Brown in *Oklahoma Frontier* (Universal 1939).

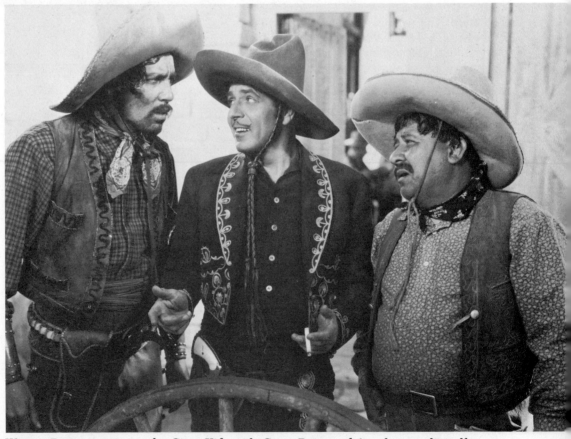

Warner Baxter, *center*, as the Cisco Kid, with Cesar Romero, *left*, who was himself later to play Cisco, and Chris Pin Martin as Pancho in *The Return of the Cisco Kid* (Twentieth Century-Fox 1939).

Bob Allen is in the fancy duds, and smiling at pal Hal Taliaferro in *Law of the Ranger* (Columbia 1937).

One of the real losers in the Western sweepstakes was Reb Russell, here with Mary Jane Carey in *Border Vengeance* (Willis Kent 1935).

While making *Robin Hood of El Dorado* (MGM 1936), Warner Baxter, playing the role of Joaquin Murrieta, had a visit from the prolific writer Peter B. Kyne, whose name probably appeared in more screenwriting credits than any other writer's during the period.

Rex Lease, *right*, makes a point with veteran cowboy star William Desmond in *Cyclone of the Saddle* (Superior 1935).

Wally Wales (later Hal Taliaferro) in a posed romantic interlude from *Breed of the West* (Big-4 1930).

How many people remember John Preston as Morton of the Mounted in *Timber Terrors* (Stage and Screen 1935)? That's Captain, King of Dogs, and Dynamite, the Wonder Horse, sharing this scene.

Robert Livingston brought his considerable talent to *The Bold Caballero* (Republic 1936), in which he played Zorro, the masked avenger. This film was Republic's first color film.

Dorothy Page, the Singing Cowgirl, gives Dave O'Brien some helpful hints in *Water Rustlers* (Grand National 1939).

Art Jarrett, Lee Powell (who was originally billed as Lee "Lone Ranger" Powell in the advertising, but was eventually forced by the copyright owners to cease and desist) and Al St. John in *Trigger Pals* (Grand National 1939).

Joan Barclay, Tex Fletcher (the Lonely Cowboy), and Ted Adams in *Six-Gun Rhythm* (Grand National 1939).

Roy Barcroft in one of my favorite portraits, from
King of the Texas Rangers (Republic 1941). Roy
had appeared in films made for many studios, but
was signed to an exclusive ten-year contract by
Republic in 1943.

5

THE DEVIL'S HENCHMEN

Although the audience's attention was primarily focused, quite naturally, on the incredible screen exploits of our favorite Western heroes, much of the success and popularity of those hour-long adventure films was directly attributable to the fine performances turned in by an excellent stock company of actors who played the heavies. One of the real pleasures most of us relished in those Saturday afternoon orgies was watching how increasingly despicable a Roy Barcroft, Kenne Duncan, Bud Geary, or Charles King could be from week to week. Space doesn't permit mention of the complete roster of this cinematic Legion of the Damned, but I would like to single out some particular favorites who brought considerable pleasure to Western moviegoers over the years.

Of all the black-hearted devils who specialized in outdoor mayhem, none looked more convincing on screen or handled his acting chores with more consummate skill than Roy Barcroft. Roy had broken into films in the early thirties doing bit parts and walk-ons (he was in Garbo's *Mata Hari*), but it wasn't until the late thirties that he began to come into his own. Harry Woods, one of the best of the badmen of the twenties and thirties, was the reigning lead heavy and Roy, who admired him greatly, frankly admitted modeling his screen characterizations after those of his idol. Alternating for several years among Columbia, Monogram, Universal, and other studios, Roy signed an exclusive ten-year contract with Republic in 1943

and became the new champion of villainy, reigning for over a decade. His versatility over the years found him doing Westerns, serials, dramas, comedies, musicals (remember him as the sheriff in *Oklahoma!*?). Then he transferred his skills to television, where he matured even further as a fine character actor. Off-screen, Roy was one of the nicest men one would ever want to meet, and I have never heard a single derogatory word ever uttered about him from the people he worked with (an extremely rare tribute, for there were plenty of bad things said about, oddly enough, the "heroes" in his films). Having a terrific sense of humor, Roy was a typical practical joker on the set, and on more than one occasion Don "Red" Barry, Bill Elliott or Allan Lane might have found their prized hair pieces (yes, they all wore frontal pieces to give them a more picturesque hair-line for the big screen) temporarily hidden by the playful bad guy. There was seldom any question in Roy's mind as to what type of role he was going to play when he received his latest script; it was very likely Sloan Nibley, a fine writer who turned out many screenplays for Republic and who is married to serial queen Linda Stirling, who originated the story of seeing Roy emerging from an office with a copy of his latest script and asking him, "Well, Roy, who is it this time? Ferguson or Slade?" to which Roy winked and replied, "Ferguson, of *course*." His mold was permanently cast.

Tom London's screen career began in the

days of *The Great Train Robbery* and continued without letup until the fifties. Another extremely versatile performer, he alternated between playing good and bad roles. Strictly cast as himself he made an excellent "brains" heavy, assigning other men to do his dirty work. With his hair whitened a little, he was the perfect heroine's father or ranch owner; his teeth out, he was a lovable old codger or happy sidekick. In superb physical shape (and quite a ladies' man off-screen even in his seventies), he was still able to ride, fight and jump around long after many of the heroes he had faced had passed from screen favor or died. Tom was another actor who was not limited strictly to the programmers; he could be found in big-budget productions as well (he played the man Katy Jurado sold her property to in the classic *High Noon*).

Trevor Bardette was quite similar to London in that he could play a wide range of roles. One of his favorite characterizations was that of the good bad man (originated in silent films by William S. Hart) who, after taking a small fling at chicanery, eventually redeems himself by sacrificing his life to save that of the hero. In *Marshal of Cripple Creek* he returned from spending time in prison to find his son following in his evil footsteps. After administering a fatherly beating, Bardette saved the boy from participating in a hold-up at the cost of his own life. When Bardette wanted to be really mean, however, he was cast in a role like that of the mysterious outlaw leader, Pegleg, in the serial *Overland with Kit Carson*.

Jack Ingram had hundreds of credits from the thirties and forties in which he was usually cast as one of the action heavies. Off-screen he was virtually a millionaire; he had parlayed his screen earnings through wise investments. Bud Geary could be seen in dozens of small roles in Twentieth Century-Fox films before he moved over to do duty mainly at Republic. An excellent stuntman, Geary handled much of his own fight work and riding. He was killed in an auto accident at the peak of his forties popularity.

Kenne Duncan, for a time, was getting more publicity than Roy Barcroft as the screen's greatest Western menace. Republic used him primarily as an action heavy, but when he moved to Columbia he got better and bigger roles in many of the Gene Autry features, and he made many television appearances. One of his highly publicized exploits was his trip to Japan, where he was photographed riding Emperor Hirohito's famous white horse. Off-screen Kenne was one of Roy Barcroft's closest friends. Bob Kortman was another successful carry-over from the silent days who made hundreds of appearances as an exceptionally convincing badman. Not only could he portray the usual shifty-eyed gunslinger, but in the thirties he often played Indian roles in features as well as numerous serials. Richard Alexander was a heavy-set player who is now best remembered for playing Prince Barin in the first *Flash Gordon* serial, but his real forte was Western banditry, and though now well on in years he still makes an occasional screen appearance as an extra. Ed Cassidy and Jack Rockwell both had impressive careers as badmen but are even more identified with the other side of the law. Between the two of them they have probably played the sheriff role more than any ten other actors in B-Western history. George J. Lewis has had one of those odd movie careers that found him alternating between playing good guys and bad guys, with an occasional Indian role thrown in for good measure. He started out as a hero in silent films and early sound serials. By the time the forties came around, he was one of Republic's best action heavies, and he made numerous serials as a thoroughly blackhearted villain with few redeeming qualities. Right in the middle of this glorious period of skulduggery, they cast George as Linda Stirling's leading man in *Zorro's Black Whip*, and he was extremely effective in this to him welcome change of pace. Unfortunately, he was back to his standard roles all too soon, and remained playing basically evil men until he had matured into better character roles. For a while he was playing in the television Zorro series and an occasional feature film, but is now quite happily retired from the screen. William Haade was one of those strange character actors who could play the meanest villain in the world and still manage to make the character funny. In one Monte Hale film he went around making hilarious wisecracks as he calmly knifed to death numerous victims. At the same time he was able to also play extremely sympathetic roles, for example, the outlaw who robbed only because he needed money for his wife's operation.

Good "brains" heavies, those men who were out to win the West only for their own interests and sent out the likes of the aforementioned henchmen to do the dirty work, were well por-

434

Here's a fearsome foursome from *Daredevils of the West* (Republic 1943): William Haade, Robert Frazer, Ted Adams, and George J. Lewis.

trayed by men like Tristram Coffin, Robert Frazer, LeRoy Mason, Francis McDonald, Kenneth MacDonald, and others. Each of these actors had his own individual style while playing outlaw leaders, but each could readily find screen work on the opposite side of the law playing doctors, lawyers, ranchers, or what-have-you with equal skill.

And of course there were the stuntmen, that rugged group of daredevils who doubled both heroes and villains in the action sequences. Almost all of the best ones, Tom Steele, Dale Van Sickel, David Sharpe, Eddie Parker, Duke Green, Ken Terrell, and Fred Graham, played regular roles as henchmen. The most famous of all these men, of course, was Yakima Canutt, who played an endless variety of badmen in the thirties. Sometimes he would be the big boss out to thwart John Wayne or Bob Steele and their like, but most of the time he was just the lead gunslinger who spent six reels wiping out the good guys only to be bested before the final fade-out.

The list goes on and on: Ted Adams, Pierce Lyden, I. Stanford Jolley, Terry Frost, George Chesebro, Stanley Price, Hal Taliaferro, Mauritz Hugo, John Merton, Lane Bradford (Merton's real-life son), Morris Ankrum, Riley Hill, Marshall Reed, Forrest Taylor, Jack Kirk, Lane Chandler, Stanley Andrews, John Cason, Rex

Lease, Robert Barron, Monte Blue, Carleton Young, Ray Teal, Robert Wilke, Glenn Strange (who made hundreds of Westerns but is better known for having played the Frankenstein Monster in several horror films), Edmund Cobb, and many more. I have tried throughout this book to include scenes which feature most of these men, but of necessity have had to omit some. But to all of them a vote of thanks for making our favorite Western heroes look so good on the screen.

Before ending this small chapter on villains, however, I must pay tribute to one special actor who was nearly everyone's choice as the favorite Western villain of all time, Charles King. It seemed that in almost every film you looked at in the thirties and early forties, there would be good old Charlie getting beaten up by Bob Steele or Hoot Gibson or Buck Jones or some other defender of justice. He'd be knocked over chairs, tables, bars, or stairs at the mere drop of an innuendo. As the years went on, King gained more weight, too much in fact, and eventually found himself playing the role of buffoon more than menace, to the chagrin of all of us. But Charles King had made his mark on screen history and in the memories of those of us who shared so many pleasant afternoons watching him die a hundred screen deaths he had so justly deserved.

Two grand old pros, Tom London, *left*, and Trevor Bardette in *Marshal of Cripple Creek* (Republic 1947).

George Chesebro and stuntman Eddie Parker in *Shadow Valley* (PRC 1947).

A trio of real menaces, Jack Ingram, Kenne Duncan, and Bud Geary, in *King of the Texas Rangers* (Republic 1941).

Edmund Cobb was a leading cowboy star in silent films and became a Western regular in films like *The Miracle Rider* (Mascot 1935).

Kenneth MacDonald was a favorite villain at Columbia, where he made films like *Valley of Vanishing Men* (Columbia 1942).

Jack Rockwell played sheriffs almost as often as henchmen. This portrait is from *The Miracle Rider* (Mascot 1935).

Jack Ingram played in hundreds of Westerns as an action heavy. This pose is from *Zorro Rides Again* (Republic 1937).

Another trio of bad hombres, Hal Taliaferro, Stanley Price and, seated, Francis McDonald. Their plotting in this scene from *Zorro's Black Whip* (Republic 1944) bodes evil to someone.

Fred Graham was a top stuntman, doubling frequently for John Wayne in big features, and played roles as a villain quite capably. This is a portrait from one of his late forties Republic features.

Edward Cassidy also specialized in playing sheriffs, but he was occasionally an outlaw. This portrait is from *Son of Zorro* (Republic 1947).

LeRoy Mason was a favorite "brains" heavy in films like *Vigilantes of Dodge City* (Republic 1944).

Roy Barcroft frequently had the assistance of top stuntman Tom Steele in films like *Ghost of Zorro* (Republic 1949).

Stuntman Dale Van Sickel, *left*, and Mauritz Hugo made a devilish twosome in *Man with the Steel Whip* (Republic 1954).

John Cason, *left*, and Lane Bradford (John Merton's real-life son), added to the villainy of many films like *Don Daredevil Rides Again* (Republic 1951).

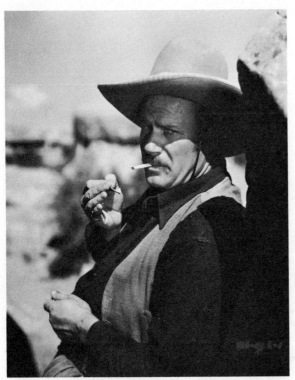

Dick Alexander was a favorite villain in the thirties and early forties. This is a portrait of him as the main action heavy in *Zorro Rides Again* (Republic 1937).

Harry Woods was a villain's villain, appearing in almost four decades of evil roles. Roy Barcroft admitted that he modeled his own screen image after that of Woods. This portrait is from one of Woods's later releases, *Short Grass* (Allied Artists 1950).

You couldn't get much meaner than the type of badman Bob Kortman usually was called upon to play. This scene is from *Zorro Rides Again* (Republic 1937).

Charles King played so many Western heavies that fans have long since lost count. Inasmuch as there are numerous pictures throughout the book with Charles as a bad guy, for a change of pace here is a scene of him in one of his zanier buffoon roles in *The Caravan Trail* (PRC 1946).

A publicity still for *The Lone Ranger* (Republic 1938). Any real Western fan worth his salt could spot, *left to right*, Lee Powell, George Letz (later Montgomery), Herman Brix (later Bruce Bennett), Lane Chandler, and Hal Taliaferro (formerly Wally Wales) behind those masks.

6
WINNING THE WEST WEEK BY WEEK

The Western, more than any other subject matter, was ideally suited to the serial format. Here was an opportunity for the studios to showcase the talents of particular Western star favorites not only once every two or three months, but each and every week for twelve to fifteen consecutive Saturday afternoons. Producing serials also offered a great financial bonus to the studios, for they could take advantage of all the great natural perils Mother Nature had to offer without having to create elaborate studio cliffhangers. After all, building tall cliffs and waterfalls could be an expensive proposition (although Republic almost wound up doing just that near the end of their producing days, when it *was* cheaper to build inside than take loads of expensive equipment and large crews on actual location).

More than half of Mascot's serial output in the early thirties was devoted to Western adventures starring some of the biggest names of silent outdoor films. Some of them succeeded partially in being good action entertainment, but most of them missed the mark. All of them lacked real creativity, and rescreening of many of the better ones shows almost tedious repetition of long, seemingly endless chases with no musical backing to make them even tolerable. Tom Tyler starred in a lackluster effort called *Phantom of the West*, which was done in ten episodes. Supposedly a mystery, the real challenge to the audience was tolerating Tom's performance. It wasn't really his fault, how-

ever, for Tom was a talented performer who had done well in features. It was actually the fault of bad direction and poor scripting, as well as inferior supporting performances. Ken Maynard did a little better job in *Mystery Mountain*, supported by comic Syd Saylor. Another mystery, this film found the cowboy star battling a black-hooded and cloaked figure known as the Rattler. Tom Mix appeared in *The Miracle Rider*, his first serial and last film. Mix fans argue pro and con about this effort put forth by their hero. Many find him old, tired and completely uninspired in his performance. Others treat him in a more kindly light, but were disappointed that he didn't contribute more effort, as well as more footage, to the film. At best the whole thing could be described as mediocre. Harry Carey appeared in three serials for the studio: *The Vanishing Legion* (good), *The Last of the Mohicans* (bad) and *The Devil Horse* (indifferent). Carey was a fine actor, but he was simply too old for all the derring-do demanded by serial script requirements. Bob Custer and Johnny Mack Brown each appeared in a minor opus, but the one star who should have made a good Western serial, Bob Steele, found himself in an aviation adventure battling a mysterious enemy known as the Black Ace. The one really important Western serial to come from the studio was *The Phantom Empire*. Not only did the film serve to give Gene Autry his first leading role and push him on the road to eventual screen stardom, but it was a superior serial adventure to boot. Gene was a singing cowboy who found himself embroiled in intrigue which led him to a mysterious underground city called Murania. Besides the standard horse-opera heroics, audiences were now treated to science-fiction escapism almost a full year before Universal was to unreel *Flash Gordon*. It might be of interest to note here that two of Republic's best technicians were involved with this film, as well as other Mascot projects, even in those days. Howard Lydecker, who did not receive screen credit until the forties, was providing special effects for Mascot, and Bud Thackery, one of the best cameramen in the business, was doing glass shots (painting special effects on glass to be placed in front of the camera and photographed along with routine scenes to enhance a visual image), among other photographic work.

The most consistent fault found with Universal serials was the constant re-utilization of silent footage in virtually all of their talking productions. Time after time the same Indians were seen being shot from the same horses in the same attacks. Not only were similar scenes used in different serials, but often they were repeated in the same serial and occasionally even in the same chapter. Economy, of course, has its place, but there are limits, and taking old mismatched footage only antagonized audiences who were jarred when they saw the grainy, jerkily reproduced scenes pop up where their current heroes should have been in evidence. Almost one-third of Universal's total serial output was devoted to Western or pseudo-Western (Northwest Mounted Police, etc.) adventures. Buck Jones starred in *Gordon of Ghost City, The Red Rider, The Roaring West, The Phantom Rider* and *Riders of Death Valley* with varying degrees of success. The earlier ventures were slightly more interesting and contained better original footage, while an effort like *The Phantom Rider* turned into an almost complete bore. Ranking close to Buck in Universal serial popularity was Johnny Mack Brown, who starred in four episodic treats: *The Rustlers of Red Dog, Wild West Days, Flaming Frontiers,* and *The Oregon Trail.* The comments on Jones's films are likewise applicable to Brown's, with the distinction that Johnny, being considerably younger, was able to handle more of his own action chores. Dick Foran, who made an entertaining series of B-Westerns for Warner Bros and subsequently made many features at Universal, was

called upon for serial duty only twice. He was the star of the "Million Dollar Serial," *Riders of Death Valley*, which also featured Jones, Noah Beery, Jr., Leo Carrillo, Guinn "Big Boy" Williams, Charles Bickford, and Lon Chaney, Jr. (a routine effort except for the exceptional cast), and *Winners of the West*, an entertaining Western about railroad-building that had, as usual, those same Indians from the silents making their interjected guest appearances. Other routine efforts included Tim McCoy's *The Indians Are Coming* (the very first talking serial); Tom Tyler in *Battling with Buffalo Bill* and *Clancy of the Mounted* (as well as several non-Western serials); *Heroes of the West* with Noah Beery, Jr., and Onslow Stevens; Lon Chaney, Jr. in *Overland Mail* (which, oddly enough, was one of the studio's better Western serials); *Raiders of Ghost City* with Dennis Moore battling a frequently camera-mugging Lionel Atwill; Bill Kennedy in *The Royal Mounted Rides Again*; and Peter Cookson as the routine hero of *The Scarlet Horseman.* Universal was the first of the big three serial-producing companies to discontinue its chapter-play output, calling it quits in 1946 after turning out sixty-nine assorted adventures. Surely they could not claim that it was an economy move, since all of the films were filled with obvious cost-cutting short cuts. Therefore we must assume, as is frequently stated, that the studio simply wanted to divest itself of the B-film stamp in general and elevate its producing image to a more sophisticated level. To be quite honest, most people probably didn't miss them at all anyway.

The percentage of Western adventures turned out by Columbia serial makers was approximately the same as Universal's: almost thirty per cent. Columbia's were similarly filled with a considerable amount of stock footage, particularly as the product of the late forties and early fifties appeared. Unlike Universal, however, Columbia had few stars of any real magnitude. William Elliott was the most popular, appearing in *The Great Adventures of Wild Bill Hickock, Overland with Kit Carson,* and *The Valley of Vanishing Men.* Elliott was an exceptionally appealing performer, excelling both in dialogue delivery and action sequences, and he became one of Columbia's better all-around Western heroes. When he moved over to Republic, again to receive high popular acceptance, he made no serial appearances, and many of his fans felt shortchanged. The Columbia Elliott serials had a considerable amount of action, but it was generally misdirected. In *Overland with Kit Carson,* for example, every chapter contained an extended sequence in which the outlaws ambushed or otherwise confronted Elliott and fought a gun battle in which literally hundreds of shots were fired with hardly anyone ever being hit. Fortunately, the location photography was extremely picturesque and that was a redeeming quality the film really needed.

The remainder of the Columbia episodic oatburners varied according to the particular talents of the leading players. Don Douglas was an odd choice to play *Deadwood Dick,* but he had a good supporting cast including Roy Barcroft, Lorna Gray, and Lane Chandler, and a great many laughs were provided by inept lines of dialogue and bad staging. *White Eagle* had Buck Jones as its star, but was a very pedestrian effort. Buck had made an earlier feature for Columbia with the identical title, and stock from this was very much in evidence throughout the entire fifteen chapters. Ralph Byrd, taking time off from playing Dick Tracy, played the comic strip hero, *The Vigilante;* Robert Kellard, who had played the hero in Republic's popular *Drums of Fu Manchu,* performed a somewhat similar chore as Byrd had when he had the comic-strip lead in *Tex Granger* (earlier, using the name Robert Stevens, he had starred in *Perils of the Royal Mounted*); Jock Mahoney, who was a superb stuntman, did three later adventures that were built almost entirely around stock footage from earlier serials (*Cody of the Pony Express, Roar of the Iron Horse,* and *Gunfighters of the Northwest,* in which he did very little extraordinary original action work, to the dismay of all his loyal followers); Clayton Moore (who reaped a small fortune from playing the Lone Ranger on television and in two feature films made in color based on the character, and who continues to this very day making personal appearances as the masked man) was only so-so in *Son of Geronimo;* Marshall Reed, who once was considered to replace Bill Elliott in the Red Ryder series at Republic but lost out to Allan Lane, got a good chance to play a hero for a change in *Riding with Buffalo Bill,* but it advanced his career very little and Lee Roberts did extremely routine duty in Columbia's final Western serial adventure in 1956, *Blazing the Overland Trail.* Columbia serials were never intended to be examples of the studio's better product. They were made for

kids, and most of them contained the very same ingredients that went into the two-reel comedies that were being turned out at the same time. If any extraordinary elements of serial virtue emerged, it was usually quite by accident, or as the result of effort expended by an exceptional director like Spencer Gordon Bennet, who knew how to make serials that could please action fans.

Republic, as might be expected, turned out the very best action serials, and fully one-third of their entire output was devoted to outdoor adventures. Their most famous serial was *The Lone Ranger,* which came out in 1938. Extensive searching by numerous investigators have failed to turn up any sign of either this serial or its sequel, *The Lone Ranger Rides Again.* All records of the films have completely disappeared from Republic files; no negatives or prints have been located, and the new copyright owners can offer no information of any value concerning the properties. The mystery was even greater than the one audiences had to solve when they attempted to guess the real identity of the masked man from among five suspects when *The Lone Ranger* first appeared on Saturday matinee screens. A large budget was expended on bringing the famous radio show to the screen, and when Republic scriptwriters got hold of the property they rewrote it to conform to their own concepts rather than those of the radio scribes. What emerged was a slam-bang action serial that retained an element of mystery in determining who the real masked man was. The suspects were five men who all had moments of screen glory either before or after this film was released: George Letz later changed his name to George Montgomery and became a big star at Twentieth Century-Fox; Lane Chandler was a popular Western star and character actor, Hal Taliaferro had been a big cowboy draw as Wally Wales and now was a first-rate character actor; Herman Brix was one of the screen's Tarzans and gained later fame as a fine actor under his new name of Bruce Bennett; and Lee Powell, who had a fine career as a serial star and might have had an even greater one had he not died serving his country in World War II. The serial met with instant success and caused Republic to do a sequel the following year. *The Lone Ranger Rides Again,* dealing with the same hot property, should have been even better than the first, considering how much the quality of production had increased at Republic in a very short period of time—but it wasn't. A detailed study of the cutting continuity (a scene-for-scene breakdown of the entire film) shows it to be merely a routine Western adventure containing only the usual Republic chases, fights, etc. (Not that *that* was bad, by any means, but audiences expected much more considering the excellent quality of the first serial.) Robert Livingston played the masked rider of the plains and turned in his usual fine performance. Livingston, who had starred in *The Vigilantes Are Coming*, an earlier serial triumph from Republic, and the Three Mesquiteers series, was an extremely competent actor and a pleasure to watch on the screen. For numerous reasons he never attained the success or stardom in the forties which he deserved.

In addition to the two Lone Ranger serials, Republic turned out quite a number of immensely satisfying Western thrillers. There were several adventures based on the Zorro character: *Zorro Rides Again*, which had likable John Carroll singing and fighting his way against the villainy of Noah Beery and Dick Alexander; *Zorro's Fighting Legion*, with Reed Hadley turning in probably the best interpretation of the masked avenger as he battled the mysterious Don del Oro; *Zorro's Black Whip*, which made no mention of Zorro whatsoever in the entire serial but which did offer the considerable talents of Linda Stirling as the Whip and George J. Lewis (in a change of pace from his usual villainous roles) playing a very acceptable hero; *Son of Zorro*, in which George Turner and Peggy Stewart were out to trap a mysterious terrorist leader known only as the Boss; and *Ghost of Zorro*, with Clayton Moore (who al-

ternated between playing heroes and villains) playing the California protector in the last serial officially based on the character. Republic had long since mastered the Western format, and almost all of their serials contained more thrills in a single chapter than the features turned out by other studios offered in their entirety. *The Painted Stallion* had magnificent photography and an excellent Western cast headed by Ray "Crash" Corrigan, Hoot Gibson, Jack Perrin, and Hal Taliaferro; *Adventures of Red Ryder* introduced Don "Red" Barry to stardom and was chock-full of excellent footage contributed by David Sharpe, who doubled Barry in a great many of the action scenes; *King of the Texas Rangers* with "Slingin' Sammy" Baugh, the famous football star, turning in an extremely bad performance as an actor but a fine job as an action star; *King of the Royal Mounted, King of the Mounties,* and *Daredevils of the West* with Allan Lane slugging his way through chapter after chapter to contribute three great action classics to the Republic hall of action fame; *The Phantom Rider* with Robert Kent masquerading as an avenging Indian God; Clayton Moore glamorizing the famous outlaw in *Jesse James Rides Again* and *Adventures of Frank and Jesse James*; and an assortment of lesser vehicles turned out in the early fifties that utilized a great deal of excellent stock footage from earlier efforts.

It has been more than two decades since I made my last weekly journey to see my Western favorites serve up their own action-packed brand of justice, but the happy memories of those days can still be conjured up in my imagination whenever I choose to recall the thrill of it all!

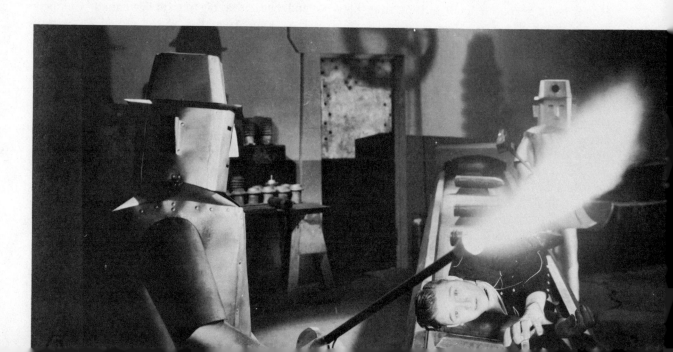

John Carroll played the dashing title character in *Zorro Rides Again* (Republic 1937).

This is one of the perils Gene Autry faced in *The Phantom Empire* (Mascot 1935).

The stars of *Heroes of the West* (Universal 1932) were Onslow Stevens, Martha Mattox, William Desmond, Diane Duval (who changed her name to Jacqueline Wells and then again to Julie Bishop) and Noah Beery, Jr.

Ken Maynard battles the mysterious Rattler in
Mystery Mountain (Mascot 1934).

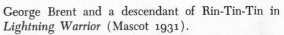

George Brent and a descendant of Rin-Tin-Tin in
Lightning Warrior (Mascot 1931).

449

Popular favorite Harry Carey and young Frankie Darro in *The Devil Horse* (Mascot
1932).

Bob Custer takes care of Richard Alexander in
Law of the Wild (Mascot 1934).

"Slingin' Sammy" Baugh, the great football star, and Duncan Renaldo, *right*, in
King of the Texas Rangers (Republic 1941).

Buck Jones in a portrait from *White Eagle* (Columbia 1941).

Trevor Bardette was the grotesque villain in *Overland with Kit Carson* (Columbia 1939).

Lane Chandler, *center*, was the third to die of the five suspects for being the masked hero. Herman Brix, *left*, and Lee Powell remained as the closing chapters of *The Lone Ranger* (Republic 1938) approached.

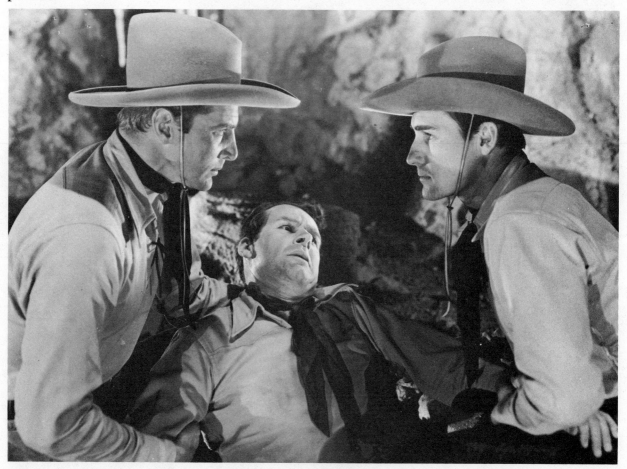

Lee Powell and Chief Thunder-cloud as the Lone Ranger and Tonto in the first serial version featuring the famous characters, *The Lone Ranger* (Republic 1938).

William Elliott, seen here with Iron Eyes Cody, was the star of *Overland with Kit Carson* (Columbia 1939).

Don Douglas was the masked hero of *Deadwood Dick* (Columbia 1940). Edmund Cobb is giving him a little help here.

Chief Thunder-cloud and Robert Livingston face
a chapter-ending peril in *The Lone Ranger Rides
Again* (Republic 1939), the second, and final, serial
based on the famous radio character.

Robert Livingston unmasked in *The Lone Ranger Rides Again* (Republic 1939).

Robert Livingston masked in *The Lone Ranger Rides Again* (Republic 1939).

Dennis Moore gives a justly deserved beating to Lionel Atwill, *left*, in *Raiders of Ghost City* (Universal 1944).

Don Terry, Lon Chaney, Jr., and Noah Beery, Jr., were the stars of *Overland Mail*. (Universal 1942).

Leo Carrillo and Buck Jones in the "Million Dollar Serial" *Riders of Death Valley* (Universal 1941), a grossly over-rated and over-publicized serial whose only real merit was the large star-laden cast.

Johnny Mack Brown in *Rustlers of Red Dog* (Universal 1935).

Don "Red" Barry, *right*, as Red Ryder delivers one to the chin of Bud Geary in *Adventures of Red Ryder* (Republic 1940).

James Pierce, *center*, and Charles King force the masked Reed Hadley into a deadly trap in *Zorro's Fighting Legion* (Republic 1939).

Tom Mix's final film was the serial *The Miracle Rider* (Mascot 1935). Here he appears with Edward Hearn in a scene from the film.

If I were Roy Barcroft, I don't think I'd turn around to get what Johnny Mack Brown is going to give him in this scene from *Flaming Frontiers* (Universal 1938).

A romantic scene you can bet serial fans would never see on the screen, a publicity shot for *Zorro's Black Whip* (Republic 1944) with Linda Stirling and George J. Lewis.

Maston Williams appears to have star Ray Corrigan at a decided disadvantage in this picturesque scene from *The Painted Stallion* (Republic 1937).

Other Western favorites who appeared in *The Painted Stallion* (Republic 1937) were Hal Taliaferro (formerly Wally Wales), Hoot Gibson, and Jack Perrin.

Tom London wants to make sure that Allan Lane is well done in the action-packed *Daredevils of the West* (Republic 1943).

Robert Kent, *right*, masked as *The Phantom Rider* (Republic 1946), rescues **Peggy** Stewart from villain-stuntman Dale Van Sickel.

Extraordinary stuntman-actor Jock Mahoney, *left*, was the star of *Cody of the Pony Express* (Columbia 1950). That's veteran character actor Tom London, *left*, and Dickie Moore showing Jock an important clue.

7

TRIGGER TRIOS

Prior to the middle thirties, audience attention at Saturday matinees was focused primarily on the exploits of a single Western hero, with the occasional assistance of a comical sidekick. Popular Western author William Colt MacDonald changed all that in 1935 when he wrote a story called *Law of the 45's*. This story was the written introduction of Tucson Smith, Stoney Brooke, and Lullaby Joslin, who called themselves the Three Mesquiteers, a Western version of the famous Three Musketeers. That same year the story was brought to the screen by Normandy Films with Guinn "Big Boy" Williams playing Tucson Smith and silent screen comedian Al St. John playing Stoney Brooke. Lullaby, for some reason, was eliminated from the screenplay. The film had some action, but is really only remembered because it was the first to introduce the now-famous characters.

That same year the real granddaddy of all the Three Mesquiteer films was made over at RKO. *Powdersmoke Range* was billed as "The Barnum and Bailey of Westerns" and featured, in addition to top-billed Harry Carey and Hoot Gibson, the greatest cast of Western "greats" ever brought together for a single film: Bob Steele, Tom Tyler, Guinn Williams, William Farnum, William Desmond, Buzz Barton, Wally Wales, Art Mix, Buffalo Bill, Jr., Buddy Roosevelt, and Franklyn Farnum. Williams played Lullaby Joslin with Carey as Tucson Smith and Gibson as Stoney Brooke. Tom Tyler, usually cast as a true-blue hero, played a sympathetic villain who wound up getting killed in a moving screen sequence.

A year later Republic became interested in the characters and bought the rights. With Robert Livingston as Stoney, Ray Corrigan as Tucson, and Max Terhune as Lullaby, the studio turned out sixteen films in a two-year period. In the first film of the series, *The Three Mesquiteers*, comic Syd Saylor played Lullaby, and in the tenth, *Trigger Trio*, Ralph Byrd replaced a temporarily ailing Livingston. Aside from those two minor switches the cast remained intact, and the series became a big money-maker for the growing Republic organization. The chemistry among the players was ideal. Livingston was perfect as the fun-loving, wisecracking, devil-may-care saddle ace who was always getting into trouble. Corrigan was similarly effective as the rugged individualist who was always getting his partner out of jams, and the comedy of Max Terhune with his dummy, Elmer, was always easy to take compared with the silliness of some screen sidekicks. The films varied considerably in quality and interest. *The Riders of the Whistling Skull* was a most unusual Western which found the Mesquiteers joining an expedition that was searching for a lost tribe and was being decimated by a mysterious killer. *Hit the Saddle* was unusual in that the young lady Livingston lost his heart to, and hoped to marry until Corrigan broke them up, was young Rita Cansino, who later changed her name to Hayworth and danced her way to screen immortality. My favorite film in the series was *Heart of the Rockies,* in which the three heroes were out to trap a bunch of animal poachers who were killing creatures on an off-limits preserve. Location photography was topnotch, and there was an excellent chase as well as an exciting fight between Livingston and Yakima Canutt.

After the sixteenth film the studio decided to move Livingston to better quality features and brought John Wayne, who had worked for the studio earlier, back to do a series of eight Mesquiteer films with Corrigan and Terhune. All eight of these films had a slickness and quality that made them rank among the very best films turned out by the studio. Almost all of them had excellent background scores with music composed especially for serials and features by, among others, William Lava.

When Wayne departed after his success in *Stagecoach,* which he made during the same period as the Mesquiteer films, Republic brought Livingston back and paired him up with Duncan Renaldo and Raymond Hatton in another series of seven titles. During 1939 Livingston had appeared in the serial *The Lone Ranger Rides Again,* a popular though uninspired sequel to the hit serial *The Lone Ranger* made a year previous. As though to use the Lone Ranger image without actually using the name, Republic had Livingston don a somewhat similar mask and ride the same kind of white horse throughout the seven films. The gimmick was a good one, and the films are immensely satisfying. Another seven-title series followed with Bob Steele replacing Duncan Renaldo and Rufe Davis subbing for Raymond Hatton; this was a little less satisfying, though still quite enjoyable. Another year passed and Republic then brought Tom Tyler in to replace Livingston for another seven films, and then, finally, the series completely ended with a final six films in which Jimmy Dodd replaced Davis and joined Tyler and Steele in some completely lackluster programmers. In all the studio had produced a total of fifty-one films in the popular series that finally ended in May of 1943.

Over at Monogram in the forties there were three very popular series which featured fighting trios. The most popular of these was, of course, the Rough Riders series, composed of eight films made in the 1941–1942 season, *Arizona Bound, Gunman from Bodie, Forbidden Trails, Below the Border, Ghost Town Law, Down Texas Way, Riders of the West,* and *West of the Law.* Starring Buck Jones, Tim McCoy, and Raymond Hatton, all eight films were real audience pleasers. Frequently the plots would tend to be somewhat similar, with Buck usually masquerading as a bandit or some other kind of social outcast in order to work his way into the good graces of whatever gang they were currently trying to bust up. Hatton played Sandy Hopkins, a character he carried over into his features with Johnny Mack Brown made at the same studio following this series. He usually sauntered into town as some kind of drifter looking for work, and Tim usually made his appearance dressed to the nines as a preacher, gambler, or other well-to-do gentleman. Eventually they all got together near the film's end and, after making up their plan of battle, shouted "Let's go, Rough Riders!" and rode off at a spirited pace to do battle with the likes of Charlie King or Roy Barcroft. Remember Buck's favorite gimmick in the series? Whenever he was getting annoyed he would pop a piece of chewing gum into his mouth. I remember how, as children, we used to jump up and down in our seats and start screaming our approval the minute we saw him go for that shirt pocket where we knew he kept that gum. Although Monogram musical scores were of a far lower caliber than Republic's, the background tracks for the Rough Riders films were a cut above the norm and were generally pleasing. All the films opened with a spirited "Rough Riders Song" sung over the main titles, and the finale of each found Buck, Tim, and Ray calling out "So long, Rough Riders" as they rode down a trail and then branched off into separate directions, again with the vocal theme in the background.

At the end of the series McCoy went into the armed forces to do World War II duty in a special capacity and the studio brought in Rex Bell to join Buck and Ray in a new string of features beginning with *Dawn on the Great Divide.* Buck wore a completely new outfit, composed of more buckskin and less denim, and looked exceptionally good, but the series died a premature death when Jones was killed in the tragic Coconut Grove fire while in the midst of a U.S. War Bond selling tour. I remember Roy Barcroft, who was one of the featured heavies in *Dawn,* telling me that when the cast went in to see the final rough cut of the film that "there wasn't a dry eye in the place and especially mine." Monogram brought Johnny

Buck Jones, Raymond Hatton, and Tim McCoy were the stars of the popular Monogram series in which they called themselves the Rough Riders.

Mack Brown over from Universal to fill the void with his almost decade-long series of actioners.

When Ray Corrigan left the Three Mesquiteers series at Republic it was with the intention of producing his own independent productions. He brought Max Terhune along with him and added John King, thus forming his own new trio, which he called the Range Busters. Distributed by Monogram, the Range Busters Westerns, though decidedly not of the superior quality of the Republic films, were entertaining and found popular acceptance. In all there were twenty-four films made in the series, which appeared on screen between 1940 and 1942. Terhune, who was called "Alibi" as opposed to his previous "Lullaby" as a Mesquiteer, was in all of the films, while Corrigan, nicknamed "Crash," and King, nicknamed "Dusty," survived until the final few films when Dennis Moore and ace stuntman David Sharpe were called in to assist in the last four titles. In *Haunted Ranch* Sharpe disappeared right in the middle of the film because he had to go into the armed forces before shooting could be completed. It was explained in the film that he had left "to join Teddy Roosevelt's Rough Riders." Veteran Rex Lease was brought in to finish the film. My favorite films in the series were *The Trail of the Silver Spur*, in which I. Stanford Jolley gave an excellent performance as the man who wore those titled spurs, and *Saddle Mountain Round-up*, which was an exciting murder mystery yarn with veteran Jack Mulhall giving an interesting portrayal.

The third series turned out by Monogram was the Trail Blazers films, which featured a notable group of performers appearing in various combinations. Ken Maynard, Hoot Gibson, and Bob Steele appeared in *Death Valley Rangers, Westward Bound*, and *Arizona Whirlwind* with so-so results. The films had a considerable amount of action, especially in the finales, which seemed to have an almost endless barrage of shots being fired. Steele, still in excellent shape, gave the best performances, while Hoot and Ken, fat and well past his prime, offered more nostalgia than anything else. Prior to these three films Ken and Hoot had teamed up to do *Wild Horse Stampede, The Law Rides Again* and *Blazing Guns*, and after the trio efforts Maynard dropped out and Hoot and Bob had Chief Thundercloud, who as Chief Thunder-cloud had played Tonto in the two Lone Ranger serials, join them for *Outlaw Trail* and *Sonora Stagecoach*. After that the Trail Blazers tag was dropped from the billing and Bob and Hoot finished their Monogram work with *Utah Kid, Marked Trails* and *Trigger Law*.

There were, of course, other groups; Dave O'Brien, James Newill, and Guy Wilkerson had called themselves the Texas Rangers, and often two stars, like Johnny Mack Brown and Bob Baker, or William Elliott and Tex Ritter, would be joined by a sidekick like Fuzzy Knight or Dub "Cannonball" Taylor, but generally when the true B-Western fan thinks of trigger trios it is the Three Mesquiteers, The Rough Riders, the Range Busters, or the Trail Blazers that come most readily to mind.

Bob Steele, Guinn "Big Boy" Williams, Hoot Gibson, Harry Carey, and Tom Tyler in the star-loaded Three Mesquiteer adventure, *Powdersmoke Range* (RKO 1935).

Harry Carey and Bob Steele in another scene from the granddaddy of all the Three Mesquiteer films, *Powdersmoke Range* (RKO 1935). Before all the experts rise up in alarm, however, I must add that *Law of the 45's* (Normandy 1935), based on William Colt MacDonald's original story, was actually the first real Mesquiteer opus; but the film version contained only *two* Mesquiteers, played by Guinn "Big Boy" Williams and Al St. John. So much for the purists.

Tom Tyler was on the wrong side in *Powdersmoke Range* (RKO 1935).

One last rare scene from *Powdersmoke Range* (RKO 1935) showing Guinn "Big Boy" Williams, veteran badman Ethan Laidlaw, Harry Carey, and Hoot Gibson. What a cast!

Max Terhune, *left*, and Ray Corrigan, *right*, successfully broke up Robert Livingston's engagement to lovely Rita Cansino (later, of course, Rita Hayworth) in the Three Mesquiteer adventure *Hit the Saddle* (Republic 1937).

Roy Barcroft, Ray Corrigan, LeRoy Mason, Max Terhune, and Bob Livingston in the Three Mesquiteer thriller, *Heroes of the Hills* (Republic 1938).

John Wayne, William Farnum, Ray Corrigan, and Max Terhune in *Santa Fe Stampede* (Republic 1938), another Three Mesquiteer adventure.

John Wayne and Raymond Hatton in *New Frontier* (Republic 1939), one more in the continuing Three Mesquiteer series.

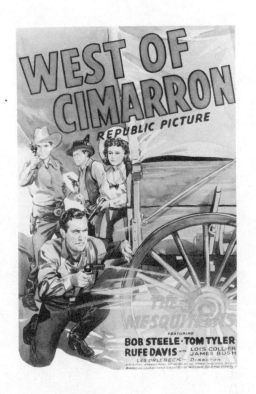

Raymond Hatton, Duncan Renaldo, and Bob Livingston as another set of The Three Mesquiteers in *Pioneers of the West* (Republic 1940).

Bob Steele and Hoot Gibson in *Trigger Law* (Monogram 1944).

Bob Livingston is behind that mask in *Covered Wagon Days* (Republic 1940). His Three Mesquiteer pals, Raymond Hatton and Duncan Renaldo, are also covered by gang leader George Douglas in the fancy duds.

477

Hoot Gibson, *left*, looks like he is about to make one of his wisecracks to Ian Keith while Ken Maynard keeps working on that safe in *Arizona Whirlwind* (Monogram 1944), one of the Trail Blazers adventures.

Bob Steele does a little clowning with the ever popular Veda Ann Borg in *Marked Trails* (Monogram 1944).

Young Don Stewart, Hoot Gibson, and Ken Maynard look approvingly at the fine work Bob Steele has done by besting George Chesebro in the Trail Blazers film *Arizona Whirlwind* (Monogram 1944).

Bob Steele, Hoot Gibson, Chief Thundercloud, and Rocky Cameron in the Trail Blazers production *Outlaw Trail* (Monogram 1944).

Glenn Strange, *left*, and Tim McCoy enjoy Buck Jones's horseplay with pal Raymond Hatton in *Down Texas Way* (Monogram 1942), a Rough Riders feature.

In the Rough Riders films Buck Jones, *right*, usually worked his way into the outlaw gangs he was trying to break up. In this scene from *West of the Law* (Monogram 1942) Buck pretty well has Roy Barcroft and Harry Woods, both standing, convinced that Tim McCoy is going to be taken care of in short order.

Buck Jones, Mona Barrie, and Roy Barcroft in Buck's last film before his untimely death, *Dawn on the Great Divide* (Monogram 1942).

Roy Barcroft loses out again to Buck Jones, this time in *Below the Border* (Monogram 1942), another Rough Riders film.

Buck Jones and Raymond Hatton in another scene from *Dawn on the Great Divide* (Monogram 1942).

Bob Steele riding hard and fast in one of his forties Three Mesquiteer adventures.

John "Dusty" King, Jack Mulhall, and Ray "Crash" Corrigan tried to solve a murder mystery in *Saddle Mountain Round-Up* (Monogram 1941), a Range Busters picture.

Guy Wilkerson, Dave O'Brien and James Newill called themselves the Texas Rangers in *Thundergap Outlaws* (PRC 1947), one in a series featuring the trio.

One of the last Range Busters films was *Two Fisted Justice* (Monogram 1943), with Max "Alibi" Terhune, David Sharpe, and John King playing the outlaw-busting trio.

The King of the Cowboys, Roy Rogers, and his queen, Dale Evans.

8

GUNS AND GUITARS

It seems a bit incongruous that in a genre that depended primarily upon real he-man action and thrills from its stars two guitar-strumming, warbling saddle serenaders should become the reigning kings of the Western film empire in the late thirties and forties—but that is exactly what happened. Gene Autry and Roy Rogers both parlayed pleasant singing voices and winning personalities into public popularity unmatched since the early days of Tom Mix's phenomenal mass appeal.

Autry and Rogers both came up the hard way, earning their chance at screen stardom by serving singing apprenticeships for several years before getting their first movie breaks. Autry began his singing career at an early age in Tioga, Texas, where, as the grandson of a Baptist minister, he performed frequent choir service. As he matured he used his singing capabilities in a variety of ways, from singing on Saturday nights at a local restaurant to appearing in carney shows, where those famous patent medicines we saw in so many B-Western plots were actually huckstered. Eventually he wound up on a local radio station and was soon discovered by a Columbia Records scout and signed to a contract. He had an appealing voice and his recordings sold well. Along with Jimmy Long he wrote "That Silver-Haired Daddy of Mine" and his recording of that song made him famous. He became a regular feature of the National Barn Dance radio program, and film producer Nat Levine offered him a role as a singing cowboy in his Ken Maynard film *In Old Santa Fe*, made in 1934. In that film Gene sang only a few brief numbers, but it was enough to encourage the studio, Mascot Pictures, to feature him as the star of a way-out serial, *The Phantom Empire*, in which Gene played a singing cowboy who discovered a mysterious underground city called Murania and had numerous adventurous escapades. He also had a chance to sing "That Silver-Haired Daddy of Mine" every other chapter or so. The die was now cast. He was put into his own series of starring vehicles released by Republic Pictures, which was a new studio formed by an amalgamation of Mascot, Monogram, and Consolidated, and became a smash hit with his very first film, *Tumbling Tumbleweeds*, released in 1935. Between 1935 and 1947 he made a total of fifty-six features for Republic, each of which made a bundle of money for the studio's coffers. I have seen all of the films either in theaters or on television, and it is amazing to notice how vastly they varied in quality and entertainment value. The studio had a habit each year of turning out set series for each star, and in the case of Autry, and later Rogers, they would produce from four to six routine efforts and then spend considerable time and expense to do a few really big shows with glossier production numbers, more exotic locations, and more involved finales. No matter, though, for all the films seemed to be met with equal enthusiasm from fans both young and old.

Although many people prefer the earlier films, I frankly find that they do not quite hold up to the excitement generated in the later more polished efforts. True, there was more location work, but Gene was still awkward before the camera, and even in his best films from the period, like *Red River Valley* and *Yodelin' Kid from Pine Ridge,* he wasn't used to best advantage. I believe Autry's best years were 1939 to 1942, when he looked, acted, and sang his very best in *Mexicali Rose, Blue Montana Skies, South of the Border, Down Mexico Way,* and others. My favorite of all the Autry films is *Mexicali Rose.* It is not, by any means, one of his most action-packed films, but it is certainly one of his most pleasant. In addition to a fine, though slightly overdone, performance by Noah Beery as a Mexican bandit who loved Autry's singing, Gene sang two of his very best songs, the title number (one of his biggest record sellers ever) and "You're the Only Star in My Blue Heaven." Another personal favorite was his 1942 film *Home in Wyomin'* which was an exciting mystery-Western that kept you guessing until the final showdown in the famous Republic "cave" sets. Other popular Autry features at the studio included *Goldmine in the Sky*, the title of another one of his smash record hits, *Melody Ranch,* in which he shared the spotlight with Jimmy Durante and Ann Miller, *Springtime in the Rockies,* and *Man From Music Mountain.*

Right at the peak of his popularity in 1942 Gene enlisted in the Air Force to fight in World War II, and when he returned four years later he found that the studio had built Roy Rogers into its new king of the cowboys. Gene made one short series for Republic in 1946 and 1947 and then left the studio he had helped in no small measure to build and went into independent production where he turned out numerous films released by Columbia Pictures. In addition, he had a popular radio show sponsored by Wrigley's gum which ran for years, and when television came into its own he produced series which not only featured himself but Jock Mahoney (the Range Rider), Dick Jones (Buffalo Bill, Jr.), Gail Davis (Anne Oakley), and even his horse (Champion). For all his shortcomings, and he frankly admits many, such as the fact that he was not a good horseman and frequently found himself falling out of the saddle in his early days (in fact, one of the most embarrassing incidents in his life occurred during one of his famous Madison Square Garden rodeo appearances right after his return from war duty when, in front of a packed house, he slipped off Champion and fell right on his rear end), and the fact that it took him years to learn how to throw an effective screen punch so that his fight scenes wouldn't have to be done in long shots with an obvious double, he was still one of the most pleasing and successful Western stars in screen history.

Roy Rogers, who's real name was Leonard Slye, decided on a show business career early in life just as Autry had, and he headed out to California from his home in Ohio to try his luck. After much the same type of exposure as Autry had experienced—singing with groups and solo, and radio appearances on the Hollywood Barn Dance show—Roy made his entrance into films as a member of the Sons of the Pioneers singing group in an appearance in *The Old Homestead,* a 1935 film featuring Mary Carlisle. After that the group appeared in *Tumbling Tumbleweeds,* Autry's first starring feature, *Gallant Defender* and *The Mysterious Avenger,* two early Charles Starrett adventures at Columbia, and several other assorted titles. In Autry's 1938 film, *The Old Barn Dance,* he received billing as Dick Weston and had a featured, though small, part. Republic was impressed with the young man and decided to build him into a new series star, introducing him to movie audiences in *Under Western Stars.* The rest is history. From 1938 to 1942 the studio featured him in a continuing string of pleasant, but generally uninspired, period films set in the old West. It wasn't until Autry left the home studio range for the Air Force that Roy was put into elaborately-mounted vehicles that would catapult him into the number-one Western star spot, from which he was never to decline. Even today, twenty years after his last starring series film made for Republic Pictures, *Pals of the Golden West* in 1951, he still holds the title of King of the Cowboys and continues to make frequent appearances on television with his wife and frequent film co-star, Dale Evans.

The early Rogers films, unlike Autry's, did not utilize his vocal talents as much as his action capabilities. In fact, in some films he only sang one or two songs, whereas in some of Autry's there would be as many as eight. The young man looked good in the saddle, and many of the production people at the studio rated him in later years right alongside William Elliott and Don "Red" Barry as a topnotch horseman. He

490

Roy in his first starring feature, *Under Western Stars* (Republic 1938).

could also handle dialogue well, and, particularly in the late forties, he was able to manage much of his action work with a high degree of skill. Prior to *Heart of the Golden West,* which was his first big production film and which, incidentally, featured both Smiley Burnette and George "Gabby" Hayes in a rare joint appearance, Roy had made thirty-one starring feature Westerns, as well as appearing in isolated features like *Dark Command* and *Jeepers Creepers,* in a period of only a little over four years. The films had titles like *In Old Caliente, Saga of Death Valley, Colorado, The Arizona Kid,* and one was hard to distinguish from another. But now the studio really duded him up in fancy dress shirts, gave him elaborate production-number backing, photographed him in picturesque locations, and stretched the running times of his features from an average of slightly less than sixty minutes to over seventy, and on an extremely rare occasion like *Bells of San Angelo* over eighty minutes. For many years during this period the Rogers films were set in modern locales in the current West. (Autry's films had similarly bounced around between period Westerns and modern-day adventures.) My favorite Rogers film in that middle forties period was *Silver Spurs,* which featured John Carradine as the main villain and which was filmed in beautiful Sierra Nevada Mountain country. In addition to several pleasant songs, there were numerous action sequences, including a spectacular wagon chase which found stuntmen leaping from a wagon in midair as it plunged over a cliff into a lake far below.

It was in 1944's *The Cowboy and the Senorita* (Herbert Yates, for some silly reason, loved to use titles like The ––– and the –––; he once wanted to call his award winning *The Quiet Man* "The Prizefighter and the Colleen") that Dale Evans made her first important en-trance in a Rogers picture, and she was thereafter to appear in more than twenty-five of Roy's later films.

After several years of these elaborate musical-Westerns, the studio began to bring in a new crop of writers who started to eliminate the musical nonsense and give Roy some strictly rugged action work to do. In *Bells of San Angelo,* writer Sloan Nibley had Roy beaten nearly to death on-screen by David Sharpe and Dale Van Sickel. Filmed at a picturesque mining site high in the mountains, *Bells* was full of red-blooded action of the kind we had not seen in Roy's earlier films. Although there were of necessity a few songs in each new title, they were kept to a minimum and Roy finished his feature film duty more as an action ace than a singing cowboy.

Again, like Autry, Roy wound up doing a very popular radio show and moving into television, where he made his own starring series of half-hour shows featuring Dale Evans and comic sidekick Pat Brady. Now he rests on his laurels and spends a great deal of time at his movie museum in Apple Valley, California, where, among such items as the original truck he first came to California in, you can find the stuffed form of his famous horse Trigger, which, although it may seen slightly grotesque, was done simply because Roy felt his fans loved Trigger so much that they would not wish to simply have him buried. Both he and Dale appear at fairs and on television whenever they feel inclined to do so, and the two extremely friendly stars are always more than pleased to talk to their many fans who visit the museum.

Between the two, Rogers and Autry made appearances in almost two hundred motion pictures—not bad at all for a couple of country boys who parlayed their voices and guitar-strumming into a movie goldmine.

Gene Autry is singing the title song in this scene from *Gold Mine in the Sky* (Republic 1938), one of his best films and most popular songs.

Roy gives Harry Woods a little aggravation in *The Ranger and the Lady* (Republic 1940) while George "Gabby" Hayes, Jacqueline Wells (later Julie Bishop), Ted Mapes, and Yakima Canutt look on.

494

Gerald Mohr, *center*, and James Bush catch Roy doing some snooping in *King of the Cowboys* (Republic 1943).

Gene exhibits a little riding skill in *Blue Montana Skies* (Republic 1939).

Roy and Dale Evans show Paul Harvey some important evidence in *Heldorado* (Republic 1946).

A nice portrait of Gene from his only non-Republic film between 1935 and 1947, *Shooting High* (Twentieth Century-Fox 1940).

Gene poses with Rudy Vallee at one of countless benefits stars of his caliber were required to attend. This one took place in 1939.

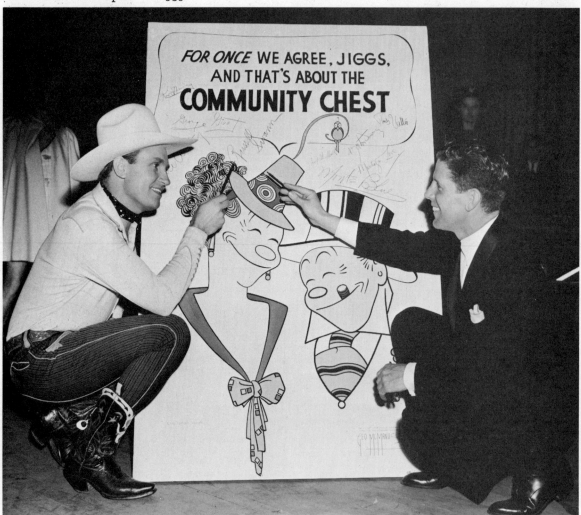

A portrait of Roy with his producer, Edward J. White, and director, William Witney, taken at a party given for Roy on his ninth anniversary as a Republic star.

Another scene at the same party shows Roy with William Elliott, studio head Herbert J. Yates, and Pat Buttram, who had made appearances on Roy's popular radio show.

Gene with Hamilton MacFadden and Kay Aldridge in *Shooting High* (Twentieth Century-Fox 1940).

Young Michael Chapin expressed in this picture what millions of fans probably had done in real life: admiration for Roy Rogers, the King of the Cowboys. This scene is from *Under California Stars* (Republic 1948).

Gene and Jimmy Durante in *Melody Ranch* (Republic 1940), another of Gene's very popular films.

Gene delivers one to the chin of Joe Sawyer in *Down Mexico Way* (Republic 1941).

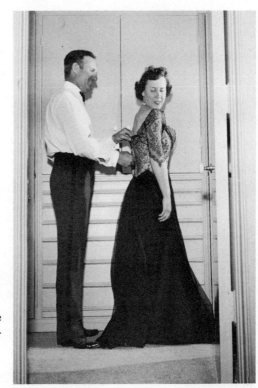

Gene and wife Ina dress for another benefit. The Autrys are one of Hollywood's happiest and longest-married couples.

In a publicity shot, Gene visits briefly with former cowboy great Tom Tyler, who was in costume for his starring role in the serial *Adventures of Captain Marvel* (Republic 1941).

STUDIO DIRECTORY
TUE SEPTEMBER 5
STUDIO A
DRAGNET
COUSIN WILLIE

NEW TIME. AIR TIME
9 00A
2 00P   6 30P
STUDIO B
FIRST NIGHTER
IT PAYS TO BE MARRIED

3 00P   5 30P
6 30P   7 30P
STUDIO C
ROY ROGERS
GREAT GILDERSLEEVE

1 00P   3 00P
STUDIO D

7 00P   9 00P

STUDIO E
BILL STULLA
JACK MC ELROY
PEANUT CIRCUS

2 30P
4 00P
5 00P
STUDIO F
KOMEDY KLUB

6 15P

STUDIO G
ONE MANS FAMILY
JASON & THE GOLDEN FLEECE   1 00P   2 00P

STUDIO H
WOMAN IN MY HOUSE   12 30P
ROSEMARY CLOONEY   3 15P   5 15P
STUDIO L
ELMER PETERSON   4 30P   5 45P
ART BAKER   4 30P   4 59P
RICHFIELD REPORTER   9: 15P
STUDIO M
KNOX MANNING   7: 45A

NBC PUBLICITY

Roy and Dale look at the NBC listings showing the time of their popular radio program.
Serial fans, that name at the bottom, Knox Manning, belonged to the man who spoke
all those forewords to Columbia serials in the forties.

Gene and leading lady Peggy Stewart in *Trail to San Antone* (Republic 1947).

Gene with Jay Silverheels, who played Tonto to Clayton Moore's Lone Ranger, in one of his late forties releases, *The Cowboy and the Indians* (Columbia 1949).

Dale Van Sickel grabs Roy to begin a brutal fight sequence in *Bells of San Angelo* (Republic 1947), while Andy Devine, *left*, and David Sharpe, holding Roy's guns, look on.

Roy's personal favorite of all the films he made was *My Pal Trigger* (Republic 1946). In this scene he is surrounded by Bob Nolan, Karl Farr, Shug Fisher, Jack Holt, Hugh Farr, and Tim Spencer.

Don "Red" Barry, Republic's first new series star of the early forties.

9

DAREDEVILS
OF THE WEST

B-Westerns attained the pinnacle of their popularity in the early and middle forties. After that, rising costs and multiple other reasons forced the genre into attrition. As was the case in the preceding decade, we once again found some old favorites still prospering, some departing; some new faces survived, at least for a while, and others perished almost before they had left the starting gate in their race for success.

Republic Pictures Corporation was now the undisputed king of the B-Western producers, and at one time held down seven of the top ten positions in the *Motion Picture Herald* annual listing of the audience's Western favorites. Don "Red" Barry was the studio's first big new series star to make an appearance in the forties. Barry, small in size but large in talent and enthusiasm, had scored well as the lead in *Adventures of Red Ryder*, a serial produced by the studio in 1940, and a series all his own was inevitable. The Barry Westerns were a cut above the routine programmers fans had been used to. Instead of stressing just the action elements, Barry's scripts called for him to do a considerable amount of acting. Frequently his films would feature him in dual roles playing both a good guy and bad guy simultaneously. My favorite in the series, which consisted of twenty-nine films, was *The Tulsa Kid*, in which he came face to face with his outlaw foster father, beautifully played by Noah Beery, in the final showdown. During this series-making period Barry was loaned out to Twentieth Century-Fox

to do a role in *The Purple Heart*. Barry says that Darryl F. Zanuck was so impressed with him that he wanted to buy his contract from Republic, but Herbert Yates refused to sell and Barry's dreams of giant screen stardom at a major studio were dashed.

Another star who achieved major success with Republic was William Elliott. Over at Columbia Bill had become a big Western and serial favorite after having appeared in numerous villain and bit roles in the early and middle thirties. Republic now featured him with George "Gabby" Hayes and Anne Jeffreys in a series of eight action-packed adventures that began with *Calling Wild Bill Elliott* in 1943. In one of the films, *Wagon Tracks West*, one of his main adversaries was Tom Tyler, who played an Indian called Clawtooth. Elliott had several things going for him: first, he had an extremely infectious and winning personality; second, he looked good on screen because he was tall and lanky and did creditably well in the action sequences, although he was doubled frequently in those Republic years by Tom Steele; finally, he was an excellent horseman, and it was a sheer pleasure to watch him ride full tilt over those Republic exterior locations. After this series of eight films Elliott did sixteen Red Ryder features and then went into big budget productions.

Sunset Carson made only fifteen features and one guest-star appearance in Roy Rogers's *Bells of Rosarita*, but he was one of Republic's best-received stars. The studio had started him out in films that top-billed Smiley Burnette like *Call of the Rockies* and *Bordertown Trail* in 1944, but Republic soon got rid of the comic, who off-screen was far from pleasant or amusing, and boosted Carson to the lead spot. It took some doing to make an actor out of the giant cowpoke. One story maintained that his delivery of lines was so bad (he ran them all together without pausing) that co-stars Tom London and Peggy Stewart actually painted a huge period on a piece of cardboard and told Carson to stop every time they held it up out of camera range and count to four before he delivered his next line. If you look closely you can see his lips moving slightly in some scenes as he did just that. But regardless of minor details like acting, Sunset was topnotch in the action category and that is really what counted with the fans. One of his films, *Santa Fe Saddlemates*, is the virtual model of an all-action B-Western. In the opening five minutes he has three fights (a test to determine his qualifications for handling a dangerous mission) and a reel or so later has another big brawl in a saloon. Finally, at the film's finale, he has a long chase followed by another humdinger of a battle with the film's villain, Roy Barcroft in a blacksmith shop. Films like *El Paso Kid, Sheriff of Cimarron, The Cherokee Flash,* and *Rio Grande Raiders* all had more than the usual share of thrills, and it was easy to see why claims were made that he was getting more fan mail from southern states than Rogers and Autry. In *Rio Grande Raiders,* incidentally, Sunset's brother was played by diminutive Bob Steele, who looked like a kid standing next to the giant star. Carson's career was finished at the studio after a succession of personal conflicts and a serious automobile accident.

In addition to these films, Republic was still riding high with its Three Mesquiteers, Roy Rogers, and Gene Autry features, but they did meet failure when they tried to star Eddie Dew in a series in which he was to play a character called John Paul Revere. Bob Livingston was brought in to take over the role after two films, but the series folded rapidly.

Over at Monogram Jack Randall, Tom Keene, and Tex Ritter were wrapping up their series with the company and a search for *new* faces found the studio turning up with *old* faces when they brought Buck Jones, Tim McCoy, and Raymond Hatton in to do the Rough Riders series,

and Ken Maynard, Hoot Gibson and Bob Steele in to do the Trail Blazers films. For good measure, they had the Range Busters as a watered-down version of the Three Mesquiteers. All three new series had thrown in the towel by 1944, and the studio signed Johnny Mack Brown, who had left Universal when that studio had decided to cut down on its B-Western output, and Raymond Hatton to star in a new series to replace the Rough Riders string of features that was broken when Buck Jones died. Brown and Hatton became the studio's bread-and-butter winners for almost ten solid years. The only other series at Monogram of any real merit was that which featured Gilbert Roland as the Cisco Kid. Roland had followed Cesar Romero, who had picked up the role after Warner Baxter had finished with it at Twentieth Century-Fox, and lent his own authentic Latin charm to the character in films like *South of Monterey* and *King of the Bandits* in 1946 and 1947.

Columbia Pictures had Bill Elliott, Tex Ritter, and Russell Hayden riding the range for them for a brief period in the early forties, but they soon departed and it was left mainly up to Charles Starrett to supply the thrills and excitement in a long string of Durango Kid vehicles until Gene Autry joined the studio in the late forties to give its Western schedule some diversity. Starrett was a pro all the way and handled a good many of his own stunts in the early days. However, as he grew older, and since he had the considerable advantage of often having his face covered by a black mask, young Jock Mahoney began to do most of the daredevil work, and it made it appear that the older Starrett became the more exciting he looked on the screen.

PRC had several lackluster series going for them featuring Bob Steele and Buster Crabbe as Billy the Kid, George Houston as the Lone Rider, and Dave O'Brien, James Newill and Guy Wilkerson as the Texas Rangers, but there was little that was good that could be said about them. Production values were almost nil and the musical background scores were so bad that most of us cringed when we heard them. Casting off his Billy the Kid tag, Crabbe did do some above-average work in a series which paired him with Al "Fuzzy" St. John, but his many fans surely must have wished that he could have made his films at another studio.

RKO continued to make good use of George O'Brien in an excellent series of features, but

510

Don "Red" Barry and his frequent co-star, lovely Lynn Merrick, in *Carson City Cyclone* (Republic 1943).

World War II interrupted him at his peak and when he returned from service his fine career was virtually finished. The studio had also started young Tim Holt on his road to stardom as a Western action star and lost him to service duty as well, but in Holt's case he was still young enough when he returned to pick up right where he left off, and he continued making Westerns until 1952.

Universal, deprived of Johnny Mack Brown, had to be content with the services of Rod Cameron, Eddie Dew, and Kirby Grant. Of the three, only Cameron really delivered the goods, and he quickly moved up the ladder to better quality features.

This period also saw isolated attempts to create new stars and series with varying degrees of success. Russell Hayden was excellent in a few Northwest Mounted Police adventures which had unusually short running times (about forty-five minutes) and were made in color. Twentieth Century-Fox put George Montgomery, who had done bit and stunt duty at Republic for several years, into new remakes of Zane Grey features like *Last of the Duanes* and *Riders of the Purple Sage*, but he quickly moved up to become a handsome leading man in the studio's

big-budget productions. The same studio also introduced a newcomer called John Kimbrough, but he was a complete failure. Republic, in addition to missing the mark with Eddie Dew, also came a cropper with Ray Middleton when they tried to build him into a new star in *Hurricane Smith*. Robert Mitchum had spent years playing bad guys in Hopalong Cassidy and Johnny Mack Brown adventures. Finally RKO tried to give him a break and featured him in the Zane Grey story *Nevada*, with Richard Martin as his sidekick. Instant stardom beckoned, though, when he was cast in *The Story of G.I. Joe*, and his B-Western career was left in the lurch.

All things considered, we were lucky indeed to have had this particular period in screen history to enjoy week after week as children. The B-Western had matured from those early days of awkward realism and was now a slickly produced commodity that fulfilled almost all our childhood demands. Perhaps there wasn't as much location work as one might have wished, but there was action in generous portions, and that was all that we Western fans asked for.

Noah Beery and Don "Red" Barry in *The Tulsa Kid* (Republic 1940), one of the best
in the series of twenty-nine Republic Barry B-Westerns.

Don "Red" Barry was once married to popular Republic leading lady Peggy Stewart.
This photograph of the couple was taken in 1942.

"Wild Bill" Elliott reaches for one of his famous reversible guns, to the consternation of Slim Whittaker, in *Hands Across the Rockies* (Columbia 1941).

"Wild Bill" Elliott and George "Gabby" Hayes search out some more action in the Republic cave sets in *The Man from Thunder River* (Republic 1943).

"Wild Bill" Elliott shows an important clue to George "Gabby" Hayes while Harry Woods, playing a good guy for a change, looks on in *Bordertown Gunfighters* (Republic 1943).

Sunset Carson was a popular series star at Republic. This scene is from one of his best films, *The Cherokee Flash* (Republic 1945).

Sunset Carson helps foil a robbery attempt for the benefit of Jack Kirk and Linda Stirling in *Sheriff of Cimarron* (Republic 1945).

Linda Stirling and Sunset Carson in *Santa Fe Saddlemates* (Republic 1945).

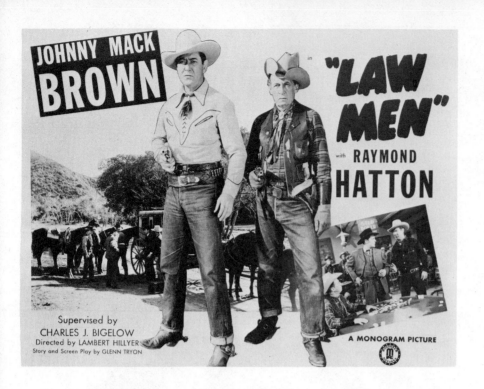

Johnny Mack Brown assists a wounded Kenneth MacDonald while pal Raymond Hatton looks on in *West of the Rio Grande* (Monogram 1944).

Charles King gets the drop on Jack Randall while bareheaded George Chesebro takes our hero's gun in *Wild Horse Range* (Monogram 1940).

George "Gabby" Hayes, my favorite sidekick. Gabby was a regular with William Boyd, William Elliott, and Roy Rogers in many of their series' features.

A rare publicity shot of Gene Autry and Jack Randall taken in the early forties.

Jack Kirk, Allan Lane, Kenne Duncan, and Tom London in *Trail of Kit Carson* (Republic 1945), one of a series of six films Lane made before taking over the Red Ryder character in 1946.

Smiley Burnette was a popular sidekick for Gene Autry and Charles Starrett, as well as a star in a few features on his own.

Fuzzy Knight was Universal's big comic sidekick, appearing with almost all of that studio's stars at one time or another, particularly with Johnny Mack Brown.

Russell Hayden and Charles Starrett in *Overland to Deadwood* (Columbia 1942).

Frank Hagney, *left*, keeps a gun on Buster Crabbe while Kermit Maynard holds his arm in *Blazing Frontier* (PRC 1941).

Dick Curtis was Charles Starrett's most frequent adversary. Here they appear in a scene from *Cowboy in the Clouds* (Columbia 1943).

Chris Pin Martin as Pancho, *left*, and Cesar Romero as the Cisco Kid in *Romance of the Rio Grande* (Twentieth Century-Fox 1941). Romero had taken the role over from Warner Baxter, who had played the character earlier for the same studio.

526

Gilbert Roland, *left*, was the third Cisco Kid when the series moved to Monogram. In *King of the Bandits* (Monogram 1947) Chris Pin Martin again played his pal, Pancho.

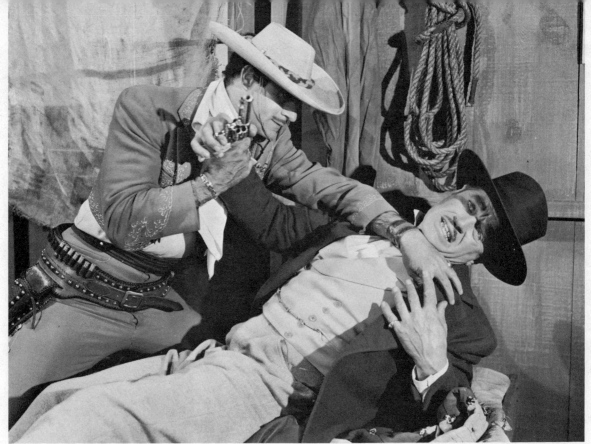

Gilbert Roland, as the Cisco Kid, battled veteran badman Harry Woods in *South of Monterey* (Monogram 1946).

Lee "'lasses" White looks like he's been in trouble again. Tim Holt, *center*, and Ray Whitley, *right*, join in the fun in *Thundering Hoofs* (RKO 1941).

Helen Talbot was another favorite leading lady in Republic B-Westerns, making many with, among others, Don "Red" Barry and Allan Lane. In this production shot from the serial *King of the Forest Rangers* (Republic 1946) she poses with visiting director Frank Borzage, ace cameraman Bud Thackery, in white shirt, and famed action director Spencer Gordon Bennet.

Linda Stirling, one of Republic's—and audiences—favorite leading ladies in B-Westerns.

Columbia's claim to the B-Western queen title was Iris Meredith.

Ray Whitley, Eddie Dew, and Rod Cameron in *Riders of the Santa Fe* (Universal 1944).

Smiley Burnette and Bob Livingston in *Pride of the Plains* (Republic 1943), one of a short series of features which had begun with Eddie Dew as the star in which the studio had hoped to introduce a character called John Paul Revere. Even with Livingston playing the role, it just didn't catch on.

Neath Canadian Skies (Screen Guild 1948) starring Russell Hayden, *left*, was one of many independent action films made during the period. That's Kermit Maynard with the rifle.

Republic tried to build Ray Middleton into a Western star in *Hurricane Smith* (Republic 1941) with dismal results.

George Montgomery, *left*, assists Francis Ford, famous director John Ford's brother, in *Last of the Duanes* (Twentieth Century-Fox 1941), one of a new series of remakes of Zane Grey stories.

RKO tried to build Robert Mitchum into a series Western star, but he went on to greater fame as a leading man before the series really got rolling. In *Nevada* (RKO 1944) Richard Martin was his guitar-strumming sidekick. Martin went on to become Tim Holt's pal in Holt's long string of popular RKO Westerns.

John Kimbrough, *right*, was another big failure as a series star. Here, in *Lone Star Ranger* (Twentieth Century-Fox 1942), he appears with Truman Bradley, *left*, and Jonathan Hale.

An interesting one-shot was *Silver Stallion* (Monogram 1941) with Chief Thunder-cloud, LeRoy Mason, and stunt ace David Sharpe.

A big failure at Republic was Eddie Dew, *right*, in two starring features. In this scene from *Raiders of Sunset Pass* (Republic 1943) he has Roy Barcroft covered.

Elliott and Peggy Stewart in *Conquest of Cheyenne* (Republic 1946). This was Bill's final appearance as Red Ryder.

10
TWENTY-THREE HOURS OF THRILLS

Every B-Western fan had his own particular favorite star or series whom he enjoyed more than any other during his young moviegoing days. For those who grew up in the twenties it might have been Jack Holt or Tom Mix or some other silent saddle ace; for thirties fans, perhaps Bob Steele, Ken Maynard, Tom Tyler, or Tim McCoy was their particular dish of oats. My moviegoing period, the early and middle forties, had numerous choices available to whet any action fan's appetite, including Gene Autry, Roy Rogers, Sunset Carson, Charles Starrett. But I found myself enjoying most the series of twenty-three features made by Republic between 1944 and 1947 based on the exploits of the famous comic-strip hero, Red Ryder. These films were the answer to an action-lover's prayer. Filmed during those glorious days at Republic when the stunt team was at its slam-bang, set-destroying peak, almost every one of the twenty-three films was loaded to the brim with exciting chases, fights, and assorted action highlights.

Republic had brought the Red Ryder character to the screen four years earlier in serial form. Donald Barry had scored a personal triumph in the John Wayne film *Wyoming Outlaw* and studio head Herbert J. Yates decided to give Barry the leading role in what was sure to be an action-packed adventure classic. Right from the start Barry rebelled against his casting. He felt he didn't resemble the character at all physically, and he did not want to work in serials, which he felt were demeaning as they

were aimed at a primarily juvenile audience. Yates convinced him to take the role, and Barry reluctantly turned in a performance that made him a star and tagged him with the Don "Red" Barry screen name, which he also hated because he really didn't have red hair. The serial did, indeed, turn out to be a huge success, due in no small part to the excellent action work turned in by stuntman David Sharpe, who doubled Barry in most of the really exciting moments of the twelve-chapter delight. The complete serial was filmed in less than a month. It had a simple plot which found villain Harry Worth out to grab valuable property which he intended to sell to a railroad for a right of way at his own price. When the serial was completed, Barry went into his own series of action features, and the Red Ryder character remained dormant until Republic could find someone new who would be able to handle the role successfully.

That chance came in 1944 in the person of William "Wild Bill" Elliott. Elliott had had a successful career for several years at Columbia where he made Westerns and serials that pleased most fans. Republic acquired his services and starred him with George "Gabby" Hayes in a series of eight exciting Western features in 1943 and 1944. Elliott was strictly playing himself, with all the gimmicks he had used at Columbia still very much in evidence, including his favorite tag line, "I'm a peaceable man, but . . ." which usually prefaced a slam-bang fight sequence. Republic decided that Elliott would do the Red Ryder character justice and immediately had him do eight features which were released between May, 1944, and May, 1945. There are those who argue, and quite justifiably, that Elliott was not really playing Fred Harman's character but only himself, and that he completely changed the comic-strip image to reflect his own image (the reversible guns, the stylized shirt, etc.). The charge is quite true, but so what? As fans who looked only for action we really didn't care about the character's name or source as long as he delivered the necessary thrills and excitement, and Elliott *did* supply just what we wanted. So while the purists cried "fraud" and grumbled, many millions just enjoyed.

The series began with two films in which George "Gabby" Hayes was still Elliott's partner, *Tucson Raiders* and *Marshal of Reno*. The former found Red and friends trying to thwart the tyranny of a villainous Governor (Stanley Andrews) and had a rousing finale in which the villains were blown up, courtesy of special-effects artist Howard Lydecker, who created a spectacular miniature for a tremendous barn explosion. In the latter Red proves the innocence of a young man who was framed for murder. The young man, incidentally, was played by Blake Edwards, who went on to become a famous producer-director. *The San Antonio Kid*, a routine effort to be sure, followed but then came *Cheyenne Wildcat*, my favorite of the sixteen Elliott Ryders. In this film Red opposed the supreme villainy of Roy Barcroft, who went around murdering his victims with thrown knives. The film had four great fight sequences, and Barcroft was dispatched in memorable fashion. During the finale, Red and Roy stage a massive brawl during which the latter throws a knife that misses Red and goes through a door panel, leaving the blade exposed. Naturally, at the end of the fight Roy is knocked against the door and killed by his own weapon. I can still see Barcroft standing silently against the door as Red wonders why his opponent has suddenly stopped throwing punches and is just staring open-eyed. Another crowd-pleaser followed immediately with the title *Vigilantes of Dodge City*, in which Red did battle with Le-Roy Mason and Hal Taliaferro, who were out to try and gain the Duchess's freight line. The Duchess was played by that fine character actress Alice Fleming in all sixteen of the Elliott films, and Ryder's constant sidekick, Little

Beaver, was played in all twenty-three features by Bobby Blake, who matured into an excellent actor in later years in such films as *The Purple Gang*, *In Cold Blood* and *Tell Them Willie Boy Is Here*. The remaining titles in the first series, *Sheriff of Las Vegas*, *The Great Stagecoach Robbery*, and *Lone Texas Ranger*, were milder in overall thrills, but were still big enough at the box-office to warrant the studio's making a second series of eight titles, which were released between August, 1945, and April, 1946. This second set began with *Phantom of the Plains* (which contained a spectacular fight sequence and stagecoach chase that ran for almost the entire last two reels of the film and which is hard to beat for sheer continued action) and continued with *Marshal of Laredo*, *Colorado Pioneers* (which featured a trouble-prone collection of scene-stealing kids), *Wagon Wheels Westward* (which had Roy Barcroft riding into a mysteriously deserted town and taking it over in order to swindle Red and a bunch of new homesteaders who were traveling there to settle down), *California Gold Rush* (which really had nothing to do with California *or* a gold rush), *Sheriff of Redwood Valley* (in which former cowboy great Bob Steele had a meaty role as a former crook who was trying to go straight), *Sun Valley Cyclone* (which purported to tell the story of how Red first acquired his famous horse, Thunder) and, finally, *Conquest of Cheyenne*, which had Peggy Stewart riding around in a newfangled horseless carriage and causing Red all kinds of trouble in one of the weakest films in the entire series.

After sixteen films Elliott had had enough of Red Ryder. He wanted better roles, and the studio obliged him by giving him big productions which may have flattered his ego but which cost him his legion of devoted Saturday afternoon fans.

The studio began auditioning new actors to fill the Ryder vacancy, including young Marshall Reed who had played numerous minor roles and did stunt work at Republic, and was featured in Johnny Mack Brown vehicles at Monogram. He might have gotten the part if Herbert Yates hadn't seen a clip from one of the six Westerns Allan Lane had turned out in 1944 and 1945. He is said to have remarked at a private screening, pointing at the screen where Lane was on view, "That's my new Red Ryder!"

For a great many people, Lane was a better physical choice to play the character of Red

Ryder. It really boils down to a matter of personal choice. I enjoyed Elliott and Lane almost equally. The first film in the series, *Santa Fe Uprising*, was released in September, 1946, and was an action-packed debut in which Lane matched wits with class-A badman Barton Mac-Lane, who was out to control a toll road owned by the Duchess, now played in these final seven features by Martha Wentworth. The finale featured a great shoot-out and fight in the famous Republic cave sets, which were located on the studio lot adjacent to the famous blacksmith shop set where so many outstanding fight sequences were staged. *Stagecoach to Denver* followed and was one of the weaker Lane entries, but the following feature, *Vigilantes of Boomtown*, had a most unusual and entertaining plot. "Gentleman" Jim Corbett (George Turner) and Bob Fitzsimmons (John Dehner) arrive in Carson City to train for their world heavyweight bout. Peggy Stewart tries to get them to leave the territory because she feels boxing is brutal and she feels people will consider the townspeople savages for tolerating the planned slugfest. Into this situation rides evil Roy Barcroft, who intends to rob the proceeds from the planned spectacle, but who is finally thwarted by Red. He fights Roy with professional boxing punches taught to him by none other than Jim Corbett. The whole thing was a lot of fun and well worth viewing. *Homesteaders of Paradise Valley* and *Oregon Trail Scouts*, two routine but entertaining features, followed. Then came *Marshal of Cripple Creek*, which is very likely the best of the Lane Ryders, and one of the best B-Westerns Republic ever turned out. The cast was loaded with pros like Trevor Bardette, Tom London, and Roy Barcroft. Bardette comes to Cripple Creek with his family in the hopes of making a fast fortune. He falls in with Gene Stutenroth, who tricks him into hijacking an ore wagon. Bardette is caught and goes to jail. In the meantime, his son arrives in town and very quickly falls under Stutenroth's influence. Red tells the bandit leader to leave the kid alone or "I'll break you

in two." Meanwhile, Barcroft winds up in prison in a cell next to Bardette and tells the latter that Red is making things tough for his son. "Why," Roy says, "he's even got him cleaning out *spittoons*." Well, that would be enough to make any man break out of jail, and Bardette does. The film ends on a frantic note with Bardette convinced that Ryder is right, and he dies saving Red's life. Ryder, in turn, goes to Stutenroth's saloon where, after telling him, "I told you if you didn't leave that kid alone I'd break you in two," proceeds to do just that in a terrific slugfest. This was entertainment to be sure, at its supercharged best. The final film in the series, *Rustlers of Devil's Canyon*, found Red combating an evil Arthur Space who was supposedly the friendly town doctor, but who was in reality the head of a gang of rustlers. With the conclusion of this final Ryder feature Lane tacked on his nickname of "Rocky" and did a long and successful series for Republic that continued into the fifties.

Republic no longer utilized the Ryder character, but Eagle-Lion turned out four features starring Jim Bannon as Red in 1949. Filmed in color, *Ride, Ryder, Ride; Roll, Thunder, Roll; The Fighting Redhead;* and *The Cowboy and the Prize Fighter* were generally awful, but Bannon, for those good old purists, did look quite a bit as you would expect a real-life Red Ryder to look.

Informed sources say that a television pilot was made with Allan Lane playing Red again, but it was never sold and I have been unable to verify the information.

All in all, those twenty-three features produced by Republic satisfied completely my enormous Saturday afternoon craving for thrills, and my memories of those films are still vivid even today. From the very first entrance of the characters (remember Red and Little Beaver walking out of a giant-sized replica of a Red Ryder book?) in the opening credits, to the final fade-out, it was polished Republic professionalism all the way—and what more could any Western fan really ask for?

William "Wild Bill" Elliott as comic-strip hero Red Ryder, one of his most popular characterizations.

Don "Red" Barry comes to the aid of Hal Taliaferro as villainous Harry Worth looks on in *Adventures of Red Ryder* (Republic 1940), the only serial to feature the Red Ryder character.

Don "Red" Barry, hairpiece and all, and Tommy Cook, as Little Beaver, in *Adventures of Red Ryder* (Republic 1940).

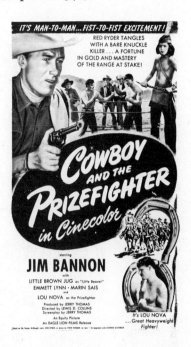

Alice Fleming was the Duchess in the sixteen Elliott Red Ryder films, and Bobby Blake played Little Beaver in all twenty-three features. This portrait was from *Marshal of Reno* (Republic 1944).

Phantom of the Plains (Republic 1945) had a finale which found Elliott battling William Haade, playing Ace Hanlon, and Ian Keith, *right*, on top of a runaway stage-coach.

Elliott gets the drop on Don Costello in *Marshal of Laredo* (Republic 1945). In the film Costello's face had been disfigured by fire, and his villainous boss, Roy Barcroft, kept flipping lighted matches at him whenever he didn't obey orders quickly enough.

William Haade, *left*, Bud Geary, and Kenne Duncan think they are going to give Elliott a good going-over in *Sheriff of Las Vegas* (Republic 1944), but I somehow feel they will be sadly disappointed.

In *Sheriff of Redwood Valley* (Republic 1946) cowboy star Bob Steele played a former bad guy now going straight. Peggy Stewart and John Wayne Wright (I wonder who he was named after?) played Bob's wife and son.

Roy Barcroft wants Elliott to get the point in
Cheyenne Wildcat (Republic 1944).

Elliott battles veteran stuntman-actor Fred Graham
in *Great Stagecoach Robbery* (Republic 1945).

A rare shot of the two Red Ryders together attending the opening of the Hitching Post Theatre in Beverly Hills. Lane was playing Red on the screen at the time.

Elliott catches up to master villain Dick Curtis in *Wagon Wheels Westward* (Republic 1945).

A new family portrait of the Ryder clan, with Allan Lane as Red, Bobby Blake as Little Beaver, and Martha Wentworth as the Duchess, from *Santa Fe Uprising* (Republic 1946).

Arthur Space, *right*, who is really the film's villain, ties up Pierce Lyden while Allan Lane supervises in *Rustlers of Devil's Canyon* (Republic 1947).

Allan Lane as Fred Harman's famous comic-strip hero, Red Ryder.

George Turner, *left*, shakes hands with John Dehner as Bobby Blake, Roscoe Karns, and Martha Wentworth look on with Allan Lane in *Vigilantes of Boomtown* (Republic 1947).

Allan Lane gives Dick Curtis back his gun after knocking him all over the place in *Santa Fe Uprising* (Republic 1946).

Allan Lane promised Gene Stutenroth early in *Marshal of Cripple Creek* (Republic 1947) that he would "break him in two" if he didn't quit his villainy. At the film's finale, Lane almost kept his word completely in a terrific battle sequence.

Allan Lane gives Roy Barcroft some friendly advice, which Roy will naturally decline to follow, in *Marshal of Cripple Creek* (Republic 1947).

Jim Bannon, *center*, made a good-looking Red Ryder in a series of four color films in 1949, but overall the features left fans cold. Emmett Lynn, *right*, was Bannon's sidekick in this scene from *The Fighting Redhead* (Eagle-Lion 1949).

Allan "Rocky" Lane was one of Republic's last big
series stars, continuing to make Westerns of varying
quality until the studio ceased production in 1953.

11
THE END
OF THE TRAIL

As the forties drew to a close, the B-Western well found itself running dry. Too many external forces were being brought in to combat the continuance of the little action gems most of us had grown up with. Costs over the years had risen spectacularly. In the thirties an hour-long film could be brought in for well under the fifty-thousand-dollar mark; now the same film would cost over a hundred thousand, and with no appreciable upgrading of quality. Also, many of the smaller theaters were folding their screens thanks to the continuing dollar squeeze, thus limiting audience attendance to an unprofitable level. An even greater element of concern to film producers was the looming specter of television, which was even then beginning to make itself felt. But the saddest of all these detrimental forces was the complete lack of vision on the studios' part in developing any really interesting new personalities to replace those who, for one reason or another, were beginning to lose their box-office appeal; while at the same time major studios were introducing a variety of screen newcomers in color presentations that were far more satisfying to general audiences.

It was Republic, as usual, who best weathered the storm until the inevitable finale. Herbert J. Yates, the head of Republic, couldn't have cared less about the Western product the studio was turning out. His big interest was in producing big color films featuring his wife, Vera Hruba Ralston. Not only were many of these films bad, but the drain of money from the studio's coffers

to produce them almost completely wiped out the company. Minority stockholders brought suit against Yates, and in one case they even forced Ralston's name to be removed from its usual place of prominence in theatrical posters and advertising. The slow deterioration of Republic over the years was not pleasant for loyal fans to watch. In the thirties the company spared no expense to shoot their low-budget films outdoors in attractive locations with a minimum of indoor studio work. Gradually, however, for reasons of convenience and economy, more and more footage was actually shot on the studio's sound stages. Now instead of long exterior chases we would see stock footage mixed with gross interior close-ups against a rear projection screen. We were exposed to a veritable plethora of fake trees, fake rocks, fake buildings. The only thing that seemed real were the players, and we sometimes had our doubts about them, too. But it wasn't a complete loss in those declining years. In all fairness it should be admitted that Republic did make a reasonable effort to try and maintain its superiority in the field it had so admirably dominated for over a decade.

Gene Autry, who had in fact put Republic on the map in the thirties, returned after World War II to find his cinema rival Roy Rogers at the top of the Western ladder, and after one short series at his alma mater he decided, for monetary and creative reasons, to transfer his allegiance to Columbia. There, under his own producing arm, he turned in some interesting and popular work until the early fifties. Rogers, on the other hand, was going through another stage in his cycle of development. He had started in a series of frontier-type period pieces, then moved into the big musical-Western production-plus category. Now he experimented with the studio's Trucolor process and somewhat more adult story lines. As an actor he had matured extremely well. He looked good, acted capably, and was an excellent horseman. Under the stimulus of fine writers and directors, Rogers inevitably gave an entertaining afternoon to his fans in film after film until he, too, left to enter television production in the early fifties.

Allan "Rocky" Lane, who had built his reputation on fast-moving serial and Western work, began his third series of familiar action pieces in 1947. The first few films were generally excellent, but the series quickly fell into the pattern of using too much stock and too little ingenuity. In most of these films he was usually opposing the villainy of Roy Barcroft, who gave a considerable boost to the overall quality of the product. Still, with all their obvious faults, the series met with commercial success, and Lane was voted into the Top Ten Western Stars listing several times.

Republic did try to bring in new faces but met little success in building them to the prominence achieved by men like Bill Elliott, Don "Red" Barry, and others. Monte Hale had played bit parts for years at the studio and was finally given a chance at stardom in a series that started out with the help of Trucolor. He just couldn't make the grade and was dropped after a few short years. However, the series did offer the frequent casting of Adrian Booth (formerly Lorna Gray) as Monte's leading lady, and that did give us some solace. Rex Allen started his career in a film called *The Arizona Cowboy*, and he quickly adopted the title as a nickname. He was a pleasant enough performer, and the studio, again, tried to give him enough good films to build him into a major star. He did achieve some success, but primarily because there was so little competition. As one of the last of the singing cowboys, he reigned until Republic closed its doors, and the lanky redhead eventually went into the lucrative field of off-screen narration, where he did many films for Walt Disney, both theatrical and television, and a long series of commercials for Purina Dog Chow. Speaking of off-screen narration, even

Rex's frequent screen adversary, Roy Barcroft, did the narration for several Disney television shows in the sixties, as well as starring in the Spin and Marty series for the Mickey Mouse Club show. As an experiment, Republic even tried to do a Western series featuring a young boy, Michael Chapin, as the star, but that series met with almost instant failure and was quickly dropped.

Over at Monogram Westerns were in even more dismal straits. Johnny Mack Brown, who had stepped in after the studio's earlier Rough Riders series had folded with the death of Buck Jones, was really beginning to show his age. He had put on considerable weight, and the scripts they were giving him to work with now were slow-moving and unentertaining. It was a shame, for Johnny had been popular since the early thirties and was one of the more convincing cowboy stars. After doing more than sixty films in the series, Johnny rode into the retirement sunset.

Monogram tried to foist two new personalities on us in those days, and the results were not good even though both actors made numerous films. Jimmy Wakely had been around in films for years with his trio doing song-fillers in the Westerns of other stars like Johnny Mack Brown and Don "Red" Barry. As a singing cowboy he was not up to par with Autry and Rogers, or even Rex Allen for that matter, and as an action hero he fell into an even lower category. Another real dud, although he did have an amazing legion of loyal fans who admired him for many of the same reasons Sunset Carson's fans had admired him, was Whip Wilson. Whip delivered lines as though he didn't know what they meant, and his whip seemed to have a great deal more personality than he had.

There were a few last-ditch Monogram stars who were able to last into the fifties, however, and who were still able to deliver convincing work. Duncan Renaldo had inherited the Cisco Kid series from Gilbert Roland and did a good job whenever the scripts would let him. Kirby Grant, who had made some films for Universal in the early forties, did a series of Northwest Mounted Police films with Chinook the Wonder Dog getting co-star billing. They were good actioners and, at least, offered some varied location work. William Elliott, who had scored immense success at Republic, now found himself doing features for Monogram (who had changed their corporate name to Allied Artists) that were an attempt to revive the action format of earlier years. The stories were generally above average, and Elliott, as always, gave very satisfactory performances. Unfortunately, Elliott wound up his screen career in a series of non-Western crime mellers instead of tall in the saddle. The studio wrapped up its B-Western production with an abysmal series of films starring Wayne Morris. Morris had enjoyed some degree of popularity in the thirties but, after returning from World War II service, found the going rough. He was most unconvincing, and nobody cared much to have a cowboy hero with a protruding beer-belly as a screen idol.

Columbia's primary contribution to the Western field was the continuing adventures of that masked avenger, the Durango Kid, played by Charles Starrett, and a few musicals with outdoor backgrounds. Starrett, who kept in excellent shape, was still effective even though the action chores were increasingly being turned over to Jock Mahoney. RKO was still turning out fine Tim Holt entries that were filmed in interesting locations and had some excellent action sequences. At the same time, other studios and independent companies turned out some real losers. Sunset Carson, having left Republic, starred in a terrible series of features that were shot in 16mm and blown up to 35mm for theaters. The stories were awful, the filming was awful, the sound was awful, and he was awful. It was a pity, for Carson had turned out some fine work at Republic when under the direction of capable hands. PRC gave us two heroes in the persons of "Lash" LaRue and Eddie Dean. LaRue talked and behaved like a very poor imitation of Humphrey Bogart. Unfortunately, he couldn't *act* like Bogart, and, like Whip Wilson, the best thing about him was his handling of the whip. Fortunately, Al "Fuzzy" St. John was along to at least give the films a few laughs. Eddie Dean had played bit parts in so many films that I am sure he lost any hope of ever achieving stardom. Usually playing badmen, he popped up in the films of Boyd, Autry, Rogers, Barry, and others with amazing frequency. When he finally did get his big chance in a series with some films made in color, the results were often uneven. When he had good character-actor support and a good script, he was tolerable, and one could even take pleasure in his singing, which was a cut above average. But when the elements of good film construction were against him, well, the less said the better. RKO tried to build James Warren into a new hero, but failed completely after only a few films.

But the shoddiest attempt to shortchange audiences was in a series of films made by two former "Lucky" portrayers in the Hopalong Cassidy films, James Ellison and Russell Hayden. Both extremely capable performers under the direction of others, they banded together and produced six films all at the same time. Utilizing one set of excellent character actors, they simply shifted them around from one film to the next with each playing a different, or sometimes the same, role. No change of costumes, no change of scenery, no solid story quality, no professional polish, no anything! While television production was soon to be similarly geared to quick production, Saturday afternoon crowds were not yet ready for this ludicrous attempt at a cinematic swindle. The chicanery was even carried over to television, where the very same films were retitled for no really apparent reason.

For a time the B-Western was a staple of early television. Fans could turn on the set and see at least two or three of their cowboy favorites each day. However, television soon began to make its own half-hour and hour-long shows, and so there was no longer any need to pay large sums of money to rent earlier, and often quite poorly produced, Western fare. Add to the question of finances the persistent appeal by parents that these early films were much too violent, with excessive and gratuitous killing, and it was only a matter of time before stations would bow to the pressure and, with rare exceptions, pull them completely off the air. On occasion you might see them pop up on a southern station or on some UHF channel (primarily because with a limited market they can be obtained very cheaply), but generally the now-aging Western fan must sit back and be content with his memories of hundreds of thrilling afternoons spent watching those favorite saddle aces mete out their own particular brand of justice. Will we ever see their like again?

Monte Hale throws a realistic punch to stuntman Fred Graham in *Son of God's Country* (Republic 1948).

Monte Hale and his frequent leading lady in his Republic films, Adrian Booth (called Lorna Gray in her earlier screen days).

Allan "Rocky" Lane in an apparently acrobatic fight sequence from *Salt Lake Raiders* (Republic 1950).

Monte Hale adds his name to those of other Republic stars in one of the studio's sidewalks. Watching are Tom London, *center*, young Bobby Blake, and Adrian Booth, who were working with him in *Out California Way* (Republic 1946).

557

Allan "Rocky" Lane met Clayton (Lone Ranger)
Moore and Gail (Annie Oakley) Davis in *Frontier
Investigator* (Republic 1949).

558

Johnny Mack Brown, showing signs of wear, keeps
apart two former Hopalong Cassidy sidekicks, Jimmy
Ellison, *left*, and Rand Brooks in *Man from the
Black Hills* (Monogram 1952).

Young Michael Chapin was one of the child stars of a brief series for Republic. Here he appears in a scene with veteran badman William Haade in *Buckaroo Sheriff of Texas* (Republic 1950).

Leo Carrillo and Duncan Renaldo as the screen's final Pancho and the Cisco Kid in *The Daring Caballero* (United Artists 1949).

Jimmy Wakely in *West of the Alamo* (Monogram 1946).

A murderous Tom Tyler, *right*, threatens young Tim Holt in *Rio Grande Patrol* (RKO 1950). Tyler was already beginning to show signs of the illness which was to shortly end his career, and his life, prematurely.

Kenne Duncan and Jimmy Wakely in *Gun Runner* (Monogram 1949).

Charles Starrett as the masked Durango Kid faces up to former Dead End Kid, William Halop, in *Challenge of the Range* (Columbia 1949).

Whip Wilson, *left*, gets a little rough with Marshall
Reed in *Night Raiders* (Monogram 1952).

Whip Wilson engages in a little playfulness with
George Chesebro in *Gunslingers* (Monogram 1950).

Rex Allen, the Arizona Cowboy, Republic's last popular series star. In this publicity still he's all dressed up for duty in *Shadows of Tombstone* (Republic 1953).

Eddie Dean, *left*, and stuntman David Sharpe, playing an important leading role this time, in *Colorado Serenade* (PRC 1946).

Rex Allen throws a pretty convincing punch to the chin of stuntman Dale Van Sickel in *Thunder in God's Country* (Republic 1951).

A few years after his starring series at Republic, Monte Hale, *left*, wound up playing villains in films like *Yukon Vengeance* (Allied Artists 1954) opposite star Kirby Grant.

"Lash" LaRue, in black, and Al "Fuzzy" St. John seem to have poor John Merton at a slight disadvantage in *Cheyenne Takes Over* (PRC 1947).

A little bigger budget was spent on *The Return of Wildfire* (Screen Guild 1948) with Richard Arlen and, *right*, Reed Hadley, but even the fact that it was in "Glowing Sepia-Tone" didn't keep it from being just a small independent B-Western with a little extra polish added.

James Warren, here in *Code of the West* (RKO 1946) with Raymond Burr, *left*, and Carol Forman, was given a buildup as a new Western series star, but he lasted for only a few films.

Russell Hayden and James Ellison shortchanged the public by turning out a whole series of films made at the same time with the same cast members being shuffled around to play different roles in each new film. The results were awful, and even Hayden and Ellison look bored in this scene from *Fast on the Draw* (Lippert 1950).

Roy Rogers was still going strong right up until the early fifties. Here he gets the drop on stuntman Fred Graham while Penny Edwards watches in *Heart of the Rockies* (Republic 1951).

Gene Autry gets ready to shoot a riding sequence for one of his later films, *Hills of Utah* (Columbia 1951).

William Elliott wound up his series career doing items like *The Homesteaders* (Allied Artists 1953). In this scene from the film he appears with Ray Walker, *left*, and Robert Lowery.

Pudgy Wayne Morris holds the dubious distinction of being the star of the final series of B-Westerns turned out by the minor studios. Here in *The Marksman* (Allied Artists 1953) he appears with I. Stanford Jolley.